D1566877

THE
PILTDOWN
INQUEST

EAST SUSSEX · Wealden District

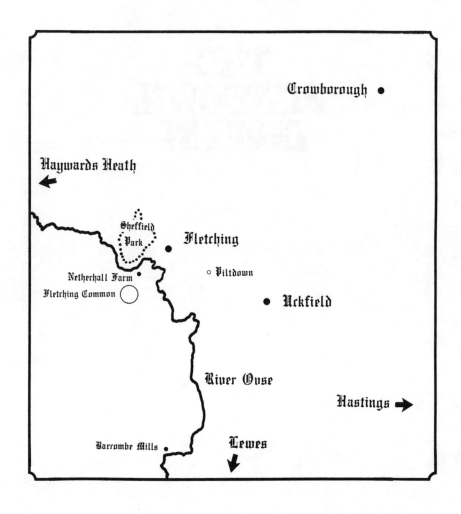

Crowborough ●

Haywards Heath ←

Sheffield Park

Fletching ●

Netherhall Farm ●

○ Piltdown

Fletching Common ○

● Uckfield

River Ouse

Hastings →

Barcombe Mills ●

Lewes ↓

THE PILTDOWN INQUEST

Charles Blinderman

PROMETHEUS BOOKS
Buffalo, New York

Credits and permissions:

Cover illustration from photo by author of Piltdown Man pub sign; permission to reproduce by Linda and Ron Hunt, owners, The Piltdown Man, East Sussex; permission by *Punch* to reproduce its cartoon; permission to reproduce cartoon Big Daddy by Chick Publications.
Geological Society of London: photos by and permission to reproduce: Piltdown gravel bed, Elephant femur with slab, Royal Academy Portrait, Sherborne horse's head, Portrait of Lewis Abbott, and Eoanthropus, Homo, Simia.
Wellcome Institute Museum: photo by and permission to reproduce: Kitchen middens.
British Museum (Natural History): photo by and permission to reproduce: Workers at pit with goose. My appreciation to the Trustees, British Museum (Natural History) for permission to reproduce pictures from its monographs "Solution to the Piltdown Problem" and "Further Contributions to the Solution of the Piltdown Problem": Misaligned molars and canine, Abrasion of cusps, Paleolithic flint implements, and Fossilized cricket bat. The photos reproduced here were taken by Professor Frank Carpenter. I also thank the Trustees for making Piltdown archival material available.
Mark Mancevice illustrated Map of the weald, Nomenclature, Critical mistake, Ecco Homo?, New finds and Eoanthropus, Beringer's lying stones, and *Homo diluvii testis*.
Charles Kidd: photo of Piltdown Man with author.

90 89 88 87 86   4 3 2 1

Library of Congress Cataloging-in-Publication Data

Blinderman, Charles, 1930-
    The Piltdown inquest.

    Bibliography: p.
    1. Piltdown forgery—History. I. Title.
GN282.5.B55   1986   573.3   86-20485
ISBN 0-87975-359-5

v

TABLE OF CONTENTS

ACKNOWLEDGMENTS

My thanks to colleagues and other friends who have helped me conduct this inquest: to Clark University Professors Ray Barbera, Fred Greenaway, Rudi Nunnemacher, and Walter Schatzberg; to Jean Perkins and Marla Wallace of the University's Goddard Library; to Inspector Richard Lacaire, Chief of Police Thomas Leahy, and FBI Agent James Ring; and to Helen Taylor, David Norman, and Ann Mitchell. I should like to thank an institution, the Mellon Foundation, for the financial support that made this project possible. Historians of the Piltdown case were generous in replying to inquiries: Peter Costello, Glyn Daniel, George Erikson, Stephen Jay Gould, John Lynch, Winifred McCulloch, A. B. Milligan, Kenneth Oakley, George Gaylord Simpson, Frederick Thieme, Sherwood Washburn, J. S. Weiner, and, especially, Ian Langham. None of these people is to be held responsible for errors in the text. Tony and Margaret Taylor, however, are to be held responsible for providing a home and friendship in Kent.

Clark University
July 1986

PART ONE

THE CRIME

CHAPTER ONE

THE PILTDOWN PIT

Thirteen centuries ago, the Saxons used the word "weald" to describe the expanse of woodland they roamed. Nowadays, the weald still holds forests, but it is also an open countryside of meadows and farms, villages and cities spread over 3,704 square miles of three counties, Kent, Surrey, and Sussex. Sussex, larger than the state of Rhode Island, was originally called Suth Seaxna lond, the land of the South Saxons. After the Saxons had settled down, a fellow named Pileca took possession of a hill, or dun, and Pileca's dun developed into Pylkedoune, whence Peltdowne in the seventeenth century. Thus from the Saxons we have the names of the places indicated in this inquest: the weald, Sussex, and Piltdown, a village near Fletching, in 1908 enjoying a small reputation in guide books as the home of a golf club and of a Church of Christ meeting house.

Before the Saxons, the land had hosted Romans, and before them, Celts, and 250,000 years before them, during the warm second interglacial period, Swanscombe Man. The Swanscombe artisan who sat by his cave knapping flint could have seen deer and beaver and other animals familiar to us, and also some animals now seen only in zoos in England—rhinoceros and elephant. A hundred million years before the rhinoceros and elephant, giant iguanadons and other dinosaurs enlivened the land.

The River Ouse still meanders over the face of this terrain, wrinkling deeper and deeper, leaving behind terraces and cutting to a bed now 80 feet below the southern wealden plateau on its way to New Haven and the English Channel. About a mile north of the river's present location, in the pleasant village of Piltdown, there lay a pit about 20 by 100 feet long and four feet deep.

The compound is still there, a cottage, a shed, some other buildings, and a dignified manor by a turnabout. The pit no longer exists, having been long ago exhausted of its gravel and filled in, though its location is noted by a memorial that looks like a tombstone. A border of shrubbery enhances the ambiance of the grave. Before 1912, the shallow pit had been as obscure as the cows that grazed nearby, nothing having ever been recorded as coming out of it except gravel left by the River Ouse of commercial use for road-building. It would become the scene of the greatest hoax in the history of science.

The hoax called Piltdown Man, bits of bone that emerged from the pit, took seven years to knit and forty to unravel. Between his debut in 1912 and his demise in 1953, Piltdown Man was considered an authentic human ancestor. He stood proud in the American Museum of Natural History's Hall of Man. Hundreds of articles and books were written about him; he was cited in thousands of scholarly and popular works; he made cameo appearances in novels and poems. Then, in 1953, he was exploded. He has since reappeared in half a dozen histories, in two British Broadcasting Corporation television documentaries, in dozens of newspaper reports. Once, for a few minutes, he agitated Jack Palance into husky wonderment on "Ripley's Believe It or Not." He continues to provide sustenance for fundamentalist enemies of evolutionary science.

Stories were made up to justify how bits of a human skull and an ape jaw found in the pit could fit together and how the bastardized ape-man could take a place alongside normal ancient people. This inquest records the stories, rationalizations, alibis, self-deceptions, hot rivalries, conspiracies, estrangements, temper, bombast, farce, melodrama, and intelligent, careful, and decent scientific discovery and interpretation. It entertains us with anecdotes about a pet goose employed as a decoy, a cabinet of secret memoranda, an elephant femur slab wrapped in swaddling clothes, a red-haired King of the Apes, Jesuitical jokes, and the tape-recorded conversation of one dead man accusing another of grievous hanky-panky.

THE COCONUT SKULL

It started harmlessly enough, though some pensive reflection should attend anyone's coming upon a piece of a smashed human skull. It started in 1908, just in time for the fiftieth anniversary of the *Origin of Species.*

Charles Dawson, a lawyer by profession, was in 1908 steward of several manors, among them that at the Barkham farm in Piltdown, and clerk to magistrates and to an urban council. A known antiquarian and amateur geologist with respectable credentials, he had spotted tiny teeth of a Mesozoic mammal never recorded in the weald before, and his talent had been immortalized in three discoveries: a reptile, *Iguanadon dawsoni;*

a mammal, *Plagiaulax dawsoni;* and a plant, *Salaginella dawsoni.* He had
six books to his credit on Sussex iron-works and pottery and on Hastings
Castle. For many years, he had been an Honorary Collector for the
British Museum of Natural History, which had accepted his stock of fossil
reptiles. A cache of natural gas he had discovered lit a railroad station and
a meeting of the Geological Society of London, of which he was a Fellow.
He was successful at his profession and accomplished at hunting down
fossils and artifacts.

Dawson often took long walks contemplating the ground, a posture
favored by gaggles of amateur archaeologists pecking at the rocks of
southeastern England. They observed strata, collected fossils, and in their
conversation in and out of local clubs, such as the Ightham Circle,
gossiped about Ice Age Man, an elusive character about whose prehistoric
existence in Britain rumors flourished.

Dawson's account of what happened at the pit begins with his attend-
ing, sometime toward the end of the nineteenth century, the Barkham
manorial court, for which he was solicitor. The session over, and just
before dinner, he went out for a stroll. He noticed some brown, iron-
stained flints on the road, flints which he had previously encountered no
nearer than Kent, five miles away. Returning to the manor house, he
asked Mr. Kenward, the farm's tenant, where those flints had come from
and was surprised to hear that the source was a gravel pit on the north-
western side of the Barkham Manor drive. After dinner, he ambled over.
The laborers shoveling out gravel responded to Dawson's inquiry about
whether they had found anything of interest in the pit; no, they had not.
He asked them to keep a sharp lookout in case something interesting
should turn up. The workmen agreed to do that. An affluent collector
such as this toff would tip handsomely. It was not until one day in 1908
that a workman (Venus Hargreaves or Alfred Thorpe) found a fragment
of a human cranium's parietal bone and gave it to Dawson.

W. J. Lewis Abbott, a local antiquarian, geologist, jeweler, and coun-
terfeiter, embellished on the story. He said that Dawson didn't know what
the piece was—a piece of coconut, an iron-stained concretion, or a fossil.
Dawson brought it to Abbott. Abbott enlightened Dawson: it had once
belonged to a human skull.

In 1955, Mabel Kenward, daughter of the Barkham Manor tenant,
told a different story, one that removes Dawson from an active part in the
first find. One day, she said, she had been sitting by a window watching
her father chatting with the workmen at the pit. When he came in, Mabel
wondered aloud why he was bringing "those old rocks in." Her father

replied that the workmen had smashed what they thought was a coconut with their pickax. He returned the pieces to the workmen, advising them to save the hoard for Mr. Dawson.

Right from the beginning of our inquest, we have to deal with different, even contradictory accounts of what happened in 1908 in that pit. The widely accepted coconut story is full of holes. If the laborers thought the thing was a coconut, they would not have brought it to Mr. Kenward. He would have had no more pleasure in an inedible and otherwise unremarkable old coconut than the navvies themselves. And if they thought it wasn't a coconut, they would have saved every splinter of it. How adult laborers in a gravel pit could have confused a human skull with a coconut is hard to explain. How Dawson could have done so is beyond explanation.

A more central mystery is whether the parietal piece, which was real, and later finds making up the Rubik cube of the cranium had come to the pit naturally generations ago or had been brought there the day before and inserted into the gravel by a villainous hoaxer. J. S. Weiner, in his 1955 *The Piltdown Forgery,* concluded that the very first fragment had been planted, as had everything else. Peter Costello guessed in 1985 that the skull might have been from a victim of the Black Death; the body could have been disposed of in or near the pit in the Middle Ages.

MODELS FOR A MANUFACTURED MAN

The parietal piece failed to impress Dawson, who waited years before going back to the pit. In 1911, from refuse heaps of gravel, he retrieved portions of the cranium's left frontal bone (which fit well with the parietal piece), left temporal, and occipital. In that they were thick and mineralized, these cranial fragments looked ancient. The supposition of great age was backed up by the discovery of a fossilized fragment of a hippopotamus lower premolar. These finds hinted at a prehistoric hominid having lived right there in the weald.

Perhaps believing that the experiment would harden relics long submerged in the often-flooded pit, or for a less honest reason, Dawson dipped the fossils in a solution of potassium bichromate. He also dipped a flint tool in this bath. The bath may not have hardened them, that flint tool being hard enough, but it did endow them with the ruddy patina expected of fossils. Sam Woodhead, public analyst for East Sussex and Hove, agricultural analyst for East Sussex, principal of the Agricultural College in Uckfield and a friend of Dawson, may have recommended undertaking this experiment at hardening, or at camouflage. Lewis Abbott said he himself had collaborated with Dawson in the skull-dipping.

Someone in 1908 who wanted to manufacture an extinct hominid had available many real specimens of what such a production should look like—its coloration, mineralization, and anatomy; and of what animal remains should be found with it, fossils of known age serving as an index to fossils of unknown age.

In 1857, an early human ancestor, the first recorded, had been blasted out of a limestone cliff overlooking the valley of the Neander in Germany. No one questioned the authenticity of the assemblage itself, limb-bones, parts of ribs and other post-cranial anatomy, and a skull cap. But because there were no index fossils, controversy did develop over dating and identifying Neanderthal Man. Opinions differed radically on whether it was a link between human beings and apes; a member of our species, though ancient: or merely a skeleton of someone who had recently passed away—an ancient Dutchman, a hermit, a cannibal, or an Irishman. Its curved leg bones suggested either rickets or equestrian training. Perhaps it had been a Mongolian Cossack who crawled into the cave and died there after chasing Napoleon around Europe. "Neander" means new man.

As fossil-hunting accelerated, relatives of the new man were found in Gibraltar, Czechoslovakia, and the Belgian site of Spy. The type had as its features thick skullbones, a flat, sloping forehead, a heavy jawbone without a chin, stout limb bones. Prominent brow ridges flowed into a single frontal torus. By 1908, Neanderthal had been accepted as either a predecessor of the human species or, in T. H. Huxley's view, an early human being.

The next find of a different hominid type validated an earlier, imaginary construction. The German biologist Ernst Haeckel directed an artist to sketch what the missing link would look like when it would be found, and he gave it a name: *Pithecanthropus alalus,* speechless ape-man. Eugene Dubois, who had studied under Haeckel, went to Java while serving as an army surgeon in the Dutch East Indies, and there, in an enviably short time, found a hominid skull cap, molar teeth, and a left femur. The skull cap was low-vaulted and thick-boned, like an ape's, its forehead sloping even more than Neanderthal's, its torus a ledge level enough to balance a cup of tea. At a cranial capacity of 900 cubic centimeters, the skull had held a brain twice the size of an ape's but below the average for a human being. The femur did not differ from that of a modern human being's.

Argument broke out about this 1891 find of *Pithecanthropus erectus,* or Java Man. Six experts, mostly German, thought the skull was that of an ape. One thought the femur an ape's; eight, an intermediate form; thirteen, human. Eight, mostly French, claimed that the fossil had come from a single individual, one authority in this group wantonly dreaming that it could have been the offspring of an indiscretion between a human being and an orangutan. The critical question was whether the skull cap and the femur, which had been found some forty feet away, had belonged to the same being. Professor Haeckel, impatient with those who refused to accept *Pithecanthropus erectus* as an ancestral hominid, advised that the strongest resistance to the idea that human beings had developed from apelike creatures came from human beings who were mentally on a par with Java Man.

Two years before the parietal fragment was found in the Piltdown gravel pit, another expedition to Java recovered bone weapons and fire-burnt wood, as well as fossils of tropical fauna, monkeys, tapirs, and a prehistoric elephant of the genus Elephas. The erect apeman had made weapons and had undertaken a successful quest for fire. The appearance in association with these remains of the index fossil Elephas dated Pithecanthropus as Pleistocene, such contemporaneity further supported by the fact that the pithecanthropine remnants were in the same state of mineralization as the elephant fossils. Frustrated by all the busy argument, Dubois hid the fossils under his livingroom floor. He had himself come to believe they were relics of a prehistoric ape.

In 1899, at Krapina in Croatia, Neanderthal fossils were found in association with Chellean rhinoceros and Mousterian mammoth, beaver, and cow. Eight years later, from a limestone grotto of a Dordogne tributary, at La Chapelle-aux-Saints in France, came a skeleton of a small elderly male. The head lay on a pillow of stones, the right arm brought toward the face, the prone body oriented from rising to setting sun. Marcellin Boule, who wrote the descriptive paper (Boule, 1971), imagined this Neanderthaler an ugly brute. Its thick cranial bones, its flat vault, its projecting torus and occipital bone, and its prognathous face would have earned it a cage in the Paris Jardin des Plantes. Near the body lay flint tools.

The next discovery occurred at Mauer, near Heidelberg. The jaw found there was like an ape's in being massive and chinless, but human in lacking the structures of an ape's jaw (the simian shelf and diastema). The molar occlusal surfaces were typically human, worn flat, as they are in our mouths, and level with each other. The articular condyle, a knob that fits into the mandibular fossa, had a completely human shape. Because the Heidelberg jaw conformed neither to Neanderthal nor to modern

T. H. Huxley's Java Man.

"The Dutchmen seem to have turned up something like the 'missing link' in Java. . . . I expect he was a Socratic party, with his hair rather low on his forehead and warty cheeks. *Pithecanthropus erectus* Dubois (fossil) rather Aino-ish about the body, small in the calf, and cheese-cutting in the shins. Le voici!" (Letter to J. D. Hooker, February 14, 1895, from Huxley [1901])

GEOLOGICAL TABLE, c. 1910: CENOZOIC ERA

Years Before Present	Period	Epoch		Index Fauna	Culture
10,000+	Quaternary	Recent			
		Pleistocene			Magdalenian
					Solutrean
					Aurignacian
			Upper		Mousterian
			Middle		Acheulian
			Lower		Chellean
		Upper		Beaver	
		Middle		Red deer	
		Lower		Rhinoceros	
				Mastodon	
				Elephas	
		Pliocene		Chimpanzee	
		Miocene		Dryopithecus	
		Oligocene		Fayum apes	
		Eocene		Lemurs	
400,000–150,000	Tertiary	Paleocene			

P A L E O L I T H I C

G L A C I A T I O N

jaws, it was given the name *Homo heidelbergensis*, important enough to be a new species, but insufficiently alien to be a new hominid genus.

Britain had many specimens to offer as challenges to those from continental Europe and Java. The first skeletal finds listed in Vallois and Movius's comprehensive *Catalogue des Hommes Fossiles* date from 1797; during the following century calvaria and other parts of human beings were exhumed from at least twenty other sites throughout England, Wales, and Scotland. In 1823, from the Welsh Paviland Cave came the Red Lady (so called because of its ochre coloration, though it was the skeleton of a 25-year-old male). In 1855, a coprolite pit in the Suffolk site of Foxhall yielded a human jawbone. In 1867 and 1873, from Kent's Cavern came a maxilla bone, the distal end of a humerus, a canine and a premolar. Antiquarians had dug up flint tools and sometimes bone and ivory ornaments as early as 1690 and from dozens of sites in the following two centuries, Sussex represented by finds at Brighton and Eastbourne.

In 1888, an early Pliocene deposit at Galley Hill, southeast of London, was found to contain a hominid skeleton. Experts involved later in the Piltdown affair commented on this find. W. J. Sollas, professor of geology at Oxford University, not believing that human beings had romped through so early a period as the Pliocene, asserted (Sollas, 1911) that the burial was recent. Arthur Keith, conservator of the Royal College of Surgeons, who thought that human beings had gone unchanged for a long time, was pleased with this combination of modern skeletal form and Pliocene vintage (Keith, 1915). Grafton Elliot Smith, professor of anatomy at Victoria University in Manchester, favored a theory that human beings had achieved a big brain before the appearance of other human parts; since the Galley Hill brain had been big, Smith fell on the side of those who thought it Pliocene. (Smith's views on Galley Hill and other hominids are most thoroughly presented in his *The Evolution of Man*, 1924.) W. J. Lewis Abbott insisted that Galley Hill Man was a Pliocene ancestor of human beings. He said that he had found prehistoric flint implements associated with the skeleton, but couldn't prove it.

Many specimens, but not one of them indisputably ancient. It was an embarrassment if not a disgrace that, while other countries had ancestors, England was poverty-stricken in its pedigree. The French were getting supercilious about all this, dismissing the English paleontologists as *chaissons de caillous*, pebble-hunters. The very names of prehistoric cultures were French—Chellean, Acheulean, Mousterian, Magdalenian.

In Oscar Wilde's *The Importance of Being Earnest*, Lady Bracknell is not pleased by John Worthing's puny birth. To his admitting that he had

been found in a handbag in the cloakroom of Victoria Station, Lady
Bracknell confesses her bewilderment:

> To be born, or at any rate, bred in a handbag, whether it had handles or
> not, seems to me to display a contempt for the ordinary decencies of
> family life that reminds one of the worst excesses of the French
> Revolution.

Jack asks what to do, and Lady Bracknell advises him that he ought

> to try and acquire some relations as soon as possible, and to make a
> definite effort to produce at any rate one parent, of either sex, before the
> season is quite over.

The Piltdown find was just such an acquisition.

HOW'S THAT FOR HEIDELBERG?

Dawson showed the pieces and spoke of them to several friends: Sam
Woodhead, who accompanied him on some of the digs; Mr. Ernest Clarke
of Lewes; W. R. Butterfield, curator of the Hastings Museum; and Lewis
Abbott, who had the fossils in his possession for a while. Woodhead
tested the cranial fragments and found them to contain phosphates and
iron, which was to be expected, but nothing organic. Organic content had
long since vanished from these ancient pieces.

These friends were not authorities. Arthur Smith Woodward, keeper
of geology at the British Museum of Natural History since 1901, Fellow
of the Royal Society, vice-president of the Geological Society (into which
he had been accepted the same year as Dawson), was a specialist in fossil
reptiles and fish, having published more than a hundred papers on the
latter, but he was also conversant with human evolution. He and Dawson
had met in 1884, and he had specified Dawson's *Plagiaulax* find with the
patronymic *dawsoni*. Woodward was the clear choice of professional
authority to consult.

About six months after the 1911 fossil-hunting season, Dawson wrote
a letter to Woodward about what he had found (the letters of Dawson
and Woodward are in the archives of the British Museum of Natural
History, Department of Palaeontology). It is a curious letter in that it
concentrates on an accounting of expenditures before it gets to the important point:

I have come across a very old Pleistocene (?) bed overlying the Hastings Bed between Uckfield and Crowborough which I think is going to be interesting. It has a lot of iron-stained flints in it, so I suppose it is the oldest known flint gravel in the Weald. I think portion of a human (?) skull which will rival *H. Heidelbergensis* in solidity. (February 14, 1912)

In the rest of the letter, Dawson remarks that he's been very busy at the office, that his clerical friend from Hastings (Teilhard de Chardin) has gone to Jersey, and that Conan Doyle is writing a sort of Jules Verne book (*The Lost World*). The first communication of this terrific find is thus sandwiched between business and personal gossip.

*By the spring of 1912, Dawson had retrieved other fossils from the pit—pieces of a hippopotamus left lower molar and of an elephant molar. In March letters to Woodward, he wrote that painters and builders were working on his house and that a visit to the pit would depend on the weather. He asked Woodward to identify one of the tooth fragments (the hippopotamus premolar) and, on March 28, assured him that he would "of course take care that no one sees the pieces of skull who has any knowledge of the subject and leave all to you." *

Dawson did not keep that promise, for in April he brought the fossils to Marie-Joseph Pierre Teilhard de Chardin, a 31-year-old Jesuit novitiate whom he had met in 1909. Workmen had alerted the solicitor that a couple of poachers in clerical garb were digging without tipping them. Dawson tracked the priests down to a quarry where iguanadon fossils had been excavated. "Mr. Dawson," Teilhard wrote to his parents about that first meeting in May 1909, "turned up while we were still on the spot, and immediately came up to us with a happy air, saying, 'Geologist?'" (May 31, 1909; Teilhard de Chardin, 1965). On April 26, 1912, Teilhard first mentions the Piltdown pit in one of his letters home. This suggests that Dawson had not told him about it for three years. In this letter, Teilhard relates Dawson's finds of flint tools, elephant and hippopotamus teeth fragments, and especially of cranial fragments.

On May 23, Dawson wrote to Woodward that he would be coming to London with odds and ends from the pit. Woodward would finally see and hold the fossils. In the display rooms at the British Museum of Natural History in South Kensington, Dawson might have passed some of the staff members who would become involved in the case—Reginald Smith, Curator of Antiquities; W. P. Pycraft, Curator of Anthropology; Frank O. Barlow, Woodward's assistant; and Martin A. C. Hinton, then a volunteer.

Dawson handed the odds and ends to Woodward. The fragment of elephant tooth, which Woodward classified as Stegodon (but which has since been reclassified as *Elephas planifrons*) had not been found in western Europe before and seemed to be of pre-Pleistocene vintage. These mammalian relics were nicely tanned, as befit specimens that had slept for hundreds of thousands of years in a gravel pit or bathed for a few hours in a chemical solution. More exciting were the cranial fragments.

"How's that," Dawson announced, one would guess in a triumphant tone of voice, "for Heidelberg?" (Dawson, 1913).

On the last day of May 1912, the trio of pebble-hunters went to dig. In a heap of gravel by the side of the pit, they found additional fragments of the parietal bone, each of the three days rendering up a piece. Woodward found a fragment that joined the occipital to the parietal bone; this was the only skull piece found in situ rather than on the refuse heaps. Teilhard, either on the first or second day, discovered another fragment of the elephas tooth. He wrote to his parents (June 3, 1912) that there was as much of a thrill in that discovery as in a hunter's bringing down his first snipe. In this letter, he referred to the skull fragment as "the famous human cranium."

The 1912 season brought forth a mastodon molar cusp, unlike anything that had ever come from such a site in Europe; and, close to a hedge, they found portions of a red deer's antler, the tooth of a Pleistocene horse, and several flints, Teilhard contributing to that hoard with a flint tool that looked like a handax (to receive the British Museum number 606). Unsure about whether the flints were rocks or actual tools, Dawson checked with the maven on the subject, Lewis Abbott, and on June 30, 1912, wrote happily to Woodward: "He says they are 'man—man all over.' "

Things were looking up. Piltdown Man was coming through as the oldest human inhabitant of England, perhaps of Europe, perhaps of the world. And even better, he had made tools, the oldest tools ever found. Interesting and remarkable, but not spectacular. For achieving prominence, something else was needed, something really unique.

′One early evening, Dawson, hacking away at the lowest stratum of the pit, a layer of sand and gravel impregnated with and cemented together by iron oxide, unearthed half of a lower jaw. ′

′By autumn, the loot from the pit consisted of fossils of elephant, hippopotamus, mastodon, red deer, horse, and beaver; flint implements; nine fragments comprising four cranial bones (frontal, parietal, temporal, and occipital); and a right lower jawbone with two intact molars, but lacking chin and articular condyle. If that jawbone went with the cranium, the contraption would have been truly spectacular. For it was the jawbone of an ape. And to have a hominid with a human head and an ape snout would turn out to be just the thing to elevate the find from an aspirant waiting in the wings to an international star. '

Woodward supervised the reconstruction of the skull at the British Museum. He and Dawson got to work on a joint paper.

DECEMBER 1912

A week before Christmas and all through Burlington House, members of the Geological Society of London listened enraptured to an autopsy of old bones and other debris disinterred from a gravel pit located in the Sussex village of Piltdown. A precocious notice in the *Manchester Guardian's* issue of November 21, 1912, ensured a packed house. Two major questions were on the minds of the auditors: When had the creature lived? Did the cranium and jaw come from a single being?

ᵈDawson described the geology of the Piltdown area and the flint implements recovered from the pit. The pit had four layers: the first, soil; the gravelly level under that contained paleoliths; those bones found in situ and nearly all the mammalian remains were in the next layer; and the bottom consisted of a mixture of clay and sand. Stratigraphic evidence indicated that the pit had originated in the Pleistocene. Paleontological evidence, the Pleistocene index fossils, confirmed that indication. Furthermore, all the fossil specimens were highly mineralized and of similar patina, as though they had shared being oxidized over a long time. They had come from two pockets—the cranial fragments, the lower jaw, and the handax that Teilhard de Chardin had found occupied or were close to one of these pockets; the other pocket disgorged most of the mammalian relics. The Piltdown hominid had whacked out tools like those of the Chellean industry.'

Other finds, from Bury St. Edmunds and Galley Hill and Kent's Cavern (and, by the time of the report, from Cheddar, Jersey, Dartford, Shippea Hill, and Ipswich) had started out with promise and ended with disappointment. ʲThis one from Piltdown seemed to have stratigraphic, geological, and paleontological authenticity. England finally had a viable competitor in the race for ancestry.ʲ

Woodward's anatomical contribution was more startling. Described by Teilhard as a very vigorous little man, with salt-and-pepper hair and a cold appearance, Woodward spoke first of points that were merely interesting—the skull was thicker than those of modern Europeans or even Australian aborigines, the latter being the then-current model of low-class humanity. He estimated its cranial capacity as 1070 cc, higher than the 900 cc of *Pithecanthropus erectus*, but lower than the cranial capacities of Geological Society members.

⟩The relatively (relative to the male cranial anatomy) small brow ridges, area of temporal muscle insertion, and mastoid processes led Woodward to decide that the living individual had been a female. Professor W. Boyd Dawkins would get a laugh from audiences he lectured to when he'd mention that the ivory texture of the female bone showed the superiority of that sex over his own!

Now came something of greater interest than a woman's skull: the cranium, though obviously human, had two apelike features: upper extension of a temporal bone structure and broad occipital bone. (The skulls of Neanderthal Man and of Java Man also had apelike features: sloping forehead and prominent brow ridge.) Then the stunner: an ape jaw!

A human head below which slung an ape jaw—that was the signature of a real ape-man. T. H. Huxley had thought the Spy skeletons brutal, and Worthington Smith in his 1894 *Man the Primeval Savage* had thought them pithecoid; the British Museum had labeled a Melanesian skull from Torres Straits the most apelike of all. Woodward specified how the jaw, in its grooves and bumps, was just like an ape's. Four features are critical in diagnosing whether a jaw is ape or human: the simian shelf, the mylohyoid ridge, the shape of the dental arcade, and the articular condyle.

1. Unlike Heidelberg's, this jaw had a simian shelf. In the course of evolution from a common ancestor, hominids had developed a chin, a truss structure compensating for progressive lightening of the jaw bone. Apes developed something different, a thin inner flange. No human being has that simian shelf; all apes do. The Piltdown jaw has it.

2. A second diagnostic feature distinguishing human from ape jaw is the presence of a mylohyoid ridge, attachment for a muscle of the floor of the mouth. All hominid jaws have it. Ape jaws lack it. The Piltdown jaw lacks the mylohyoid ridge.

3. A third differentiating diagnostic feature is the shape of the dental arcade, which is divergent in a human mouth (distance between canine teeth is less than that between rear molars), parallel in an ape's. Since only part of half a lower jaw had been found, no one could know just how wide or of what curvature the entire jaw had been.

Could the creature talk? The cranial capacity, three times that of an ape, hinted that it was advanced enough to speak. Woodward informed

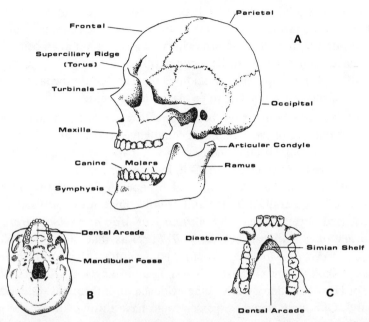

Nomenclature of skull and jaw. (A) Profile view of human skull and jaw. (B) View of human skull from beneath. (C) Ape lower jaw.

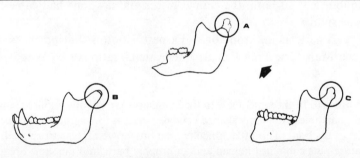

The critical mistake. The jaw should have guided choice of condyle. But instead of reproducing the condyle of an ape jaw, B, for the missing piece, Woodward chose a human condyle, C, that would fit into the mandibular fossa of the skull, thus creating Piltdown Man, A. If Woodward had chosen B, there would have been no *Eoanthropus dawsoni.*

his audience that the divergent arcade of the Piltdown jaw was wide enough to allow for speech. This was circular reasoning, since Woodward had designed the reconstruction to be more divergent than an ape's.

4. The fourth diagnostic feature is the articular condyle, the knob that fits the lower jaw into the mandibular fossa. This structure, Dawson guessed, had "rotted off." Therefore it had to be designed. Only two

options were available: the condyle could have been designed to be compatible with the jaw fragment, that is, apelike, in which case it would not have fit into the mandibular fossa, which was that of a human being; or it could have been designed to be incompatible with the jaw fragment but compatible with the human cranial housing. They chose the latter option and reconstructed the condyle to be like a human being's.

The jawbone could have been immediately consigned to a source different from that of the cranium. It could have been a real ape's jawbone that had accidentally been found next to a real ape's skull. But England, a land attractive to Saxon, Roman, Celt, hippopotamus, rhinoceros, mastodon, and elephant, had been shunned by ape. A fossil tooth found in Essex had been identified by the authoritative anatomist and paleontologist Richard Owen (in his 1884 *Antiquity of Man as Deduced from the Discovery of a Human Skeleton at Tilbury*) as that of an Old World monkey, *Macacus pliocenus* (Owen), and Abbott's collection included a monkey's skull that he claimed to have dug up in England. But these finds had not been considered convincing evidence of anthropoid residence in England. Of course, some trespasser could have thrown an old ape jawbone into the pit (that crazy excuse would many years later be used to explain how the jawbone got into the pit). Therefore, and this was a tremendous leap of faith, the cranial pieces and jawbone had come from the same source.

The American anthropologist Earnest Hooton, having nicknamed Piltdown Man "The First Female Intellectual," rationalized Woodward's choice:

> In order to fit the simian jaw to the human socket we must model upon the mandible a humanly shaped condyle which is incongruous with the rest of the bone. This little difficulty need not, however, embarrass us. If nature puts conjoined human and anthropoid parts into the same organism, some compromise has to be made at the junctures. (Hooton, 1931)

The little difficulty would swell into a big controversy.

The two implanted molars, apelike in their cusps and proportions, were at the same time the most human feature of the jaw. Since the human jaw can move in a rotary way, side to side as well as back and forth, the surfaces of its molar teeth tend to be flatter than those of ape molar teeth. In "The Piltdown Skull," Dawson expanded on this point that the molar teeth were worn as flat

> as in primitive races of men who carelessly grind up minute quantities of

grit with their food, and this is a characteristic which has only been met with in man. It is believed that the long canine teeth of the apes would prevent the particular grinding motion by which the molars acquire this process of wear.

Everything was so unusual as to be incredible. The finds of mastodon and elephas were firsts for Southern England. The combination of human cranium and ape jaw was a first for the whole world. The creature was chimerical, like a satyr. Yet there he was. From the Piltdown grave, his final resting place, had been exhumed a good part of his skull and most of half a jaw, with a couple of teeth in it. The resurrection men had fit it all together, and that full skull staring at the members of the Geological Society was powerful, though silent, witness. An apeman could well have looked like that; and if he could have, why should he not have? An additional mark of authenticity was given when Woodward dubbed the contraption *Eoanthropus dawsoni,* another tribute to its discoverer, like *Iguanadon dawsoni.* He was even fleshed out in the *London Illustrated News* and elsewhere so that everyone could see what he looked like as he squatted, hacking out tools.

Dawson disliked the "artistic efforts":

I was very disappointed with the Eo. bust. . . . It represents a common type among the Sussex agricultural labouring class and [?] by no means the lowest stages.

The Americans are evidently not used to see the type and imagine it to be very savage in appearance. I think there is yet scope for further artistic efforts. Perhaps an india-rubber balloon stretched over the plaster cast might inspire a sculptor. With such a thick skull, Eoanthropus might well have done without such a head of hair. (October 8, 1915)

While German paleontologists were gloating over the 1907 discovery of Heidelberg Man and French paleontologists were reveling in a frisson of pleasure brought on by the 1908 discovery of the ugly, elderly gent at La Chapelle, a manufactured Englishman was on its way to a ditch 70 miles south of Piccadilly Circus. Just how the hoax was done has been explained and will be summarized later; but who did it and for what motive remains a mystery. In 1896, Worthington Smith had written, "Bad fortune seems to attend nearly all discoveries of very ancient human relics." The Piltdown case underscores that dismal appraisal.

CHAPTER TWO

THE RISE OF PILTDOWN MAN

THE EARLIEST MAN?

REMARKABLE DISCOVERY IN SUSSEX

A SKULL MILLIONS OF YEARS OLD

On November 21, 1912, the *Manchester Guardian* thus scooped its competitors in an exclusive story that had been sneaked out through the veil of secrecy lowered by the Piltdown scientists. On December 19, the *Times* of London gave its imprimatur:

A PALEOLITHIC SKULL

FIRST EVIDENCE OF A NEW HUMAN TYPE

From across the ocean, the *New York Times* trumpeted in one daily headline after another:

PALEOLITHIC SKULL IS A MISSING LINK

MAN HAD REASON BEFORE HE SPOKE

DARWIN'S THEORY IS PROVED TRUE

Initially, the find had been of interest only to a neighborhood. It rippled to touch a wide populace throughout Europe and the United States and to overwhelm some people in the professional communities of museums, universities, and scientific societies. Eoanthropus appeared in professional journals and commanded headlines in great newspapers because people have always been interested in their descent from dust or ape and because he satisfied nicely some cultural biases and idiosyncratic theoretical expectations.

Articles came out in the *Daily Telegraph,* the *Literary Digest,* the *American Review of Reviews,* and in many other periodicals. W. P. Pycraft wrote an article for the *Illustrated London News* (December 28, 1912), its frontispiece an assertively prognathous Man of Sussex. Impressed by the "incontrovertible" evidence, Pycraft fantasized on what the creature must have looked like. "He was a man of low stature, very muscular, and had not yet attained that graceful poise of the body which is so characteristic of the human race to-day." Piltdown Man knew how to make a fire and a handax. He gamboled about the Sussex countryside as naked as a monkey, flashing an admirable pair of canines. His cranium could hold two pints of Carlsberg beer.

Provincial as well as national and foreign newspapers told the tale of Piltdown Man. On February 1, 1913, the *Hastings and St. Leonards Observer* ran a short article, "Pre-Historic Man. The Newly-Discovered Link in His Evolution." The author, Lewis Abbott, takes credit for targeting Sussex as the territory for exploration, for inspiring Dawson to look into wealden flint-gravels and spreads, and for helping Dawson understand what had been found. Abbott relates the "cokernut" story, alludes to a row of human jaws before him, and defines the teeth as essentially chimpanzoid. The discovery at Piltdown, he boasts, proved the accuracy of his prediction that the Pliocene ancestor would be found in the weald.

Two weeks later, the same periodical transcribed the Piltdown case into doggerel like that of an Old English bestiary, the description followed by the moral:

> Now for the moral of my tale:
> We little humans in this vale
> Of joys and fears our short lives pass,
> And then we're blotted out alas!
> Perchance in a thousand years,
> Our skulls may be unearthed—Our fears,
> Our hopes, our aspirations may
> Be analyzed, some future day,
> By some keen-brained geologist,
> Who'll hold our jawbone in his fist . . .
> Dawson, we owe you a debt
> And hope that you will dig up yet,
> In research geological,
> Our tree genealogical. ("H.R.H.")

In the winter months of 1913, Dawson displayed a cast of the Pilt-down skull in his Uckfield law office and gave interviews to reporters. He tried to fashion his own model of the skull, using water-colors for different shades. As winter greened into spring, plaster casts of fragments and of the reconstructed skull with its detachable jaw were distributed to anato-mists, geologists, and other naturalists, many of whom got involved in arguments about the most credible reconstruction. Teilhard advised that the various reconstructions added nothing definite to the case. He urged the fossil-hunters to look for more pieces, and they did. They found a lulu.

FIGHTING TEETH

One of the big questions of the find was the age of Eoanthropus. Most opted for Pleistocene, some for Pliocene, a few joy-killers for merely modern. The second big question was whether Eoanthropus was human only in its skull, the jaw having accidentally been inhumed next to cranial fragments, in which case Eoanthropus was an oddity hardly worthy of notice even by the provincial papers; or whether it was a single individual composed of a human skull and ape or apelike jaw, in which case it was the most important hominid discovery ever made. Arthur Smith Wood-ward dismissed the criticism that the skull came from a human head and the jaw from an ape's mouth. The combination of human and ape fea-tures, he said in his address to the Geological Society, had been "long previously anticipated as an almost necessary stage in the course of human evolution." Tradition had it that as ancestral brains approached the modern, ancestral jaws retained, in Darwin's phrase, "fighting teeth." The canines withered as the brain blossomed and took over the functions (eating, threatening, courting) previously assigned to the teeth. The brain led to fire and tools, weapons, and, in the male sex, masculine wiles. A canine tooth had been fabricated for the reconstructed skull. It would have been satisfying to find the canine tooth of the pit's jaw.

Scientists and the laity came to visit the pit. Arthur Conan Doyle, interested in the mysteries of science as well as the science of mysticism, saw in the Piltdown story the fibers of strangeness he was weaving into his novel *The Lost World.* He entertained Dawson at his home in Crow-borough, and offered to drive Dawson anywhere in his motorcar.

No explorations were conducted during the winter months of 1912-1913 while the reconstructed cast with its reconstructed canine made the rounds. In February, Abbott's article on the finds appeared in the *Hast-ings and St. Leonards Observer,* the article in which, among other things, he predicts that "in all probability the missing teeth were essentially chimpanzoid." In March, Abbott surprised Dawson by telling him that the Geological Association was planning an excursion to the pit. It took place on July 12, 1913. Abbott, preening himself on having instigated Dawson to look for a likely site, or on having pushed him into that very pit, approved of the progress of civilized opinion. He looked forward to the newspapers, national as well as local, giving the Geological Association excursion the publicity due such an event. He encouraged the extensive dissemination of photos.

The fecund pit had more treasures to deliver during the digs of the 1913 season: another fragment of the elephant tooth that fit with previous fragments; and Dawson found nasal bones and another small bone thought to be a turbinal (a support of nasal mucus membranes). The bones were delicate, the turbinal so fragile that it crumbled upon being handled. Later, Mrs. Smith Woodward glued the pieces together. These were the only parts of Eoanthropus's face ever recovered.

The summer of 1913 produced two finds of interest to reinforce the authenticity of Piltdown Man. Dawson, alert to the possibility of discovering Eoanthropine remains elsewhere, went exploring. With his usual wizardry—he could spot bits and bones invisible to most mortals, such as the arrowhead that escaped the notice even of Conan Doyle at his home—one evening at some unnamed "new place, a long way from Piltdown," he picked up a frontal bone fragment, described as being not thick and with a brow ridge curving from slight at the edge to prominent over the nose. The base of the nose being rotten, he asked Woodward (June 3, 1913) how to go about gelatinizing it to firm it up. He also says that he intended to look out for Woodward and bring the piece of skull to him, "but don't expect anything very sensational." Nothing more is heard of this new find from a new place, but Dawson would continue looking elsewhere for descendants of Eoanthropus until he found or manufactured one.

The next find was sensational. Teilhard had come from Canterbury to visit Dawson at Castle Lodge, in Lewes. They toured the countryside during the weekend of August 8-10, 1913, at which time Dawson may have escorted Teilhard to Site II, and they may have found fossils there. On that supposition rest some of the accusations against one or the other or both of them. Toward the end of the month, Teilhard stopped off again to visit Dawson and the pit. After breakfast, Teilhard went off with his host and Smith Woodward to dig. Recounting what happened, he wrote to his parents that they had been joined by "a pet goose, who would not leave us while we dug, alternately cute or bad-tempered towards us, and always ferocious to passers-by" (September 10, 1913).

In *The Earliest Englishman,* Woodward said that Teilhard seemed to be weary as he sifted in his clerical garb. Woodward told him to calm down for a while. Picking at a spoil heap of rain-washed gravel, Teilhard found an inch-long fossil, colored a blackish brown on its sides and, like the molars, a reddish-brown on its occlusal surface. "It was a moment of grand excitement," he wrote home. He had picked up a canine that was just like the one the British Museum technicians had designed in their reconstruction of the skull. This would have the dubious honor of becoming the most talked-about tooth in history.

A few days later, Teilhard stayed with Woodward in London, and at a party met *"un certain Gregory"* (William King Gregory, of the American Museum of Natural History) and W. P. Pycraft. The gentlemen may have passed around the canine with the brandy. The pattern of its wear, its relatively short root, the tip of which had been broken away, and its size were all humanlike; but it was simian in its upper surface, inclination, and projection. Woodward assigned it without hesitation to the jaw, which he had assigned earlier, with similar bravado, to the cranium. Everyone congratulated Teilhard on his sharp eyes.

In a letter to Woodward (September 2, 1913), Dawson confided his annoyance that someone had leaked the news of the canine find to the *Express.* He preferred favorable reviews by Pycraft and Lankester and a good report in the *Times.* At the September 1913 meeting of the British Association for the Advancement of Science and at the April 1914 meeting of the Geological Society, Woodward exulted on the fighting tooth so wonderfully appropriate to the jaw and cranium of *Eoanthropus dawsoni.*

In its notice, *Nature* (September 25, 1913) welcomed the canine tooth as "definite proof" justifying Woodward's having given Piltdown Man its own genus. The April 1914 issue of the *Quarterly Journal of the Geological Society* carried Dawson and Woodward's collaborative "Supplementary Note on the Discovery of a Palaeolithic Human Skull and Mandible." Dawson was responsible, as he had been in the previous year's address, for the geological report. He described the layers of the pit, discussed the flints found in the fourth layer, the incisor of a beaver, and the latest hominid remains, nasal and turbinated bones. He also mentioned a pelecypod embedded in a chalk flint, *Inoceramus inconstans.* Woodward's anatomical analysis followed. The new bones were like those of Melanesian and African noses. The canine belonged to the mandible, in the socket of that right lower jawbone (had there been a socket). "It probably, therefore, came into place before the second and third molars

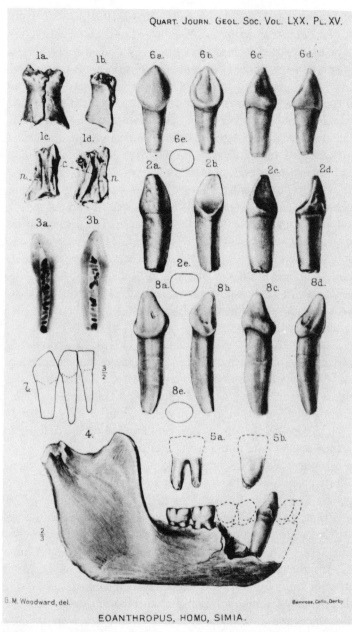

G. M. Woodward, del.   Bemrose, Collo., Derby

EOANTHROPUS, HOMO, SIMIA.

Eoanthropus, Homo, Simia. (1) Views of nasal bone. (2) Views of canine tooth. (3) Radiogram of canine tooth showing grains in pulp cavity. (4) Jaw bone with molars and canine tooth installed. (5) Impression of cavity for molar roots. (6) *Homo sapiens* milk-canine. (7) *Homo sapiens* milk-canine and milk-incisors. (From *QJGS* 70 (April 1914), Plate 15.)

as in Man—not after one or both of these teeth, as in the Apes."

The canine did present a few disconcerting problems, which could be explained away for a while. X-ray analysis showed that the pulp cavity contained 19 sand grains. Nothing troubling about that, not in 1913, for the canine had presumably undergone fossilization, sand grains seeping in over the millennia as the earth rolled on from Elephas to Edward VII. X-ray analysis also showed that the upper canine had tormented this lower tooth into being simply worn down, as though it were an old tooth. But the pulp cavity was large, a sign of its having been a young tooth.

The X-ray analysis also showed something else, a very rare circumstance: as the Piltdown coterie's dental consultant Dr. Underwood put it, the wear had gone so deep as to break through the tooth into the pulp cavity itself. No one had ever seen anything like that. The tooth therefore could have been temporary or permanent, from the mouth of a child or a senior citizen or a middle-aged person, erupting before or after the first molar, and dated as Pliocene or Pleistocene.

Dawson, in a letter written years after its discovery rationalized the disharmony between a young pulp cavity and an old tooth:

> The pulp cavity of the "Eo" canine is certainly large. It does not seem to have occurred to anyone that as one end is open, the walls of the cavity may have been the subject of post-mortem decay, and that bacteria may have cleared away the comparatively soft walls during a prolonged soakage in water and sand.
> I think I have noticed this in fossil teeth and broken bones. You have plenty of material to describe this. (February 6, 1916)

CRICKET, ANYONE?

The gravel pit, which had become bountiful after its initial stinginess, had few more fossils to yield, a piece of rhinoceros tooth found by Davidson Black, an assistant to Grafton Elliot Smith, who would in the 1920s achieve fame for his excavation of Peking Man. Then Dawson found a fossil as important as the canine and even more delightful. In the summer of 1914, digging in rich soil under a hedge bordering the pit, he seized upon a piece of a fossilized elephant's thigh bone. Arthur Keith identified the exact spot as being near the refuse heap where cranial fragments had been found and also near the pocket that had contained the jawbone. Covered with the yellow clay representative of the deepest layer of the pit, this fossil slab, taken out in two parts, looked like a tool of some kind, but a more sophisticated tool than any made by low-brow Neander-

Fig. 1.—*Section of gravel-bed at Piltdown (Sussex).*
Approximate scale =1/24 of the natural size.

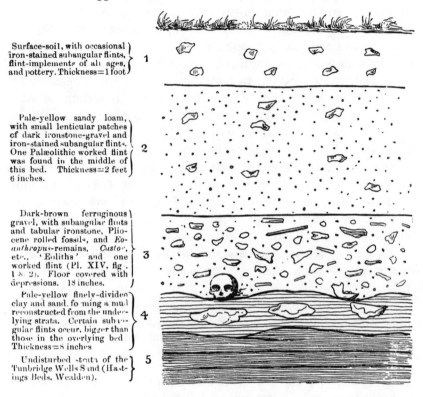

Surface-soil, with occasional
iron-stained subangular flints,
flint-implements of all ages,
and pottery. Thickness=1 foot ⎫ 1

Pale-yellow sandy loam,
with small lenticular patches
of dark ironstone-gravel and
iron-stained subangular flints.
One Palæolithic worked flint ⎬ 2
was found in the middle of
this bed.   Thickness=2 feet
6 inches.

Dark-brown   ferruginous
gravel, with subangular flints
and tabular ironstone, Pliocene rolled fossils, and *Eoanthropus*-remains,   *Custo°,*
etc.,   'Eoliths'   and   one ⎬ 3
worked flint (Pl. XIV, fig.
1 & 2). Floor covered with
depressions.   18 inches.

Pale-yellow finely-divided
clay and sand, forming a mud
reconstructed from the under-
lying strata. Certain suban- ⎬ 4
gular flints occur, bigger than
those in the overlying bed.
Thickness=8 inches

Undisturbed strata of the ⎫
Tunbridge Wells Sand (Hast- ⎬ 5
ings Beds, Wealden).   ⎭

Section of Piltdown gravel bed; approximate scale = 1/24 of natural size. (From *QJGS* 70 (April 1914), Figure 1.)

thalers. It was the only Lower Paleolithic bone implement ever found anywhere, a remarkable artifact from the hairy hands and two-pint head of Eoanthropus.

Accepting an invitation from Woodward to dine at the Geological Club on December 2, 1914, the day of another presentation to the Geological Society, Dawson wondered whether Woodward had included in his paper reference to the microscopic structure of the bone implement and whether Woodward could undertake a comparison of this fossil with the femur of Pliocene or Pleistocene Elephas. He recommended an illustration "to point out the most probable region of the femur from which the fragment was derived, making a diagram of a femur with the outline of the implement dotted upon the surface for demonstration"

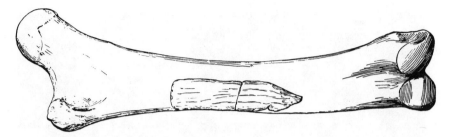

Elephant femur with slab. Hinder view of femur; 1/8 natural size. (From *QJGS* 71 March 1915.

(November 21, 1914). This was done.

A description of the latest bonanza from the pit edified the Geological Society meeting of December 2, 1914: rolled fragments of highly mineralized rhinoceros and mastodon teeth and the femur implement covered with firmly adherent yellow clay. This bone was "much mineralized with iron oxide, at least on the surface, and it agrees in appearance with some small fragments of bone which we found actually in place in the clay below the gravel." It was probably, or so Woodward said, dug up by workmen from the bottom layer of the pit and thrown under a hedge eventually to be found by the diggers (Dawson/Woodward, 1914).

One panelist said that the instrument had been used as a club. Another said that thongs had been attached to it. Mr. Reginald Smith noted that it "would rank as by far the oldest undoubted work of man in bone" and considered the possibility that it had been found and whittled in recent times. It was, he said, an "interesting problem" and would provoke "an ingenious solution." The French archaeologist Abbé Henri Breuil would later comment that a giant beaver had gnawed it into its present shape. To some observers, it resembled a cricket bat.

Discoverers and defenders of Piltdown Man posed for a Royal Academy portrait in 1915. The third member of the trio of diggers, Teilhard de Chardin, couldn't be there because he had been inducted into the French Army and was occupied with tasks more urgent than sifting gravel heaps. However, those who were able to make the session were joined by Woodward's reconstructed skull and by a basketful of relatives of that skull. The pit would give birth to no more fossils.

A MAN FOR ALL SEASONS

Three reasons are available to explain the success of the Piltdown hoax—the state of physical anthropology before World War I (under which one

John Cooke, R. A., Royal Academy Portrait. In 1915, the partisans of Piltdown Man gathered to celebrate his arrival. On wall: picture of Charles Darwin. Standing (left to right): F. O. Barlow, G. Elliot Smith, C. Dawson, and A. Smith Woodward. Seated: A. S. Underwood, A. Keith, W. P. Pycraft, E. R. Lankester. (From archives, Geological Society of London.)

might place the fact that many authorities, in England as well as elsewhere, had to rely upon analysis of casts rather than of the actual fossils); the anatomical, chemical, and paleontological knowledge and skill of the hoaxer; and the circumstance that Piltdown Man conformed to general cultural expectations and satisfied specific theories. The first two reasons are less critical than the third—the forgeries (for several clustered under the rubric "hoax") fit in well with cultural biases and theoretical assumptions.

Victorian and Edwardian anthropology was explicitly racist, drawing a hierarchy down from white European to Australian bushman and African black wrestling for a place on the lowest rung of the human ladder. Piltdown Man became, for most British commentators, the standard-bearer of a moderate ethnocentrism.

The investigator could ascertain a specimen's place on the ladder by tracing correlations between discernible physical structure and the cognition, the rationalizations, the dreams that kept the brain roiling. Craniometry was the pseudoscientific corollary of phrenology; in Victorian phrenological texts, such as the Fowlers', the noble brow of a humanitarian signaled the goodness within, while a sloping forehead, heavy brow ridges, and pronounced occipital marked a malefactor—just as, in Chaucer, the amorous proclivities of the Wife of Bath had their physical expression in a gap between her upper incisors. Long before his remains were blasted out of a cliff, people knew that Neanderthal Man would look like a brute with an elongated head, heavy brows, a weak chin, and the posture of a pugilist.

Unlike the Neanderthal ignoramus, Eoanthropus, like modern Europeans, had been educable. That conclusion derives from the theory then called paedogenesis (neoteny today) that ours has been a victorious species because human beings retain infantile features of the anthropoid fetus and infant, such as globular cranium, incomplete closing of sutures, and a straight face, all contributing to keeping human beings educable. In the *London Times's* December 19, 1912, issue, the article "A Palaeolithic Skull" mentioned that Frank Barlow, Woodward's assistant, had reconstructed a skull that seemed to be like that of a young chimpanzee, with globular cranium and orthognathous face, while other cavemen's faces were prognathous, like those of grown-up apes. Dawson also made this point.

Two different theoretical approaches to the human lineage were followed by different theorists. The minority party, led in England by W. J. Sollas and (for a while) Arthur Keith and in the United States by Aleš Hrdlička, proposed that a single line led to human beings, Neanderthal Man a stage in our lineage. Most paleontologists believed that there had been several hominid lines; this party tended to erase Neanderthal Man from our lineage, and insult him while doing so. Marcellin Boule was as passionately hostile against having Neanderthal Man as our ancestor as others were about having an ape. He described the La Chapelle Neanderthal of 1908 as the slouching troglodyte familar to us as the malefactor of countless modern horror movies. Boule took the skull of Piltdown Man as evidence of a human ancestor not only better-looking than Neanderthal Man, but also more fit. Neanderthal Man, he said, had gone extinct. As for Java Man, to Boule he was a gibbon.

Arthur Smith Woodward agreed with Boule on the idea of branching hominids, that Piltdown Man was better, and that Neanderthal had gone extinct, though he disagreed on Boule's severance of jaw from skull. After the expected review of the history of the find and the expected inventory of the fragments, *Nature* noted (on December 19, 1912) that, though Eoanthropus did have some simian features (a low and broad occipital and the apelike mandible), it was sufficiently advanced to be ancestral to the human species itself:

At least one very low type of man with a high forehead was therefore in existence in western Europe long before the low-browed Neanderthal man became widely spread in this region. Dr. Smith Woodward accordingly inclines to the theory that the Neanderthal race was a degenerate offspring of early man and probably became extinct, while surviving modern man may have arisen directly from the primitive source of which the Piltdown skull provides the first discovered evidence.

The notion that Europeans were mentally more advanced than non-Europeans, a notion agreeable to Europeans, received support from many sources, including the Bible. Tennyson back in 1850 expressed this general cultural bias when he eulogized European Man as "the heir of all the ages, in the foremost files of time." Almost without exception, European anthropologists for generations preceding the Piltdown finds agreed with that. Commentaries on Piltdown Man did not improve the hopes of non-Europeans to share common humanity with Europeans. The commentators did not look out their windows at English countrymen for examples of throwbacks; they looked overseas. The strategy was to emphasize the simian nature of the skull and the human nature of the jaw by finding comparable features in benighted colonial subjects. The process elevated Piltdown Man from a link between ape and human being to a link between African black (or similar "low" people) and European white.

Thus Dawson thought that the molar occlusal surfaces were as flat as those of savages, who uncouthly allowed grit to get into their mouths; and when the nasal bones were recovered, Woodward compared them to those of Melanesian and African people's. Professor A. F. Dixon would later (*Nature,* July 12, 1917) inquire into whether the lower jaw's "ape-like peculiarities have not been over-emphasized in the various reconstructions of the entire skull. The author believes that it is possible to reconstruct the lower jaw on more distinctly human lines than has been proposed hitherto."

Pycraft illustrated his article "The Most Ancient Inhabitant of England" (Pycraft, 1912) with a series of drawings showing that the chimpanzee has no chin and the Caucasian has a well-developed chin, the African Kaffir's slight chin occupying a middle position. Another picture lines up jaws in this order: chimpanzees, Torres Straits Islander, and European, showing a progressive increase in enlargement of the mouth cavity, larger mouths being better vestibules for speech than the parsimonious dental arcade of ape or New Guinean.

The Manchester anatomist Grafton Elliot Smith drew a different genealogy: the Piltdown brain led in one direction to Neanderthal and other primitive extinct and extant peoples (Tasmanian, Australian bushman, Negro), and in another direction to more advanced races (Caucasian). As late as 1939, Sir Arthur Keith wrote (Keith, 1939): "Certainly the prognathism is marked, and although such a full muzzle has never been seen before in a skull that is human, yet the degree of prognathism is not beyond the range found in Australian and African skulls."

In sum, the lower jaw satisfied a general cultural bias of lay and scientific people; it showed Eoanthropus to be like the apes and their lower-rank human counterparts. But the skull showed that this English ancestor was a high-brow, properly unlike the continental and Java cretins. Piltdown Man thus vitalized English national morale and undercut Belgian, German, and French pride of ancestry.

Though Piltdown Man did not illustrate everyone's theory, he had a protean adaptability to many different cultural biases and professional traditions. In an act of retrospective prediction, Darwin had suggested that our ancestor was arboreal, tailed, with prehensile toes and imposing canines, that he was a monkey, and that he came from the African veldt rather than the Sussex weald. The commentators neglected those details, extrapolating only the one about fighting teeth to force a parallel between Piltdown Man and Darwin's guess.

The biases distorted many theories of minor importance and at least three proposed by the most prestigious supporters of Piltdown Man. George Grant MacCurdy, a professor at Yale University, had worked out a "law of mammalian paleontology." As he defined this in *Science* (July 31, 1914), "the permanent teeth of an ancestral race agree more closely in pattern with the milk-teeth than with the permanent teeth of its modified descendants." One would expect in an ancestor not just generalized fighting teeth but fighting teeth that looked like modern baby teeth. The infantile features of the Piltdown canine illustrated that law. "If a comparative anatomist were fitting out Eoanthropus with a set of canines he could not ask for anything more suitable to the tooth in question," wrote MacCurdy.

Woodward and Dawson assumed that the earliest hominid would be Pleistocene; they therefore focused upon the Pleistocene fossils as confirmation. Arthur Keith and Lewis Abbott, however, had theorized that the earliest hominid had been a Pliocene production; the pit supplied evidence for that. An extensive and often acrimonious debate was conducted in those years about whether certain rocks had been flaked by natural action or by prehistoric artisans. These eoliths were (and are) abundant at the Piltdown pit. Abbott thought that Piltdown Man had made them.

The geologist J. Reid Moir believed that the human species had originated in England. He wrote on flint implements retrieved from Kent, Salisbury, and East Anglia. After the finds at the pit, he was satisfied that the eoliths had been made by "the Piltdown person," and took it as proof that our origin was not in misty Asia but on the solid bedrock of England (Moir, 1913, 1917). Lewis Abbott's theory also insisted upon England as the site of the origin of our species. W. J. Sollas, professor of geology at Oxford University, inclined to the theories that human intellectual prowess had appeared early and that structurally the earliest hominids manifested features of both human being and ape. He had seen such features in the Neanderthal specimens (Sollas, 1911). In 1915, the second edition of his *Ancient Hunters* appeared, featuring *Eoanthropus dawsoni* as a rival to Heidelberg as the oldest known European. He praised Woodward, for Teilhard's discovery of the canine tooth vindicated the Woodward-Barlow method; that tooth agreed "in a remarkable manner with the tooth inserted in the restoration, differing only in being a little smaller, more pointed, and less obliquely inclined."

At the very top of the hierarchy of British science stood two people whose authoritative support of Piltdown Man's authenticity helped to legitimize the fake: Arthur Keith (Scottish) and Grafton Elliot Smith (Australian). Arthur Keith, conservator of the Royal College of Surgeons, was a luminary whose acceptance of Eoanthropus as authentic brightened its chances in the world.

Keith, by six years the elder of the two, would write more pages on Piltdown Man than would anyone else. Born in 1866, he graduated at 22 with a medical degree from the University of Aberdeen. Thus starting out his professional career as a physician, he soon revealed a more abiding interest in research than in medical practice. He proceeded through the corridors of the scientific establishment from Fellow of the Royal College of Surgeons to senior demonstrator of anatomy at London Hospital to head of that department. Research, papers, and books on human embryology, cardiology, and anthropology preceded his taking the position of conservator of the Royal College of Surgeons Museum in 1908. His *Introduction to the Study of Anthropoid Apes* had been published in 1897.

Keith thought that human beings had existed with about the same cranial capacity and face since the Pliocene. This theoretical bias encouraged his accepting Galley Hill Man as a credible prehistoric hominid buried during the Pliocene or early Pleistocene. The fact that the skeleton had a globular skull competent to room a brain of modern grandeur, far from dissuading certification, encouraged it. But Keith had few allies eager to accept Galley Hill Man as an ancient burial. Lewis Abbott was one of the few. He therefore looked forward to a specimen that would better illustrate his theory.

Rumors had reached Keith before the Geological Society meeting in December 1912 that the British Museum harbored interesting hominid fossils dug up from a gravel pit in Piltdown. He was jealous because he had hoped that the Royal College of Surgeons would have been chosen as the repository for such fossils of ancient man. Woodward allowed him to visit the fossils for twenty minutes. Given his theoretical assumption that the earliest hominid would be very like the latest, one would expect that he would disagree with the Woodward-Barlow model's showing a cranial capacity of only 1070 cc.

He also disagreed with the reconstruction of the jaw, believing that Woodward and Barlow had made it too apelike, the canine tooth so massive that it would have inhibited the free lateral motion of human mastication. After Teilhard had found a real canine, Keith changed his mind: though perplexing, it was more reasonable to assume that the jaw had belonged to the possessor of the cranium than that a coincidence had occurred. But the canine hadn't come from that jaw. The jaw's third molar had not yet erupted, which meant that the jaw was young. The wear of the canine suggested that it was old and therefore that it had come from some other eoanthropine specimen's jaw.

He disagreed on some other, less important points. He argued that the skull should have been reconstructed as symmetrical and that its bearer had been male. But he was mostly gratified by Piltdown Man and decided to write a book on it. The book appeared in 1915, *The Antiquity of Man,* its cover embossed with a gilt portrait of Piltdown Man, his favorite hominid occupying a volume and a half of the text. He deplored the delapidation of other ancient hominids into gravel to mend roads.

He made a reconstruction to rival that of Woodward and Barlow. He adjusted the angle of the cranial bones to open the skull for an additional 400 cc of brain, and he curved out the dental arcade more toward human divergency. The Keith reconstruction then was of a Piltdown Man more modernly human than the Woodward-Barlow model. To counter criticism, he submitted to a test: he put together pieces of a skull that had been whole and had been measured before being fractured; his guess that the original had had a cranial capacity of 1415 cc was almost exactly right (it had contained 1395 cc of brain).

The second high authority supporting Piltdown was Grafton Elliot Smith. Born in Australia, Smith had begun his research on the brain while studying for a medical degree at the University of Sydney. He lived in England for a while before taking a post, in 1900, at the Government School of Medicine in Cairo, shortly before Teilhard de Chardin arrived in that city. His work in Egypt included the autopsy of mummies and investigation of the pyramids, and he became deeply interested in Egyptology. He theorized on cultural diffusion, that civilization had radiated out from Egypt, a theory attested to, in his opinion, by congruent practices all over the world in embalming and monument-building.

In 1909, two years after election to the Royal Society, Smith returned to England, where he continued work on Nubian skeletons and, as professor of anatomy at Victoria University, Manchester, on neurology. He was well known in his own time for his studies of Egypt, his theory on the diffusion of culture, and his research on the evolution of the brain. Pugnacious and witty and learned, he was as ready to defend Eoanthropus as his hero, Thomas Henry Huxley, had defended Darwin.

Piltdown Man satisfied the theories of Lewis Abbott and of Grafton Elliot Smith better than it did anyone else's. In 1912, at the Dundee meeting of the BAAS, Smith, then president of the Anthropological Section, hazarded a prediction: available evidence sketching human genealogy back a million years shows that, in human evolution, the unquestionable and tangible factor is the "steady and uniform development of the brain along a well-defined course throughout the primates right up to man." The brain came first, developing toward humanness before the hands did, before the advent of upright posture, before speech. Thus, if a very early hominid should be found, it would have a brain halfway between a pithecanthropine's and a modern human being's. It would also be apelike. It could very well have large canines.

After the Geological Society announcement of December 1912, Smith acknowledged that he had predicted Piltdown Man's cranial anatomy "some months before I knew of the existence of the Piltdown skull, when I argued that in the evolution of the development of man the brain must have led the way." He found the association of a human skull that had primitive simian features with an ape jaw of advanced human features just right and commended the Woodward-Barlow reconstruction for its design of a brain of only 1070 cc.

He was delighted by later finds also, especially by that of the canine tooth.

Just as the young child still uses its teeth for purposes of attack, so in the dawn of human existence teeth suitable for offensive purpose were retained long after the brain had attained its distinctively human status and had made the hands even more serviceable instruments for attack. ("The Piltdown Skull," 1913)

His talk to the Literary and Philosophical Society of Manchester on the controversies (summarized in *Nature,* December 18, 1913) was picked up by *Current Opinion* (also December 1913), "The Controversy over the Discovery of 'Dawn Man,' " which solved the controversy by stating that it was permissible to associate a human skull and ape jaw. Evolutionary theory had prepared us for just that.

An example of how Eoanthropus could be shaped to fit different theoretical assumptions comes through in a dispute between Arthur Keith and Grafton Elliot Smith, a dispute that thrilled the pages of scientific journals for three decades.

At a meeting of the Royal College of Surgeons, at a Royal Society meeting, and in the exchange of views in *Nature* throughout 1913 and 1914, Keith and Smith (Smith seconded by Woodward and Dawson) argued about whether the Piltdown cranial capacity had been 1350 cc or 1070 and about the shape and symmetry of the brain. They continued reviewing the Piltdown material for the rest of their lives, Keith returning to a final reconstruction twenty years later. He confirmed a cranial capacity of 1350 cc but deduced that the brain had been, like the modern, asymmetrical. Smith defended the virtue of Eoanthropus in interviews, articles, letters, monographs, books, writing more pieces on Piltdown Man than anyone else did, and revising his defensive tactics as paleontologists found new material and formulated new theories. Though the two continued to disagree, they held fast to the belief that Piltdown Man was an authentic hominid. Both were knighted for their services to the nation.

Dawson carefully observed the quarrel between Keith and Smith. In letters of 1913, he recognized that "it will be very awkward if a considerable error has been made about the capacity of the skull," arguing that the thickness of the cranial walls necessitated a low cranial capacity; that Keith was unfair, holding a grudge against Woodward, going about "looking for trouble." He recommended Smith's interpretation as a "splendid manifesto." Still on the prowl for other missing links, Dawson thought he had found one in the camp of the enemy, Arthur Keith. "Since I last saw you," he wrote to Woodward, "I have been writing on the subject of 'the 13th dorsal vertebra' in certain human skeletons, which I believe is a new subject." He sent along the results of this investigation, asking Woodward to introduce the paper to the Royal Society.

I am very anxious to get it placed at once because I have had to work the photographs under the nose of Keith and his assistant. I gather from the latter person that Keith is rather puzzled as to what to make of it all, and I want to secure the priority to which I am entitled. (May 12, 1912)

Human beings don't have a 13th dorsal vertebra.

The synopsis of where Piltdown Man stood at the end of 1912, that drawn by Smith in his December 1913 talk to the Literary and Philosophical Society of Manchester, is useful because it shows what most British scientists believed at the time and because, by negating each of the statements, we can arrive at an equally clear understanding of what no one believes anymore.

1. The fossils were almost certainly Pleistocene.

2. The jaw was not an ape's for it contained human teeth.

3. The skull was that of a primitive human being.

4. The canine discovery settled once and for all the validity of Woodward's reconstruction of jaw and teeth.

5. The brain capacity of Eoanthropus was no more than 1100 cc.

6. Eoanthropus was a legitimate new genus, ancestral to Heidelberg and to modern human beings.

A good deal of luck attended the rise of Piltdown Man—a geological survey of the Piltdown area had come up with a mistaken Pleistocene age; Sam Woodhead had analyzed the cranial fragments for organic content, finding none; but he had failed to analyze the jawbone. X-rays had been taken of the molar roots, but at the wrong angle. That investigators had limited or no access to the real fossils meant that they would miss gross points, such as the disharmony in weight between cranial pieces (which were well mineralized) and mandible (which wasn't). The hoaxer may not have been a genius; but he knew his subject well enough to produce a plausible phony with intriguing connections to Neanderthals, pithecanthropines, apes, and contemporary citizens. Scientists had fun in tracing out these connections. Cultural biases of phrenology and racism warmed the climate for acceptance, and those theories promulgated by esteemed scientists (Woodward, Moir, Sollas, Keith, Smith) as well as by those occupying a lower professional level (Butterfield of the Hastings Museum, Pycraft of the British Museum) and those of productive amateurs (Dawson and Abbott) were bolstered by *Eoanthropus dawsoni*. But not everyone approved.

CHAPTER THREE

THE SKEPTICS

In 1914, Arthur Keith said "the Piltdown remains have been universally accepted as ancient and authentic." People familiar with the case today assume that, in 1914, Piltdown Man was in fact universally accepted. But that is not the way it was.

BRITISH SKEPTICS

Most British scientists accepted the fossil as a very old and singularly single hominid being, but not all. The finders themselves did not accept everything uncritically. Dawson didn't believe that the eoliths in the pit had been instruments made by *Eoanthropus,* despite pressure from Lewis Abbott to interpret them as such. Woodward intermittently distrusted his earliest Englishman. Piltdown Man did not fit into accepted evolutionary models. In a paper read before the Geological Society on April 29, 1914, Woodward said that in the gradational series from the fossil primates *Mesopithecus* to *Dryopithecus* to Heidelberg Man "there appears to be no place for a stage resembling that of any adult existing Ape. It is difficult even to understand how *Eoanthropus* can be one of the series" (Woodward, 1914).

What the third digger, Teilhard de Chardin, thought about the fossil's authenticity, his letters do not reveal. If either Dawson, Woodward, or Teilhard were the Piltdown hoaxer, then of course whatever faint skepticism they expressed was just part of the charade.

E. Ray Lankester, director (1898-1907) of the British Museum (Natural History), a professional biologist and an esteemed popularizer of science, supported some aspects of the find and denied others. After the first Geological Society meeting on the discovery, Lankester admitted the importance of the find, but then said that having visited the pit and examined skull fragments and jaw, he was not certain that those remnants had been the apparatus of a single individual, and he would draw no conclusion about their age. In "The Missing Link" (Lankester, 1915), however, he came out for unity of cranium and jaw but did not believe that Eoanthropus had made the tools. He remained baffled.

Arthur Keith, uneasy about the fit between so apelike a jaw and so human a skull, was among the hundred or so Geological Association members who toured the pit in July 1913. He and a Major Marriott went to visit a bank clerk and ornithologist named Harry Morris. In his autobiography, Keith recalled that Morris was so annoyed at the "acclamation" given to Dawson and his own "neglect" that he gave expression to a "sour" skepticism about the whole affair. Morris did not tell his visitors that he had been writing memoranda to himself and hiding them in a cabinet full of flints.

A *British Dental Journal* article, "The Piltdown Skull" (1913) punned, "Veritably a bone of contention, this interesting anthropological document is still a matter of lively discussion." Two events illustrating this remark constitute the most important documents of British skepticism about Piltdown Man.

The first was a single column article that appeared in *Nature* in November 1913. David Waterston, a professor of anatomy at King's

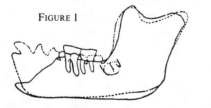
FIGURE 1

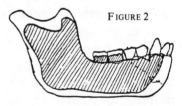
FIGURE 2

Waterston's jaws. These two drawings illustrate David Waterston's. contention that the lower jaw found in the pit was an ape's. Figure 1 imposes a radiogram tracing of a chimpanzee jaw (broken line) upon the unreconstructed Piltdown jaw (continuous line). Figure 2 imposes a tracing of the reconstructed Piltdown Man jaw upon the jaw of a chimpanzee (shaded). (From Waterston [1913].)

College, took issue with the supposition that the skull and jaw had belonged to the same individual. According to Waterston, radiograms taken of the mandible proved it to be simply an ape's.

> No human mandible is known which shows anything like the same resemblance to the chimpanzee jaw in outline and in all its details. Of

the molar teeth, I need only say here that not only do they approach the ape form, but in several respects are identical with them. The cranial fragments of the Piltdown skull, on the other hand, are in practically all their details essentially human. If that be so, it seems to me to be as inconsequent to refer the mandible and the cranium to the same individual as it would be to articulate a chimpanzee's foot with the bones of an essentially human thigh and leg. (Waterston, 1913)

The analogy is not dramatic but the point is clear enough: the supporters of Piltdown Man's authenticity had made a bad mistake. If Waterston's view was correct, then Piltdown Man would have been only an old human skull accidentally allied with an ape's jaw, of no more significance than any of the other hominid fossils dug up in the United Kingdom.

The next skirmish is a one-act farce, the protagonist a dental anatomist anxious to prove to a panel of Piltdown fans that the canine tooth could not have been as described. The skeletal summary given below can be fleshed out with images of panelists yawning, grunting, and now and then displaying their own canines.

Scene: Odontological Section of the Royal Society

Date: January 24, 1916

Speaker: Dr. Courtney W. Lyne

Title: The Significance of the Radiographs of the Piltdown Teeth

Panelists: Dr. Arthur Smith Woodward, Professor Arthur Keith, Professor Arthur Underwood, Professor Grafton Elliot Smith, Mr. Pycraft, et al.

Dr. Lyne noted that in all animals from iguanadons and salamandrine labyrinthrodonts to dogs and chimpanzees and people, the pulp invariably diminishes with advancing age. The large pulp (and heavy dentine formation) of the Piltdown canine tooth indicated that its possessor was young. Yet the sagittal sutures of the skull had closed, which indicated that the being was mature. Dr. Lyne marveled at this prodigy, mature in the head and juvenile in the tooth.

He expressed his bafflement at the next incongruity, between the mandibular fossa, of a kind that would hold a free-swinging human jaw, and the canine, which being raised above the level of the other teeth would have prevented such rotary freedom. Even worse, in the reconstruction the canine was already raised high, which meant that the permanent tooth replacing it would have projected even more, more than in any known anthropoid: "The act of yawning with such articular mobility and with projecting canines would be one which Piltdown Man would not be likely to indulge in with pleasure."

In human beings, the permanent canines erupt before the permanent molars; a study of Piltdown dentition shows that its permanent canines erupted after the permanent molars. The Piltdown canine was a milk tooth, as shown by its large pulp; in the orangutan's mouth, the milk canine is still in place when the second permanent molar has erupted. Since in the Piltdown jaw, the canine was a milk tooth and the molars permanent, the sequence of eruption demonstrated that the jaw was an ape's and not a person's. Lyne suspected that the canine did not belong to that jaw and that that jaw did not belong to that skull. But he had hopes for future clarification of this exceedingly strange contraption: "The loom of Time may yet weave for us the sure features of this creature."

Woodward rose for the first rebuttal: It was impossible that a unique primate skull would be found in the same deposit as a unique primate jawbone and a unique primate tooth.

Keith acknowledged that the pulp cavity does steadily decrease with age, that there was a problem of compatibility between human mandibular fossa and ape canine, and that the degree and kind of wear of the canine were out of keeping with the other fragments. But you can't argue against the empirical evidence.

Underwood proposed that the canine was not a milk tooth, but an elderly permanent tooth, so old that its surface tissue had been worn away and a hole punctured right into the pulp cavity.

Smith wryly observed that Keith had opted for a canine older than the molars and that Lyne had opted for one younger. Lyne had forgotten that no fossil apes had been found from Pleistocene England. He drags in a hypothetical ape.

Lyne retaliated that the unfortunate animal could not have shut its mouth.

The establishment, through *Nature,* reiterated the litany of defense (a Piltdown note, June 8, 1916):

We are of opinion that future discovery will show that all three specimens are, as Dr. Smith Woodward inferred, parts of one individual, or at least of individuals of one species. A closer acquaintance with the anatomy of anthropoid apes will reveal many similar incongruities in their structure. If mankind has been evolved from an anthropoid stock the occurrence of a combination of human and anthropoid characteristics in earlier or dawn human forms, such as occur in Eoanthropus, is just what we ought to find.

YANKEE SKEPTICS

It certainly wasn't enough to cause even a hairline fracture in the Anglo-American alliance, but the controversy taking place in paleontology assumed the dimensions of a fight between English *Nature* and American *Science*. *Nature* had backup from the British Museum of Natural History. But *Science* could look over its shoulder and see a comforting platoon of skeptics inducted from the Smithsonian Institution, the American Museum of Natural History, and Yale University.

A research scientist at the Smithsonian Institution undertook the most exhaustive and destructive analysis of the creature. Its result could have been the decisive dissociation of cranium and jaw and the evaporation of Piltdown Man.

Gerrit S. Miller, Jr., in his "Jaw of the Piltdown Man," published in November 1915, did not try to unravel the Piltdown knot. He cut it. Having borrowed casts of the Piltdown fossils from Aleš Hrdlička, Miller proceeded to compare the mandible with those of 22 chimpanzees, 23 gorillas, and 75 orangutans, a populous apiary. He began the process of dissolving Piltdown Man as a unified being by expressing his disappointment that the condyle was missing: "Deliberate malice could hardly have been more successful than the hazards of deposition in so breaking the fossils as to give free scope to individual judgment in fitting the parts together." Miller categorized three kinds of evidence authenticating Piltdown Man.

1. The distributional evidence showed that no ape fossils had ever been found in England, from which one could deduce, as Smith and Gregory did, that the jawbone therefore had to be human. Miller said that an ape could have existed in England, the paleontological record is scanty, and a tooth that was like the first molar of a chimpanzee had been found in 1895 in Taubach, Saxe-Weimer.

2. The paleontological evidence was that the relics had been found close together. But finding relics close together does not compel the conclusion that they had come from the same source.

3. The third kind of evidence, the anatomical, took up most of Miller's analysis. This analysis is extremely detailed and without flab; its style is sharp, clear, at times elegant; and its thesis, hindsight proves, correct. Miller's procedure foreshadowed that of the paleontological sleuthing of mid-century.

Anyone could have seen, and everyone did see, that the jaw owned a simian shelf but not a condyle. Miller did not focus on such gross structures. He measured the curvature of the dental arcade and jaw, the borders of the molars, the smoothness of the enamel, the elevation of the mylohyoid ridge, the very cusps and the depressions between them, and he concluded that in every specific diagnostic feature the jaw was not like that of an ape's.

It was an ape's.

There was a sentiment in the scientific world that what Woodward and company had wedded, nobody ought to sunder. Miller split the contraption apart and told a new story. He assigned the cranium to a hominid Eoanthropus all right, but the jaw, which was in the regular flattening of the molar occlusal surfaces too highly unusual even for extant chimpanzee teeth, to a British extinct Pliocene ape, for which he invented the name *Pan vetus.*

Unlike Courtney Lyne, whose critique was pummeled into dust, Miller was influential. George Grant MacCurdy of Yale University had said in an *American Anthropologist* article in 1913 that he believed southern England to be the locale for prehistoric hominids; Sussex valley deposits were just the place, and so he had been prepared for Piltdown Man, skull and jaw intermediate between Heidelberg and a young chimpanzee. But after Miller's iconoclastic exploit, MacCurdy wrote "Nature has set many a trap for the scientist; but here at Piltdown she outdid herself in the concatenation of pitfalls left behind" (MacCurdy, 1916): parts of a human skull, apelike lower jaw and canine, flints of pre-Chellean type, some Pliocene fossils, some Pleistocene. Like Miller, MacCurdy discounted proximity:

> Association can never be made to take the place of articulation; and so far as Piltdown is concerned, nothing short of the actual articulation of the mandible with the skull should have sufficed to outweigh the lack of harmony existing between these parts.

He classified the cranium as *Homo dawsoni,* a member not of a new genus but merely of a new species; and the jaw and canine as part of a fossil chimp. His analysis relied on Lankester, Waterston, continental paleontologists, and Miller. The conclusion of the article was a salve to calm the sting hurting British fans: "As for the man of Piltdown, he still exists and is quite as ancient as he was before the revision, which is saying a good deal; even if he is robbed of a muzzle that ill became him." He would later replace the muzzle.

Miller also influenced staff members of the American Museum of Natural History. In one of his letters home, Teilhard de Chardin wrote that he had met a "certain" Gregory while staying with Woodward in London. In 1914, William King Gregory published an article that repeated the hoary paleontological syllogism: no apes had existed in Pleistocene England; an ape's jawbone had been found in an English Pleistocene deposit; therefore the jawbone was consistent with the cranium.

But anatomical reasoning suggested it could not be. The uninhabited alveolus for the third (and missing) molar suggested that that molar would have been too large for a human mouth. The inner side of the chin region lacked genial tubercles (genial not meaning friendly, but pertaining to the chin; and tubercles meaning small tubers, or bumps) for attachment of the genioglossus muscle of the tongue. The canine did not seem to belong to that lower jaw. Perhaps it was not a right lower canine, but a left upper. And, if that was so, then "its wearing surface is such that the first lower bicuspid which occluded with it must have been elongate and prominent and much more anthropoid than human in shape." Gregory was also troubled about what he thought the most controversial part of the Piltdown find: the size of the braincase.

This skepticism was invigorated by Miller's analysis. For the *American Anthropologist*, Gregory wrote a "Note on the Molar Teeth of the Piltdown Mandible" (1916). Paying his respects to Miller, he argued in favor of a "generic identity" between the Piltdown jaw and teeth and those of a chimpanzee. Gregory listed MacCurdy and W. D. Matthew as American skeptics. Gregory, Matthew, and C. R. Eastman co-authored a short article, "Recent Progress in Vertebrate Paleontology." Matthew here called Miller's argument "irrefutable." "It is hardly to be expected, however," they warned, "that this conclusion will be readily accepted by the European writers."

Gregory's boss, Henry Fairfield Osborn, president of the American Museum of Natural History, was also a mild skeptic at that time. His *Men of the Old Stone Age* (1915) described the small and broad nasal bones as typically human, like those of primitive Malay and African faces; the jaw typically ape, except for its molar teeth, though even these "approach the dentition of the apes in their elongate shape and well-developed fifth cusps"; and Piltdown Man unrelated to Heidelberg or Neanderthals or "any of the existing species of man." It was a side-branch and went extinct. In the reconstruction by Professor J. H. McGregor, which Osborn reproduced, a better synthesis of human and ape was achieved by placing the canine as left upper, curving the dental arch, and deepening the chin, reducing the beastly prognathism of Woodward's reconstruction.

Osborn was unsure whether Piltdown Man was a unified being. Seemed as though the jaw was that of an ape, the skull that of a Britisher. The Britisher Arthur Keith didn't care for the compliment. "From a British point of view," Keith wrote in his 1917 review of Osborn's *Men of the Old Stone Age,* "our author is all at sea as regards the discovery of Piltdown." The cranium and jaw agree in their texture and fossilization and size, and the teeth, Keith under pressure asserted more strongly than usual, are "as unlike chimpanzee teeth as teeth can be." He chided that Osborn could not blame his British allies "if they fail to give his judgment that due which his great services to palaeontology should naturally demand from them" for he "has done less than justice to the work and opinions of his British colleagues." In a review of Keith's *The Antiquity of Man* (1915), the American anthropologist William Wright complimented Keith for his willingness to sacrifice theory to facts, but declined to compliment Piltdown Man for anything. To the other incongruities, Wright added one between molars that are human and a canine that is simian.

Miller's argument seduced an English authority into the camp of the skeptics—P. Chalmers Mitchell, who rejected the new hypothesized ape but approved of Miller's confirming "the doubt already stated by many investigators" about compatibility of jaw and cranium. W. J. Sollas, however, maintained that since the two parts had been found rubbing elbows with each other, and agreed nicely anatomically, the chance of their having come from different sources was "unworthy of serious consideration." W. P. Pycraft cooked up the most peppery rebuttal to Miller and spiced it with rhetoric about the American's dogmatic statements, warped judgment, and distortions of fact. It is obvious, his January 1917 article in *Science Progress* insisted, that the Piltdown jaw was more like a human's (e.g., the Kaffir's) than like an ape's and that the Piltdown molars showed a surface at right angles to the vertical axis of the tooth, a feature of human teeth. The three tubercles on the Piltdown molars, the thickening of the enamel, and the wear on the molar occlusal surface are all more human than simian. Miller's reply to Pycraft's reply demonstrated that the tubercles, enamel thickening, and occlusal wear are features of orangutan molars.

CONTINENTAL SKEPTICS

In continental Europe, Piltdown Man was tolerated in the professional literature without great enthusiasm. Professor MacCurdy, in his 1924 review (in *Human Origins*) of continental reception, generalized: "Objections soon came from France and Italy."

G. Sergi's "La mandibola umana," *Revista di Antropologia* (1914) accepts Piltdown Man as authentic. Other Italian writers were respectfully but steadily skeptical. Influenced by Miller, V. Giuffrida-Ruggeri wrote in his 1918 *L'Uomo Attuale una Specie Collettiva* that Piltdown Man was a doubtful specimen. It took some virtuosity to connect a human cranium with a monkeylike jaw, *"nonche il canino"*—not to mention the canine. No one could know what it all meant. The most thorough of the Italian works was Nello Puccioni's *Appunti in torno al frammento manibolare fossile di Piltdown (Sussex)* (1913). Puccioni was discontented with Woodward's reconstruction of the jaw because it was neither simian nor Neanderthal. Too crude to harmonize with the relatively fine features of the cranium—*"né carne né pesce,"* neither fish nor fowl, it remained questionable whether it could enter the family of the Hominidae. He cites Lankester and Waterston in support of his opinion that the jaw and the cranium belonged to two distinct individuals. A Spanish work, Hugo Obermeier's *El hombre fosil,* also questioned the feasibility of imposing harmony.

R. Anthony, in a *Revue anthropologique* article of September 1913 *("Les restes humains fossiles de Piltdown")* took Keith's side in the dispute about cranial capacity, but said he would prefer Piltdown Man as a member of our own genus *(Homo dawsoni).* In 1912, Boule shared the opinion of Dawson and Woodward on the unity of Eoanthropus. Then he read Miller. In his 1915 *La Paleontologie humaine en Angleterre,* he recommended that, since the jaw was exactly that of a chimpanzee, it should be removed from the cranium and given the name of a hypothetical extinct ape, *Troglodytes dawsoni.* He professed his duty to be that of a skeptic concerned about the integrity of his science.

A Dutch commentator, Professor H. V. Buttle-Reeper, in *Man and His Forerunners,* maintained that Piltdown Man was Neanderthal, its front teeth more human than Woodward had assumed. A Danish commentator, M. Ramstrom, influenced by Miller, in 1919 published "Der Piltdown-Fund," which swirls in the complex riddles of uncertain discoveries, incomplete reports, and antagonistic interpretations. Ramstrom can't figure any of it out. "Who is right?" he queries. "Who stands on firm ground?" "This, then, is the real evidence?" After praising the dynamic and purposeful research, he leaves us with an intriguing diagnosis: "Probably some of the conclusions and theories are correct; one just doesn't know which ones."

An objective poll of the international scientific community in the four years after the Geological Society announcement fails to validate the widespread opinion that this community was fooled by Piltdown Man. Some, mostly British, were impassioned advocates, such as Keith, Smith, Sollas, and Pycraft, seconded by some continentals. But many continental, and most American, scientists were skeptical.

In the winter of 1912-1913, Woodward exhibited the reconstructed skull to the International Congress of Medicine, which met in Dublin. The *Dublin Daily Express* on August 13 inferred that a serious mistake had been made in the interpretations of Pithecanthropus and Eoanthropus. "Both creatures present curious combinations of ape-like and man-like features; but as the points that are man-like in the one are ape-like in the other, and vice versa, it follows that their claims to stand in the line of human ancestry would be mutually destructive." Pithecanthropus is probably the valid ancestor, for the Piltdown skull is only that of a human being, at best a racial variety *(Homo piltdownensis)*. Labeling it as a new genus (Eoanthropus) involves "great biological heresy." Professor Keith is mistaken in trying to force the lower jaw into conformity with the skull and in claiming a great antiquity for the combination. "It is certainly strange," this remarkably prescient report continued, "that if the Sussex skull belongs to a race that had inhabited Western Europe for a million or a million and a half years down to the birth of modern man, we have no other skull of the type it represents to match the Piltdown specimen."

As though in direct response to that, from the debris of another site rose the Son of Piltdown Man.

CHAPTER FOUR

BETWEEN THE WARS

Without being oversentimental, we can sympathize with the many experts conned by Piltdown man. And we should keep in mind that Woodward and the others did exemplary work in their sciences. The American paleontologist George Gaylord Simpson, in reply to my inquiry about his views on Piltdown, reminded me that Piltdown was the only great mistake of Woodward's life. Simpson, who knew Woodward, said he was happy that his friend had never known that Piltdown Man was a hoax and disgusted that Woodward is remembered for the mistake and not for his scientific successes (Private communication, September 21, 1984).

The find of a second eoanthropine elsewhere, some months after the pit had gone sterile, was a blow to skepticism. As Woodward and Sollas emphasized, a coincidence of human skull and ape jawbone could have happened at one site; but for it to happen again elsewhere strained incredulity. The period between the world wars served up, year after year, one hominid fossil after another, each of which should have sent Piltdown Man packing. Yet his defenders held on with a tenacity that does not evoke respect. What happened between the wars is not complimentary to Woodward, Hooton, Smith, or Keith.

At Barcombe Mills, near Piltdown, Dawson found fragments of several cranial bones and a molar tooth stained the same color as the Piltdown remains; but all these were modern. Still, he was lucky or crafty. The Sussex weald is not littered with old bones. When he went visiting other sites with Woodward (as he did in 1914), he never found anything. He did find important things at another site, and they are known, but just where and with whom are not known.

PILTDOWN MAN, JR.

Dawson did not identify the site that was the birthplace of Piltdown Man, Jr. Sheffield Park, fields and a superb garden, two miles north of Piltdown Common, has regularly been assumed to have been that site. A footnote in H. J. Osborne White's 1926 *Geology of the Country Near Lewes* corrects this wrong assumption:

> In response to an enquiry, Sir A. Smith Woodward states (in let. 28th Oct. 1924) that the situation of this field was never revealed to him, but he is satisfied that it is "somewhere on Mr. John Martin's Netherhall farm . . . near Chailey (or Fletching) Common."

At the beginning of 1915, Dawson wrote to Woodward:

> I believe we are in luck again! I have got a fragment of the left side of a parietal bone with portion of the orbit and root of nose. Its outline is nearly the same as your original reconstruction and being another individual the difference is very slight. (January 9, 1915)

He also found a fragment of an occipital bone.

Seven months later, Dawson casually informed Woodward of a subsequent find at Site II, an eoanthropine molar tooth "just the same as the others as to wear." The booty included a fragment of a rhinoceros molar as well, an index to the dating of the human pieces.

In October 1915, Dawson became ill with septicemia, and by February 1916 was to have an injection of serum that he thought would make him "worse, temporarily." The treatment was not successful; he lingered on for another six months and died in August 1916. Throughout this time, Woodward did nothing about reporting the confirmatory find of the new ape-man. On February 28, 1917, he finally announced Dawson's discovery to the Geological Society. Thus, more than two years went by from the time of Dawson's first mentioning the Site II frontal bone to the announcement, while defenders and skeptics bashed each other over Piltdown Man, unaware that another waited in the wings to play out his filial role.

In his "Fourth Note on the Piltdown Gravel, with Evidence of a Second Skull of *Eoanthropus dawsoni*" (1914, the year the pit went sterile), Woodward shaped the isolated molar tooth into a weapon against Miller. Comparison of this new tooth with corresponding molars of "a Melanesian, a Tasmanian, and a Chimpanzee, of approximately the same

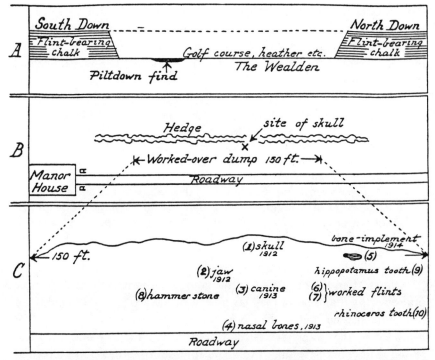

The Pit in its environs. After converting, Osborn wrote "The Dawn Man of Sussex," which pictures the pit: (A) Lateral view, the pit between the downs. (B) Overhead view of pit between roadway and hedge. (C) Close-up overhead view, with some finds and dates. (From Osborn [1921].)

size" showed that it was essentially human. The portion of frontal bone was as thick as the comparable piece from the Piltdown pit's cranium. Grafton Elliot Smith composed an appendix for Woodward's paper on the endocranial cast of the Piltdown skull.

Meticulous Ray Lankester demurred again. He thought it possible that the piece of frontal bone and the molar had come from the same individual whose cranium and jaw had been found in the pit. He did not speculate on how the pieces had traveled.

Piltdown Man, Jr., frontal and occipital bones and single molar, snared three American skeptics. After a service at Westminster Abbey in 1921, Henry Fairfield Osborn made a pilgrimage to South Kensington to visit the relics from the pit and Site II. Woodward removed them from a steel safe—protection from German bombers past and future—and placed the Piltdown men on the table. Osborn spent two hours closely examining the family resemblances of Senior and Junior. He recanted, the experience expressed by a prayer from Princeton college days to the effect that, though it appeared paradoxical, "O Lord, it is nevertheless true," confessing the awesome conversion to readers of his 1921 "The Dawn Man of Piltdown, Sussex":

> If there is a Providence hanging over the affairs of prehistoric men, it certainly manifested itself in this case, because the three minute fragments of this second Piltdown Dawn Man found by Dawson are exactly those which we would have selected to confirm the comparison with the original type, namely: (1) a first lower molar tooth, (2) a bit of bone of the forehead near the right eyebrow, (3) the middle part of an occipital bone of the skull. Both the grinding tooth and the eyebrow region are absolutely distinctive. Placed side by side with the corresponding fossils of the first Piltdown Man they agree precisely; there is not a shadow of difference.

No story in the history of anthropology, Osborn exclaimed, is more praiseworthy than that of the Dawn Man of Sussex. In his mea culpa for past infidelity he said he had been wrong about the canine, too—that belonged to the lower jaw; he had been wrong about Woodward, and Woodward could have said, I told you so. Osborn settled on Piltdown as closer to the human line than was Neanderthal (Osborn, 1928).

In 1922, Osborn interpreted a single tooth found in Nebraska as that of a new anthropoid, which he named *Hesperopithecus haroldcookii,* and which turned out to be the tooth of a prehistoric pig (Blinderman, 1985).

In that year, too, George Grant MacCurdy, who was at our last view of him an ally of Miller, went on his pilgrimage to South Kensington. Although repeating his dictum that "association can never be made to take the place of articulation," he now contended that "the Piltdown lower jaw is seen to be intermediate between the lower jaw of Heidelberg and that of a young chimpanzee." What led him to this revision was the improbability of another accidental association of parts at Site II; association at two different sites can be made to take the place of articulation. As for the simian shelf that had not appeared in any hominid jaw before, well, "one must invoke a wider range of individual variation within the genus Homo (Eoanthropus included) than has hitherto been considered ample" (MacCurdy, 1924). Piltdown Man, Jr., also converted William King Gregory (Gregory, 1929).

In 1924, upon retiring from the British Museum of Natural History, Sir Arthur Smith Woodward bought a home in Haywards Heath, Sussex.

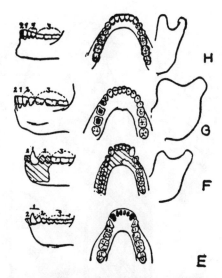

Gregory: Evolution of Primate Jaw. W. K. Gregory, like Osborn, moved from skepticism about Piltdown Man to a belief in his authenticity. (F) Piltdown jaw between (E) human-like anthropoid jaw and (G) primitive human jaw. (H) Modern. (From Gregory [1929].)

From his home, Woodward wandered out to the pit, dug, sifted, and satisfied his nostalgia for the gravel by peering at it through a magnifying glass. The Piltdown romance still had powers to charm. It had been a splendid episode, the hours of hard labor rewarded by the excitement of another bony fragment, the friendship, above all the putting together of pieces of a missing link so credible that opposition like that of Osborn, MacCurdy, and Gregory shook in its foreign boots.

Woodward often talked with the novelist Ernest Raymond about the good old days, about the "brown old coconut" that had grown into so fruitful a tree. H. G. Wells had estimated in his *Short History of the World* that by 1920 more than a hundred papers and books had discussed Piltdown Man. The Sussex hominid may then have received as much attention as all other fossil hominids put together.

Woodward fondly recalled that time when a member of a Lewes audience, upon being shown a slide of Piltdown Man, shrugged away the wondrous creature with a "You could meet chaps like that in Lewes any day." Though Sir Arthur persevered for years with his pick, his sieve, and his magnifying glass, the pit had gone out with Dawson. Woodward and Raymond found an unremarkable trilobite and a bone fragment of some contemporary animal. Seven years after he had moved to Sussex, Wood-

"THE CEREBRAL FORMATION INSIGNIFICANT; THE
JAW SUPERB"

Party Politician: "See how even in this distant progenitor of ours we may trace those traits which, evolving through the ages, reach their almost divine development in us." (From the *Herald* (Swansea, Wales); reproduced in *American Review of Reviews* ["England's Most Ancient Inhabitant," 1913].)

ward found a sheep's tooth.

No books entirely on Piltdown Man came out in the 1920s (or 1930s), but he was a minor object of attention in the third and expanded edition of Sollas's *Ancient Hunters* (1924), a little more important in Smith's *The Evolution of Man* (1924), and still the major character of Keith's *The Antiquity of Man* (2nd ed, 1925). These books, of course, all upheld him. But attacks were coming from two directions: from fundamentalism and from science. In the scientific community, from 1917 to mid-century some investigators continued the approach that Miller had taken in performing an autopsy upon the remains. More important, however, were fossil hominid finds that showed Eoanthropus to be not an anomaly, but a mistake.

A GENTLEMAN OF QUALITY

Priority in a public statement that Piltdown Man was a hoax may go to an American fundamentalist. The Bible not only does not say anything about transmutation of ape into human being; it explicitly rejects the theory that kinds (or species) can evolve into other kinds. Apes are apes and people are people, and an ape-man is as incredible as a merman.

Who would want an ape or an ape-man for an ancestor anyway? Apes could be seen at their disgusting antics in any zoo. And people of the first generation of the twentieth century had many examples of what we would be like if we had that depraved ape within us, examples (a small selection) from Tennyson, Robert Louis Stevenson, and the Italian criminologist Cesare Lombroso, who scientifically proved that the ape throbs in the atavist of enormous jaws, strong canines, and prognathous snout, prognathism appearing in 95 percent of criminals.

The ape-man crawled his way from a cave in the Neander valley through a descriptive paper by T. H. Huxley, who once publicly claimed that he would prefer to have an ape for a grandfather than a certain bishop, into Lombroso and out of *Criminal Man* into the novel *McTeague* by Frank Norris. The hero's jaw is "salient, like that of the carnivora." Fighting teeth are the central symbol of this naturalistic novel. Trina's birthday gift to McTeague is a "tooth of a gigantic fossil, golden and dazzling," hung outside as an advertisement for the dental office; in a brawl, a character bites McTeague's earlobe; and McTeague himself, to extort money from Trina, to punish her, or just for the sheer joy of it, bites Trina's fingers so zealously that they have to be amputated.

Piltdown Man's features, a thick skull, a prognathous jaw, and fighting teeth, made him the darling of the evolutionists, but the bête noire of the fundamentalists, for whom an ape-ancestor lacked sects appeal.

In 1922, Alfred Watterson McCann, a nutritionist, wrote a book attacking the degrading theory of human evolution as it had been put forward by those arch perverts, Huxley and Darwin, and their followers. *God—or Gorilla,* dedicated "To all lovers of truth," is a dry run for the turbulent Monkey Trial that would soon dazzle the citizens of Dayton, Tennessee, and entertain the rest of the world. McCann did not approve of Henry Fairfield Osborn's having installed Eoanthropus in his Hall of Man exhibit at the American Museum of Natural History:

> Seemingly, it is taken for granted that the disgraceful history of the Piltdown Man . . . has been so far forgotten as to make it safe to present his "restoration" to this generation as a gentleman of quality rather than as the discredited hoax he has been shown to be. . . . With these fragments, which a juggler could conceal in the palm of one hand, the scientists "reconstructed" the Piltdown Man.

He didn't follow through on this. Had he done so, the scientific community would have ignored him anyway. Like fundamentalists before, then, and now, McCann relished playing evolutionists against one another, a ploy irritating to evolutionists. He refers to W. D. Matthew, Aleš Hrdlička, and, of course, Gerrit Miller, in his contention that the jaw is that of a newly discovered species of extinct chimpanzee. It had never been used in human munching. "The Piltdown remains," McCann generalizes, and one cannot fault him on this, "disclose the ease with which 'missing links' between apes and men can be fabricated by resort to wide stretches of imagination in support of preconceived opinions."

I have come upon a couple of references from the period between the wars that brought up the possibility of Piltdown Man's being a hoax, and then dropped it. But, so far as I have been able to discover, no one before McCann and no one for many years afterward came out and said in print that Piltdown Man was a hoax. To Alfred Watterson McCann may (it's uncertain whether by "hoax" he referred to fragments or to theories) go whatever reward attends the first person to label Piltdown Man a hoax.

"(OBVIOUSLY OF CRUCIAL IMPORTANCE)"

Remains brought from pit and field stimulated the defenders of Piltdown Man to stretch their imagination in fitting together what really did not fit, geologically or anatomically. Similar nimbleness was called for from the 1920s to the 1940s because of the discoveries of new hominid fossils, australopithecines from Africa, more pithecanthropines from Asia, a specimen of uncertain genealogy from Sussex, and many Neanderthals. All of these were incompatible with Eoanthropus. These hominids should have posed a fatal challenge to Eoanthropus. But as they were dug up, one after another, the further discussion that skeptics had called for was constantly postponed. Defenders of Piltdown Man declined to give up their defense. Instead, they either said nothing or made up stories. It is so awkward an episode that even an evolutionist can feel a twinge of respect for McCann's diatribe. First the finds, and then the stories.

Of minimal importance during these years was the unearthing of a female skull in excavation for the construction of a new Lloyd's of London building. With four cranial fragments were found, and exhibited in March 1925, mammoth molar teeth and a femur knob, a rhinoceros ulna, pieces of a red deer, and part of an ox skull.

In the same year, far from the City of London, far off in southern Africa, Raymond Dart, a former student of Grafton Elliot Smith, met the Taung baby. Although only the lower jaw and the front part of a skull, this David would make the Piltdown Goliath tremble. In his paper on Australopithecus, Dart described the southern ape as more human than was Eoanthropus, whose simian shelf "scarcely differs from the anthropoids." Dart did not solve, nor introduce, the obvious problem that this raised: Australopithecus had a cranium like an ape's, but a jaw more human than Piltdown's. The idea held by so many, that the earliest hominid would have a large brain and an apelike snout, was precisely reversed by the Taung tot.

Teilhard de Chardin was in China with Davidson Black, also a former student of Grafton Elliot Smith. Teilhard had been centrally involved with Piltdown, Black peripherally. (In 1914, he had found a piece of rhinoceros tooth in the pit.) Along with an international crew, Teilhard and Black went spelunking in Choukoutien, outside of Peking, and uncovered a population of *Sinanthropus pekinensis,* which resembled (and ultimately would be incorporated with) *Pithecanthropus erectus.*

The eoanthropine arrangement consisted of an apelike jaw and a very human cranium. The australopithecine arrangement consisted of a humanlike jaw and an apelike cranium. The sinanthropine arrangement consisted of fully human leg bones, human dentition, and a cranium not fully human, but football-like, vaulted as though it were from one of Lombroso's criminals. Something was very wrong with all this.

Near Dartford, on the south bank of the Thames, in 1935 and 1936, a dental anatomist named Alvan T. Marston dug up a hominid occipital and left parietal, Elephas relics, and hundreds of flint implements. Stratigraphic analysis led him to conclude that the hominid, called Swanscombe Man, had lived 225,000 years ago and thus was "definitely a precursor of the Piltdown type." But the skull seemed to be *Homo sapiens.* It didn't make much sense, however, to place the more primitive Eoanthropus, with its apelike jaw, as having lived later than Swanscombe Man. From 1937 onward, Marston kept demanding that an inquiry be made into the status of the Piltdown skull. Suspecting that the canine had come from an ape's jaw, he conducted the outrageous experiment of fitting the canine into an ape's jaw. It fit. He went on to say that the mandible was just like that of a female orangutan.

The new hominids did not sufficiently impress the pro-Piltdown party. When attacked, this party simply affirmed the humanity of the specimen from Piltdown and denied it to the specimen from Africa and sometimes even to the specimen from China. A typical example of this response is *The Pedigree of the Human Race,* by Harris H. Wilder, professor of zoology at Smith College. Wilder's knowing of Dart's finds failed to stop him from criticizing Miller for dissociating cranium and jaw. There was the Taung baby with its humanlike jaw. And there was Piltdown Man: "Any ape-like characters of the jaw, although extremely interesting, are to be expected."

Wilder's book appeared in 1926, a bit early for anyone to have grasped the full impact of the new finds. But as late as 1931, when ignorance of the new finds could no longer be an excuse, Earnest Hooton chivalrically came to the aid of a lady under seige. "Dame Eoanthropus: The First Female Intellectual," a chapter of his *Up from the Ape,* traces the story of the finds; calls the elephant thigh-bone artifact remarkable; expresses agreement with Lewis Abbott, "an authority on the geology of the Weald," on dating the remains as Pliocene-Pleistocene; concedes that the jawbone has a simian shelf and that the canine tooth is like that of a female chimpanzee; and goes on to justify the unity of cranium and jawbone. The incongruity of the jawbone's made-up condyle with the rest of the piece is only a little difficulty. The "Piltdown Lady" had acquired "a big brain without losing anything of her jaw worth mentioning." Hooton thought that the Piltdown Lady was more like the ancestral form of European grand dames than anything so far discovered.

Robert Broom and Louis Leakey found more australopithecines. Broom as late as 1950 still believed that Eoanthropus was a unified being, its simian shelf an example of convergent evolution. Leakey used Piltdown Man for calibration of his fossil finds, for example, on the prolongation of nasal bones (though he would later claim he knew Piltdown Man was a hoax).

Were we to anticipate Sir Grafton Elliot Smith's changing his mind, we would be disappointed. The cerebellum of the Lady of Lloyd's, he admitted, was like that in *Homo sapiens* "as well as, curiously enough, in the Piltdown cast." This additional example of the Piltdown cranium's total humanity meant nothing. Smith comes back to Piltdown Man in *The Evolution of Man* (1924), *Search for Man's Ancestors* (1931), and *Discovery of Primitive Man in China* (1931).

Smith took cognizance of the profound skepticism of German anthropologists who "have either refrained altogether from referring to the Piltdown discovery (which obviously is of crucial importance) or have stated that the issue is so doubtful as to be excluded from the argument." In a review, he generalizes on "the widespread suspicion of the authenticity of the Piltdown Man as a valid genus," the "chief reason for the lack of agreement in human palaeontology."

Though that skepticism was muted in England and the United States, one example worth mention is Aleš Hrdlička's "The Skeletal Remains of Man" (1930). Having published two long articles in 1922 and 1923, Hrdlička, curator of physical anthropology at the U.S. Museum of Natural History, returned to puzzle over the incongruities between cranium and jaw, such as the latter's having a simian shelf, an old hat of a subject by then but still attractive enough to provoke a new appraisal:

> The specimen is not heavy in weight nor massive in structure; it is marked in fact by relatively moderate build, strikingly at odds with both the first and second Piltdown skulls which in all their parts are decidedly thick. There is no perceptible correspondence between the jaw and the skulls.

But, then, its molars were like those of modern humans, or fossil humans, or Dryopithecines. As for Site II, perhaps some mistake had been made. The isolated molar seemed to have come from the Piltdown jaw itself. Like Lankester, Hrdlička did not speculate on how the pieces had gotten from Piltdown to a site elsewhere.

He was also concerned about the circumstance that "neither the skull fragments nor the easily damaged nasals or turbinal show injuries or wear from being rolled in the gravel. Neither are there any gravel marks on the pieces of the second cranium." Like so many others, Hrdlička came close to whispering fraud, but said, "Here is an enigma which needs, it would seem, some further discussion." Unfortunately, he was not himself prepared to give it that further discussion. In fact, as Frank Spencer points out, he "surprisingly accepted the jaw as an authentic fossil whose morphology was commensurate with its suggested geological age" (Spencer, 1984).

No one has attempted the monumental task of working out the damage done by Piltdown Man as scholars whose names are unknown to us, and middle-level scientists such as Professor Wilder, and those at the top of the hierarchy, such as Hooton, Smith, and Keith, tried to design a rational scheme of human descent by calibrating the new hominids on how well they lined up with the faulty yardstick of Piltdown Man. A couple of examples will indicate what I mean. The Piltdown specimen having proven that an ape jaw could function in a human skull, Smith mistakenly imposed simian features upon the pithecanthropine jaw. One of the world's leading primate anatomists thus was deceived by Piltdown into making a gross anatomical error. To almost everyone else, it seemed clear that Peking Man is cousin to Java Man. But Smith maintained that Peking Man is cousin to Piltdown Man. One of the world's leading advocates of evolution was thus led by Piltdown into making a gross theoretical error.

Giving Piltdown Man a relative would serve to substantiate his reality. Arthur Keith, correctly and temperately enough, expressed doubt about the alleged consanguinity between Peking Man and Piltdown Man. This treason, as Smith saw it, so angered Smith that he wrote he would hesitate to use Keith's book in his courses. Their estrangement was complete.

One more example of how following the Piltdown will-o'-the-wisp led Smith to stumble into error is provided by a geological revision of the age of the pit. A resurvey of the River Ouse in 1926 showed that the terrace on which the pit is located had been formed after the Pleistocene. This meant that Eoanthropus was contemporaneous with the post-Pleistocene hominids entering the human family. But none of those had a jaw like that of Eoanthropus. This again should have induced Grafton Elliot Smith to give up his disastrous trek after Piltdown Man. But it didn't. Paleoanthropology was plunging into incoherence because of Piltdown Man. Here's Smith's response to that: "The tempting task now for the first time becomes possible of achievement, of creating a solid and coherent foundation for a real science of human palaeontology."

English texts of the 1920s accepted Piltdown Man as authentic, for example, M. C. Burkitt, *Prehistory* (1921), and E. Cecil Curwen, *Prehistoric Sussex* (1929) and *The Archaeology of Sussex* (1937). In his books, Curwen subscribes to the accepted Piltdown story, as does J. Reid Moir in *The Antiquity of Man in East Anglia* (1927), which, while asserting that the Piltdown find "is of great importance," devotes only one page to it, and in that page notes that the canine teeth stick up above the level of the molars, a simian rather than human feature.

But the voice of skepticism, with a pronounced German accent, continued to be heard in the scientific literature. The German articles blackballing Piltdown Man's application to the club of Menschenwerden tend to be long. Heinz Friederich's *Schaedel und Unterkiefer von Piltdown ("Eoanthropus dawsoni Woodward") in neuer Untersuchung* (1932), 62 pages, finds insupportable the evidence for the belongingtogetherness of cranium and skull: the cranium is entirely human and recent; the jaw stands in the closest proximity to that of a female orangutan and should be named *Boreopithecus dawsoni.* The introduction to this book was by Franz Weidenreich, who agrees with its skeptical propositions. The next year, Hans Weinert published his *Das Problem des "Eoanthropus" von Piltdown,* 76 pages comprising a perfect study in confusion. Separating the fossils into human skull and ape lower jaw would be a comfortable solution; but they belong together. How can one explain that simian lower jaw? By labeling it a throwback, that's how. Weinert brings up a more sensible explanation of similarities between the cranial fragments of the two sites: those assumed to have come from Site II really came from Site I. Someone goofed in the inventorying.

With all its gravel gone, the pit had been filled in, grassed, and ennobled with a wooden memorial. On July 23, 1938, Keith unveiled the stone replacement. The eulogy, or epitaph, is as stonily oblivious of reality as were the sponsors of the event:

> Here in the old river gravel
> Mr Charles Dawson, F. S. A., found
> the fossil skull of Piltdown, 1912-1913.

"The Weald was then alive," Keith reminisced in his address, "with antiquaries searching for the handiwork of ancient man," and Dawson had been first among them. Like Smith, he went toddling off cliffs following that alluring Piltdown phantom ("The Piltdown Man Discovery," *Nature,* July 30, 1938). Here's Keith's 1938 theory of human evolution:

> We now know that when the Piltdown type was being evolved in England—or at the Western end of the Old World—a totally different type had come into being in the Eastern lands of the Old World. The Eastern types had low receding foreheads, modelled as in the gorilla and chimpanzee. The Western or Piltdown type differed; it had a relatively upright and high forehead, modelled not on gorilla lines but rather on those of the orang. While the Eastern forms retained in their shape of head the low squat type of the chimpanzee and gorilla, the Western or Piltdown type tended to assume the higher vaulted skull seen in modern races. There is no denying that in many of his features Piltdown man foreshadowed some of the structural modifications we find in modern races of mankind.

The *Nature* article on the unveiling quoted Woodward as happily speaking of the discovery's "growing in magnitude and importance."

While the Piltdown pit was receiving the homage of a nation in the summer of 1938, Keith completed his final reconstruction of the skull. He underlined the skull's apelike features as though no one had ever done that before. In 1939, he wrote that he had nothing to add to his 1915 conviction that the skull and mandible formed part of the same head, except that he was, after 24 years, more firmly convinced of that.

Les Premieres Hommes (1943), a paleontological survey by F. M. Bergounioux and André Glory, classified Piltdown Man with Neanderthals. The authors saw the fossil as a unified being and referred to the debate's having lost its virulence. But while Bergounioux and Glory were giving the debate its last rites, Piltdown Man having conquered, Franz Weidenreich, another participant in the Choukoutien spelunking, knocked Piltdown Man out of the tree:

> I am only wondering why, if a human vault, a simian mandible and an anonymous "canine" were combined into a new form, the other animal bones and teeth found in the same spot were not added to the *"Eoanthropus"* combination; I do not believe in those miracles whether offered by anti-Darwinian or Darwinians. The sooner the chimaera *"Eoanthropus"* is erased from the list of human fossils, the better for science. (Quoted in Howells, 1959)

In 1937, Weidenreich had compared radiograms of the Piltdown jaw with that of an orangutan. In 1946's *Apes, Giants, and Man,* Weidenreich wrote, "All that has been known of early man since the discovery of the Piltdown fossils proves that man cannot have had an ancestor with a lower jaw of a completely simian character." The skepticism that had irked Grafton Elliot Smith grumbled into sarcasm under Weidenreich.

Dawson had died in 1916; Abbott in 1933; Sollas in 1936; Smith in 1937; and Woodward in 1944. As new hominids came on the scene, new scientists were there to greet them. Marston in 1947 pointed out that potassium bichromate could effectively alter the gray-tan of cranial bones to the rust of fossils. In 1948, Woodward's *The Earliest Englishman* was published. In his introduction to this memoir of the Piltdown saga, Keith came out again for the integrity of the fossils, though he also said, ominously, "The Piltdown enigma is still far from a final solution." By 1949, Marston was demanding, "Let the mistake be recognized—let it no longer be defended." In 1950, Keith, in his autobiography, proclaimed Eoanthropus as the most important and instructive of all ancient homi-

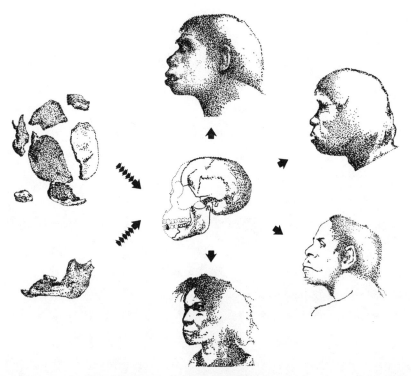

Ecce Homo? After Woodward assembled human cranial fragments and an orangutan jaw into Piltdown Man, artists fleshed out the reconstruction: from top to bottom of crescent, these portraits are adapted from A. Forestier, *Illustrated London News* (1912); J. H. McGregor, in Osborn (1915); A. S. Woodward (1948); and Maurice Wilson, AP (1951), two years before the exposé disassembled Piltdown Man.

nids, its authenticity beyond question.

A year after the publication of *The Earliest Englishman,* an inquiry began that would uncover what Lyne, Waterston, Miller, Hrdlička, Boule, Marston, Friederichs, Weidenreich, the Taung baby, Peking Man, Swanscombe Man, and Neanderthals (from Rhodesia, Palestine, the Crimea, Spain, from France's Fontechevade, Germany's Ehringdorf, Yugoslavia's Krapina, Italy's Saccopastore and Quinzano, and a Neandertalnik from Teshik-Tash, U.S.S.R.) had failed at, the final proof that Eoanthropus was not earliest, not English, not man, and not even real.

CHAPTER FIVE

EXPOSÉ

ᐟAt a meeting of the Geologists Association in 1947, Alvan T. Marston delivered a paper on the Piltdown mandible and canine tooth, both of which he described as pure ape. During the ensuing discussion, Kenneth Oakley, of the British Museum of Natural History's Geology Department, suggested that it might be feasible to subject the Piltdown fossils to a test for fluorine content. This test would be the undoing of Piltdown Man.

Fluorine had first been detected in teeth in 1802. By 1844, it was known that teeth and bones absorbed the element from an environment that had it. Absorption of fluorine changes the phosphate hydroxy-apatite (the main component of teeth and bones) to fluorapatite. The test can't determine an absolute date, but can reveal whether two relics in the same fluorine-rich environment have been there for the same amount of time. If two or more pieces from the same site were to contain radically different amounts of fluorine, that would mean that they had arrived there at different times. If they show the same amount, then they could have been deposited together.ᐧ

The femur, skullcap, and tooth from Java checked out as having the same amount of fluorine, which was not inconsistent with the thesis that they had all come from the same possessor. Applied to Galley Hill, the test showed that the skeleton contained the same amount of fluorine (0.3 percent) as post-Pleistocene fossils, and had not, therefore, been a Pleistocene burial. The Swanscombe skull and accompanying Elephas relics had absorbed the same amount of fluorine (2 percent) since they had come to rest on the Thames bank in the middle of the Pleistocene. The test knocked out the antiquity of hominid fossils from Bury St. Edmunds, Dartford, Baker's Hole, and London.

ᐧIn September 1948, the British Museum's Department of Geology gave permission for Oakley and his associates to drill into Piltdown Man.

This wasn't as much of a desecration as drilling into the Crown Jewels, but the fossils had been protected from German bombs during two wars, from being molested by inquisitive scientists for forty years, and even from the public, who viewed not the fossils themselves, but casts.

'The drill bit into the mammalian fossils. The pit was shown to have contained populations from different ages: the older, Lower Pleistocene, or Villafranchian, was represented by the mastodon and elephas fossils (2-3 percent fluorine); the more recent, Middle or Upper Pleistocene, by deer and beaver fossils (less than 1.6 percent). It bit into Eoanthropus, cranium and jaw. Eoanthropus checked in at 0.2 percent.'

Piltdown Man was thus deposed as the earliest Englishman, genealogical priority going to Marston's Swanscombe Man. But the conclusion that the cranial and jaw fragments had about the same amount of fluorine in them suggested that all the parts had slept in the pit through the same long night, absorbing fluorine at the same rate. This result did not coerce the conclusion that the two parts had belonged to one individual, but it did not deny that. Oakley wrote in January 1949:

> ᐟ The results of the fluorine test have considerably increased the probability that the mandible and cranium represent a single creature. The relatively late date indicated by the summary of evidence suggests moreover that "Piltdown Man," far from being an early primitive type, may have been a late specialised hominid which evolved in comparative isolation.ᐟ

In a collaborative paper that year, Oakley and C. Randall Hoskins again gave heart to Piltdown fans: the cranial and jaw fragments could well have come from the same individual. Pleased with the settling of one of the big Piltdown problems, the age of Eoanthropus, Marston remained dissatisfied with the conclusions about the other big problem, the unity of Eoanthropus. Piltdown Man still hung tenaciously onto both his head and his jaw. In June 1949, Marston read a paper, "On Piltdown Man," to the Royal Anthropological Institute; the paper was incorporated into an article, "The Relative Ages of the Swanscombe and Piltdown Skulls, with Special Reference to the Results of the Fluorine Estimation Test," published a year later (Marston, 1950). He went over the history of the finds, anatomical and geological difficulties, the growing skepticism about Piltdown Man's authenticity, still arguing

> It is evident that many mistakes have been made concerning Piltdown Man—many mistakes by many highly qualified and highly placed men. To err is human and none of these men have been divine.

The British Museum of Natural History continued to display Piltdown Man as though he were one being. In September 1949, Kenneth
Oakley read a note to an anthropological meeting at Newcastle; this note,
from Robert Broom, the famous finder of australopithecine remains,
stated Broom's conviction that the canine tooth "is not at all anthropoid.
. . . The author now has scarcely any doubt that the Piltdown mandible
belongs to the same individual as the associated brain case." As for the
simian shelf, Broom thought that a specialization due to parallel evolution.

Vallois and Movius were compiling their *Catalogue des Hommes
Fossiles.* Oakley wrote the section on "Royaume-Uni" fossil remains. For
the Piltdown fossils, he listed the bones; dated them as contemporary with
deer and beaver fossils; and noted that Site II was probably Sheffield
Park. He rejected any validity to the conjecture (which Weinert among
others had offered) that the bones from Site II had belonged to the skull
from Site I, that possibility being to Oakley "infinitely remote." He also
gave an inventory of the various taxonomies proposed for Eoanthropus:
(1) those who thought that skull and jaw belonged together called the
whole thing *Eoanthropus dawsoni,* though Kleinschmidt had in 1922
recommended *Homo sapiens dawsoni;* (2) those who separated the two
gave different labels to cranium (Miller, *Eoanthropus dawsoni;* Marston,
Homo sapiens) and to jaw (Miller, *Pan vetus;* Friederichs, *Boreopithecus
dawsoni,* and we could add Boule's *Troglodytes dawsoni*). This exuber-
ance of taxonomic labeling reflects a good deal of uncertainty about what
any of it was.

The *Catalogue,* with Oakley's tacit acceptance of Piltdown Man as
authentic, was published in 1952. At a Wenner-Gren International Symposium in June 1952, Oakley told his colleagues that Piltdown Man had
lived not a million years ago, as Osborn had estimated; not even 200,000
years ago, Keith's estimate; but only about 50,000 years ago. But Eoanthropus had lived. To the American anthropologist Ruth Moore, the
test proved that "there has been no miracle mixing of bones. . . . Oakley
emphasizes that it is still possible that the remains represent two creatures,
though this does not now seem likely" (Moore, 1953). Hans Weinert
found support for his theory: that the two parts belong together, the lower
jaw as hominid as the cranium, but an atavistic structure.

Oakley's continued defense of Piltdown Man's integrity and rationalizations like Weinert's atavistic jaw and Broom's convergency of shelf strut
failed to discourage the skeptics. At a 1950 talk to the Oxford University
Anthropological Society (Daniel, 1983), Oakley described his test and its

results. In the audience sat J. S. Weiner, of the Department of Anatomy of Oxford University. The two met each other for the first time and discussed the Piltdown problem. Later, Wilfred Le Gros Clark, a colleague of Weiner in the Department of Anatomy, discussed it with Oakley. Weiner had his doubts about the accuracy of the first test—based on small samples, it could not detect minute differences in fluorine content.

Ashley Montagu's contribution (Montagu, 1951) severed cranium and jaw. Marston returned to the fight with his 1952 "Why the Piltdown Canine Tooth and Mandible Could Not Belong to Piltdown Man." As 1953 approached, at an international congress held in London, no one read any papers on Piltdown Man. He was welcomed with a degree of hospitality not seen since Banquo's ghost came to dine.

JUST A MISTAKE

The team of Weiner, Oakley, and Le Gros Clark went to work refining and reapplying the fluorine test. Here are the results:

	Piltdown pit fluorine content %
Cranial fragments	0.1
Jaw	0.03
Elephant, mastodon, rhinoceros	1.9-3.1
Hippopotamus	0.05

ᵠStratigraphic analysis going back to Dawson's day and the earlier fluorine test had suggested that elephant, mastodon, and rhinoceros had lived earlier than other fauna whose remains were found in the pit. The new test, showing these fossils having a greater concentration of fluorine, validated those suggestions. No surprise there. Eoanthropus had already been shown to be recent.ᵥ

But the figures showed something troublesome: a difference in fluorine content between cranial fragments and jaw. Apparently, Eoanthropus was, after all of forty years of controversy, composed of parts from two different beings, one of whom (she of the cranial fragments) had lived before the other (he or she of the mandible).

Piltdown Man was certainly an enigma. He could not have been old, because the fluorine test dated him well after the Middle Pleistocene. He had about as much fluorine in him as did the scientists probing him. Yet he could not have been recent, with so primitive a jaw. He could not have been two beings: the major paleontological authorities, extinct Woodward, Smith, Sollas, and Osborn and extant Keith and Hooton and others had affirmed him to be unified. Yet he could not have been unified, since the cranial bones contained a higher content of fluorine (at 0.1 percent) than the mandible (at 0.03 percent). How the piece of hippopotamus tooth, with so much less fluorine than pieces from the other fauna, had come to land in that pit was a minor problem compared with the new and more accurate results finally realizing the hopes of Miller and other skeptics: the dissociation of cranial and mandibular fragments. Having once started, the investigation drove on.

The fluorine test was applied to the fossils from Site II:

	Site II Fluorine Content %
Cranial fragments	0.1
Molar	0.01

Another dissociation: the cranial fragments were from an individual who had lived before the one represented by the molar. The Site II molar could have come from the jaw at Piltdown, as Lankester, Hrdlička, and Weinert had intimated. Since it could not have transported itself from Site I to Site II, it must have been carried there.

ʲDawson's friend Sam Woodhead, invited by the solicitor to analyze the cranial fragments, had detected no nitrogenous content in them. He did not analyze the mandible, perhaps because, or so thought Le Gros Clark, he didn't want to mutilate the delicate jaw bone; or because he felt no need to do so, the cranial fragments taken as representative of the entire hoard; or because he was the hoaxer. Had he tested the mandible, he would have found that it did contain nitrogen; such a disparity—top inorganic, bottom organic—would have split the contraption right away.

In the course of drilling the mandible, Oakley saw that the material slivered off, as though from bone, while the cranium powdered, as rock would. He also smelled burning bone, the same odor that most of us know from having our teeth drilled. And an examination of the canine and molar teeth showed that, as Oakley and Hoskins noted, "below an extremely thin ferruginous surface stain their dentine was pure white, apparently no more altered than the dentine of recent teeth from the soil." The jaw seemed to be more like new bone than old stone. ˀ

Unlike fluorine, the organic element nitrogen is released over time. The less nitrogen, the older the fossil.

Nitrogen content: Site II

	%		%
Mandible	3.9	Turbinal	1.7
Canine	5.1	Molar	4.2
Cranial pieces	up to 1.9	Frontal bone	1.1
Nasal bones	3.9	Occipital	0.6

These results speak for themselves. Your present guide hears this:

1. The frontal bone from Site II, with a residual nitrogen content of 1.1 percent, falls within the range of the Piltdown cranial pieces. It seemed to have come from the same skull as those and it junctured well with the Piltdown cranial fragments.

2. The molar from Site II probably came from the Piltdown mandible. It was the right size, and close enough in chemical content.

3. The canine probably did not.

4. The Site II occipital bone aligns with nothing and came from a different human being. In fact, it occupied the same occipital region as that of the Site I piece.

5. The Piltdown nasal bones have the same nitrogen content as the mandible. However, nasal bones are part of the skull, not the jaw, and the nitrogen content of the nasal bones is so much higher than that of the cranium that it could not very well have belonged to that cranium. Its source was someone else's head.

6. The bone called a turbinal could have come from the Piltdown face.

Organic carbon, which like nitrogen dissipates over time, was high in the jaw and teeth, in the nasal bones, and in the turbinal, but lower in all the cranial fragments from the sites. Other tests conducted for collagen, ash, water content, and specific gravity reinforced each other, showing that Piltdown Man was a diverse population: the Piltdown cranium and the Site II frontal fragment from one individual; the Site II occipital from another; the nasal bones from a third; the mandible and isolated molar from a fourth; the canine from a fifth. The Barcombe Mills material, three skull fragments and a molar, had their sources in the heads of two people who contributed nothing to the Piltdown assemblage.

Piltdown Man was, as the skeptics had long hoped he would be, abolished.

THE MALTESE HIPPOPOTAMUS

The mammalian fossils came in for their share of the fun. Almost all of them had emigrated to Piltdown. Oakley thought that all of them had. In 1968, he wrote, "I must point out that after establishing this primary fact [that the jaw was of a modern ape], a thorough investigation of the specimens in the succeeding year enabled us to show that they had *all* been faked or 'planted' and not a single fossil bone or tooth had genuinely occurred in the Piltdown sites." The beaver may have swum in the Ouse and the deer may have locked antlers with a rival on its banks; but the mastodon and rhinoceros molars had come from the Red Crag deposit, in East Anglia. That was a short journey, though how they had accomplished the trip was mysterious. The elephant femur may have also undertaken a short journey, from the Thames terrace, or from a few hundred miles away, the valley of the Somme in France.

A test for radioactivity of the Elephas molar fragments (labeled by the British Museum as E596, E597, and E620), which Woodward thought very singular finds, sent the Geiger counter into a tumult.

Radioactive Counts per Minute

Red Crag (England)	6-15	E596	203
Siwaliks (India)	8-19	E597	175
Algeria	15-18	E620	355

Only one site in the world could bombard these fragments with so much radioactivity: Ichkeul. They had trekked a long way from northern Tunisia to southeastern England.

As for the hippopotamus, fossils of its extinct form had been reported, rarely, from British sites. But the fragment of a hippopotamus molar had the low fluorine content, and the creamy color, of similar teeth from the Mediterranean. The Piltdown pit's hippopotamus tooth fragment was traced to a limestone cave in Ghar Dalam, Malta. Thus the Piltdown assemblage had something to say for itself: it was a cosmopolitan crew, from East Anglia, the Thames terrace or Somme valley, Tunisia, Malta; and, it would soon become clear, Borneo, home of that old man of the forest, the orangutan.

Somehow, all these animals had wandered, like elephants trudging to an ancestral graveyard, from various sites in Europe and Africa. Or maybe a person or persons unknown had inadvertently dumped them into the pit and onto the field, where they were later found and misunderstood. Or had done it advertently.

SKULLDUGGERY

It was all very untidy. Every test that established date, composition, or source, unleashed more problems. Another series of tests proved that Piltdown Man was not a mistake in interpretation (though it had enough of that), but a hoax.

Kenneth Oakley, who was born in 1911, the year that Dawson undertook a systematic search of the pit, was one of the trio undertaking a systematic search of the Piltdown assemblage. He was joined by J. S. Weiner and Wilfred Le Gros Clark and other investigators. It is not clear just who or what stimulated the hypothesis that Piltdown Man was not a mistake, but a deliberate hoax. The different accounts of how the exposé was initiated provide a nice symmetry to the different accounts of how the fossils were first found.

Kenneth Oakley recalled that the results of the 1949 fluorine test implying that Eoanthropus was recent aroused an instinctive reaction that it was also bogus. But he did not share that suspicion with the readers of his published pieces on the test. According to Le Gros Clark, the molar teeth started people thinking of fraud: in the British Museum's first (1953) monograph on the exposé, he wrote: "It was because these features appeared to lend such strong support to the hypothesis of artificial abrasion that it was decided to re-examine all the Piltdown material for further evidence of faking." J. S. Weiner gave a different account of the beginning that led rapidly to the end. During a paleontological conference, he had dinner with Oakley and the American anthropologist S. L. Washburn. They chatted about the unusual circumstance that no one knew the exact location of Site II. Weiner began to attend to the whole tangle, the anomalous and increasingly tenuous position Piltdown Man held in the sequence of human evolution; the early test results showing disparate ages of the fossils; the hints that an intimate, not to say indecent, relationship obtained between the Site II molar and those in the Piltdown jaw; the question about whether Piltdown Man was one being or a composite. Perhaps the jaw, which seemed to be that of a modern great ape, was in fact that of a modern great ape? But, if so, how had it gotten into the pit? And if an ape jaw, from where did it get its human dentures?

In his popularized version of the investigation, *The Piltdown Forgery* (1955), Weiner wrote:

A modern jaw with flat worn molars and uniquely worn-down eye tooth? That would mean only one thing: deliberately ground-down teeth. Immediately this summoned up a devastating corollary—the equally deliberate placing of the jaw in the pit. Even as a mere hypothesis this inference could at once dispose of two of the most intransigent Piltdown posers: how the jaws and teeth had ever got there and how the teeth had come by their remarkable wear. But the hypothesis of a deliberate "salting" of the Piltdown gravels clearly carried much wider implications, and the idea was repellent indeed.

The patinas on the fossils ranged through a colorful spectrum, yellow, brown, orange, rust, red. Some of the fossils had taken on color naturally— the mastodon and rhinoceros tooth fragments were hued like their peers in the Red Crag site. The original cranial fragments may have had a rust color, but no one could be sure because Dawson had said that he (and Abbott added himself) had dipped those fragments in potassium bichromate in the belief that the compound would harden the fossils. So it was expected that these pieces would have chromium on their surface. But other fossils should not have had any traces of chromium. They could not have absorbed chromium from a site that did not have any. A patina of chromium was detected on the faunal teeth, the mandible, and one of the flints (E606, found by Teilhard de Chardin).

The fossils had been stained through submersion in potassium bichromate prior to their discovery, unless some wise guys at the British Museum did it after Woodward delivered immaculate pieces there.

The staining gave the fossils an appropriate and deceptive patina of mineralization and speeded up oxidation brought about by other means. Leaving no stone unturned, the investigators subjected the fossils to X-ray analysis. X-rays passed through bone crystals will defract them at a characteristic angle: this angle is distorted by sulphate in the bone crystal. The hoaxer had dipped many of the fossils into a sulphate solution (and some of them into both potassium bichromate and iron sulphate solutions) to dress them in rust, the rust of iron oxide. But in this process, phosphate in the bone was replaced by sulphate from the solution; and bone apatite converted to gypsum (the same gypsum used in fertilizers and in plaster of Paris), and the presence of that gypsum was additional evidence of fraud.

Apatite stems from the Greek *apate,* fraud. The German descendant *Apatit* means the deceptive stone (because it looks like other minerals).

The staining had left 7 percent iron throughout the width of the cranial fragments; 8 percent on the surface of the jaw, falling to 3 percent within a few millimeters, the iron sulphate solution not soaking in deeper than that. This was additional evidence, if any were needed, of incongruity between cranium and jaw. In 1960, Ashley Montagu wondered whether the hoaxer had renovated the cranial bones by thickening them artificially. After all, that fellow had falsified just about everything else; why not the cranial bones? Montagu gave an old skull a bath in potassium hydroxide and found that it swelled. But Oakley disagreed: the cranial bones were already slightly mineralized and these sub-fossils had the same thickness as many other skull bones in the British Museum. Frank Spencer recently (1984) diagnosed the skull as suffering from the osteoporosis of Cushing's syndrome. The cranial fragments had from the beginning been recognized as belonging to a human skull, though the idea that the occipital bone was apelike turned out to be, like all the other propositions about the apeishness of the skull, hokum. The Piltdown skull was that of a 40-year-old woman, its coronal and sagittal sutures having closed in her advanced age.

The occlusal surfaces of the molar teeth and canine had been painted with red sienna, the sides of the canine with Vandyke brown. The canine is one of the more intriguing of all the deceptive stones in this lapidary. It was fake from top to bottom and side to side. Its appearance on August

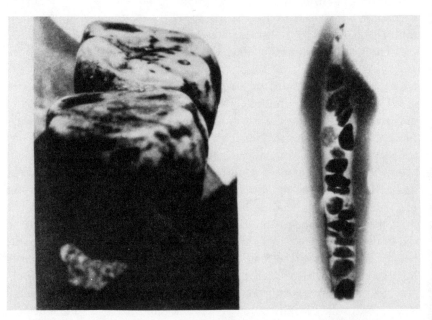

Misaligned molars and canine tooth. By filing the molars into two different planes, the hoaxer left a clue for detection. Nobody detected this in 1913. The radiogram of the canine tooth shows internal grains, a large one plugging the hole filed into the pulp cavity. (From Weiner et al., 1953, Plate 3.)

30, 1913, with features seemingly halfway between ape and human being, stifled some hostile criticism and led to much admiration not only of Teilhard's sharp eye but also of Woodward's talent at prophecy. The dental consultant, Dr. Underwood, put down his colleague Dr. Lyne, who was upset by signs of adolescence and maturity in a single tooth. The investigation of 1953 supported Dr. Lyne's position: the canine tooth had recently erupted in some jaw, its large pulp cavity a sign of its youthfulness. Its crown looked old because of artificial aging, that is, because it had been filed down. Crisscross scratch-marks were seen in 1953.

The hole penetrating into the pulp cavity had been taken as evidence of the tooth's maturity. But the inventor of the canine had filed away too merrily, right into the pulp cavity, and then had filled the hole with a material like chewing gum. The surface of the tooth had been so well abraded that dentine was exposed. Yet X-ray analysis showed no sign of secondary dentine formation. The 19 sand grains in the pulp cavity were unnaturally loose rather than compact and unrepresentative of the mixture of different sizes in the pit itself. They had been inserted into the cavity. The root may have been broken to make it shorter than an ape's canine root.

Whenever Arthur Keith felt uneasy about Piltdown Man, he looked for solace to the molar teeth. They always came to our aid, he sighed. The molar teeth had been abraded, filed down, and smoothed out with acid, but they had not been filed on the same plane, one inclining obliquely to the other. Miller and Marston had both simulated how such flatness could be achieved by taking a file to chimpanzee teeth, though when they did that neither one anticipated being on the trail of hokum.

Le Gros Clark studied a sample of 137 ape jaws and 200 human jaws to define acceptable boundaries of molar teeth features. He showed that the Piltdown molars could not have grown in any mouth, ape or human. Pycraft, in an excess of devotion to the Piltdown jaw, had once pointed out that the angle formed by the molar's occlusal surface and by its side was a sharp right angle, as in human teeth. Le Gros Clark cleared up Pycraft's confusion: The edge of human molars is beveled.

Weiner performed the same filing operation and was especially proud of his artificially abraded canine in his faked fake jawbone. William Howells (1959) narrates a believable scenario about Weiner's renovation:

> He was delighted. He took the "fossil" into Le Gros Clark's office, put it on the desk, and said with a great air of innocence: "I got this out of the collections. What do you suppose it is?" Sir Wilfred, not an unperceptive man, perceived exactly what it was, and exclaimed, "You can't mean it!"

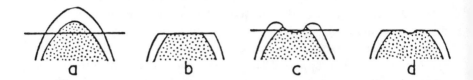

Diagram illustrating the peculiar type of abrasion on the cusps of the Piltdown molar teeth. In (*a*) is shown a schematic section through an unworn cusp. If this were subjected to artificial abrasion in the plane indicated, the appearance shown in (*b*) would be produced, i.e., a flat area of exposed dentine (stippled) flush with the surrounding enamel; such an appearance is seen on the antero-internal cusps of the Piltdown molars. In (*c*) is shown a schematic section through a cusp partially worn by natural attrition, illustrating the concavity of the dentine depressed below the surrounding enamel. Artificial abrasion in the plane indicated would produce the appearance shown in (*d*), i.e., a depressed "dimple" in the center of a flat area of dentine flush with the surrounding enamel; such an appearance is seen on the antero-external cusps of the Piltdown molars. (From Weiner et al., 1953.)

A miscellany of other clarifications came out of the analyses. The flint tools had originated in sites on the Sussex chalk Downs. They too had not been in the pit for longer than a little while. They could have been taken from a "neolithic block" and made to look older. The elephant femur bone implement had been faked too, with a modern metal knife. Oakley whittled one just like it. The turbinal was not a turbinal, but slivers from the limb bone of a small animal.

As for Piltdown Man's origin, he had at first been generally accepted as a Pleistocene product, or even Pliocene. The early stages of the investigation showed that he was no more than 50,000 years old; but radiocarbon dating brought him and the jaw closer to our own time. It showed that the skull had been in the head of a woman who lived no more than 630 (+ or - 100) years ago and who may, therefore, have been a contemporary of Geoffrey Chaucer. The jaw bone was that of an orangutan, dated as having swung from tree to tree 500 (+ or - 100) years ago; that ape then could have been a contemporary of Shakespeare. Where the hoaxer had located a five-hundred-year-old orangutan jawbone remains unanswered, though some guesses will be considered later. Ultimately, it had to come from the East Indies, where such fossil fetishes are venerated by Dyaks.

A small casualty of the whole affair was Ruth Moore's *Man, Time, and Fossils*. This book has the misfortune of being the last defender of Piltdown Man's authenticity. Apparently, the manuscript was in press just as the news of the exposé broke. Moore finds Piltdown Man important because he shows, or his large, modern head shows, that modern man is more recent than paleontology had assumed.

> To date the arrival of modern man at about fifty thousand years ago instead of the one million previously set for him shakes anthropology, history, and the theory of evolution.

Man, Time, and Fossils came out in 1953. So did the British Museum's *The Solution of the Piltdown Problem.*

EPITAPH

With the breaking of the news came headlines as sensational about the death of Piltdown Man as they had been back in 1912 about his birth. The *Observer* reported on the history of suspicions and the various tests for fluorine, organic carbon, nitrogen. From the *Manchester Guardian,* November 23, 1953:

FEATURES OF THE PILTDOWN SKULL "DELIBERATE FAKES"

Professor Weidenreich, the paper reported, saw Piltdown as having violated a law: the larger the braincase, the more reduced the jaw. And in a later edition, the *Guardian* paralleled the death of the Piltdowner with the rise of the Swanscomber. An article in the *Times,* November 21, 1953, headed

PILTDOWN MAN FORGERY
JAW AND TOOTH OF MODERN APE
"ELABORATE HOAX"

not only gives a summary of the coconut story and the exposé, but also pinpoints a suspect: Charles Dawson, who chose Teilhard de Chardin and Arthur Smith Woodward as his instruments because they were unimpeachable authorities. The *Times* blithely yanked victory from the simian jaws of defeat:

> That the deception—whoever carried it out—has, though cunning and long successful, at last been revealed is a tribute to the persistence and skill of modern palaeontological research.

Two days later, November 23, another blare of headlines in the *Times:*

MORE DOUBTS ON PILTDOWN MAN
SECOND DISCOVERY SUSPECT
IMPLEMENTS STAINED ARTIFICIALLY

Piltdown Man, Jr., turned out to be as spurious as his dad. The next day, in the same paper, still another report, "Early Man," this on how the exposé affected modern theories of evolution. It cleaned up a mess. In the *Times* of November 26, a letter appeared from one L. M. S. Kramer: "Sir—May we now regard the Piltdown Man to be the first human being to have false teeth?"

The *New York Times* was right there with her English sister on November 22, 1953:

PILTDOWN MAN IS EXPOSED
JAW AN APE'S
SKULL FAIRLY RECENT

This article reported that Earnest Hooton had expressed "shock and dis-belief" at the implications of the hoax. However, Hooton didn't really seem all that jolted by the loss of his Lady Eoanthropus, the world's first female intellectual. "It doesn't disturb our ideas of human evolution at all," he maintained. "If it is right that the head is a fake, it loses all significance and removes a very puzzling link." The results of the investigation, he went on, "impugn the honesty" of Sir Arthur Smith Woodward.

Five months later, in April 1954, Hooton published fuller comments on the Piltdown exposé. He expressed reservations about the accuracy of the tests and a hope that he might live to "witness the discovery even of an authentic Eoanthropus—jaw, brain case, and all." Here he rejected the insinuation that Smith Woodward "could have had anything to do with the perpetration of this alleged fraud. Nor would I have believed it of Dawson, whom I never knew." While Hooton does not advise anyone to be reckless, he also does not advise any paralyzing caution. Sherwood Washburn, on the other hand, draws this lesson: "There never was enough of the fossil to justify the theories built around it."

A few days after news of the fraud broke, on November 25, 1953, members of the House of Commons had just finished a flurry of brief comments on the persecution of Catholics in Poland, establishment of an atomic energy corporation, and the Report of the Royal Commission on Capital Punishment, when Brigadier Clarke drew attention to the terms of a motion before them:

That this House has no confidence in the trustees of the British Museum, other than the Speaker of the House of Commons, because of the tardiness of their discovery that the skull of the Piltdown Man is a partial fake.

The motion did not have much chance for passage. Among the trustees of the British Museum were not only the Speaker of the House of Commons but also the Prime Minister, the Lord Chancellor, and the Archbishop of Canterbury. The Speaker queried the seriousness of the motion and made the excuse, one would suppose amid poorly suppressed hilarity, that the honorable trustees "have many other things to do besides examining the authenticity of a lot of old bones." Another member warned that there were enough skeletons around without getting into skulls. Mr. Beswick then queried what had happened to the Dentists Bill, to which Mr. Crookshank replied that he had no announcement to make other than that that was not a fake, to which Brigadier Clarke begged leave to withdraw his name from the motion "in view of the excellent answer which I have received."

Like other scientific hoaxes, Piltdown has not been a topic of much interest to novelists. He appears in Jessica North's *Mask of the Jaguar* (1981) and in Angus Wilson's *Anglo-Saxon Attitudes* (1956), one plot of which is the discovery of an old English Christian tomb that contains an intrusive idol from a pagan cemetery. Professor Pforzheim complains about his discipline: "Alas, we historians have so little scandal. We are not paleontologists to display our Piltdowns." Sir Edgar complains about the investigation: "We pursue humane studies, we're not technicians. All this spectrographic analysis and fluorine tests and what-not. There's no place for 'sweetness and light' in all that."

The liturgical phrase *hoc est corpus meum,* "here is my body," whelped three degraded offspring, hocus-pocus, hoax, and hokum. The body of Dawn Man and almost all his dawn buddies had been brought to Sussex, renovated, planted, discovered, and acclaimed in a case of scientific hocus-pocus that finds no parallel in the history of paleontology, or biology, or science. The fake muddied the theory of human evolution for four decades, catching in its swirls many of the best scientists of England. The questions of where the fossils originated, of what was done to them, and of how they succeeded in fooling so many people so much of the time were answered thirty years ago.

Our inquest has so far explored how the Piltdown bauble came to be hung on our genealogical tree in the Christmas season of 1912; why it

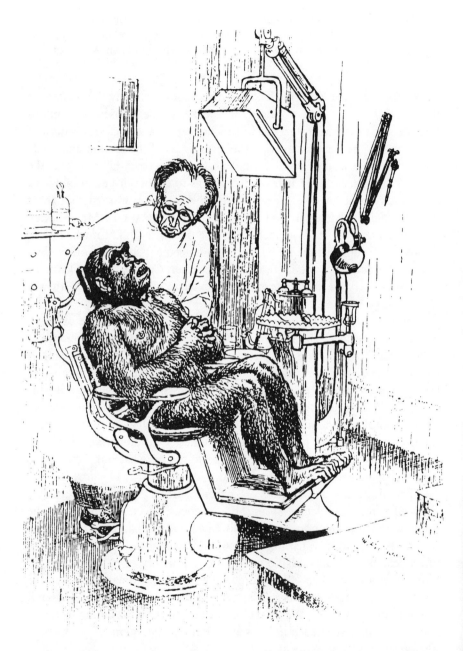

"This may hurt, but I'm afraid I'll have to remove the whole jaw." (From *Punch,* December 2, 1953.)

remained there for forty years; and what blew it off. As we approach the pit's fiftieth memorial anniversary, perhaps the only time in history that a hoax has been memorialized as a national monument, the questions of why it was done and who did it have still not been answered. It's possible that someone other than those identified in the literature as hoaxer created the coconut, such as J. Reid Moir or A. S. Kennard or someone whose name is not even known. Maybe the hoaxer was an Edwardian Flint Jack, one of the workmen digging up gravel, a scion of the de Vere Cole group (mentioned by Daniel, 1972), or an English schoolboy fooling around— the contribution of H. J. Fleure.

Dawson imagined that English delinquents might have lived close to the pit. He wrote to Woodward,

> I hear that some of the youths about here are preparing all sorts of prehistoric surprises for future diggings! Also that a deformed hare's skull is being pickeled [*sic*] for presentation to me—my clerks have warned me of these "goings-on." I have no doubt the young Kenwards are in it. (January 1, 1912)

The present owner of Barkham Manor suggested to me, one would hope as a joke, that the past tenant of Barkham Manor, that is, the elder Kenward, did it as a joke.

Identification of the young Kenwards as the Piltdown hoaxer would be the most satisfyingly comic conclusion to the inquest and would, not incidentally, resolve several problems (the carelessness of some of the forgeries, accessibility to the pit over seven years, and motive). Some of the forgeries were beyond the knowledge and skill of schoolboys. To historians of the case, the true culprit or culprits are in this lineup, listed alphabetically:

Abbott, W. J. Lewis   Hinton, Martin A. C.
Butterfield, William R.   Smith, Grafton Elliot
Dawson, Charles   Sollas, W. J.
Doyle, Arthur Conan   Teilhard de Chardin, Pierre
Hewitt, John T.   Woodhead, Samuel

The following section begins with a profile of the Piltdown hoaxer, a generalized sketch, and then tests how well each of the suspects merges into that sketch.

PART TWO

THE CRIMINAL

CHAPTER SIX

PROFILE OF A HOAXER

The first hint that the fossils might be fraudulent became public in a 1914 article by W. K. Gregory, "The Dawn Man of Piltdown, England."

> It has been suspected by some that geologically they are not old at all; that they may even represent a deliberate hoax, a negro or Australian skull and a broken ape-jaw, artificially fossilized and "planted" in the gravel bed, to fool the scientists.

Gregory didn't think it was a deliberate hoax. From a *Scientific American Supplement* of the same year:

> Of first importance is the question of the age of these remains, and in considering this the suggestion that has been made that there was anything in the nature of a "plant" or a hoax may be disregarded in view of the circumstances of the discovery.

But both these found the topic too hot or vaporous to handle.

After the exposé, many people came forward to say that they had known all along that Piltdown Man was a hoax. A. S. Kennard teased that he knew the identity of the hoaxer, but wouldn't tell. Robert Essex's naming the hoaxer "X" wasn't all that helpful. Martin A. C. Hinton knew back in 1913 that a hoax had been perpetrated, but didn't let on until fifty years later, and named no one. In 1970, Kenneth Oakley reported that Gerrit Miller had asked Remington Kellogg, director of the Smithsonian Institution, back in 1915 to see if the Piltdown teeth had been fraudulently altered and that, by 1930, Miller was sure some of the features of the Piltdown jaw were "the result of fraudulent alteration"; but he never made his suspicion public. C. P. Chatwin, of the British Museum, knew it too; he also kept quiet. Ditto for Teilhard de Chardin. And for Sam Woodhead. Peter Costello reports that Professor Frederick Wood-Jones said that "if it had not been for the outbreak of the Great War, there would have been a terrible scandal about Piltdown."

Ronald Jessup's 1970 *South East England* tantalizes us with: "Neither Dr. Weiner nor the present writer feel able to name the probable perpetrator of the forgeries, but Mr. Raymond leaves but little to the reader's imagination." Since Dr. Weiner had come as close as close can be to naming Charles Dawson as the hoaxer, this remark is puzzling. The diligent tracker of the Piltdown criminal rushes to Ernest Raymond's *Please You, Draw Near* (1969), to flush the quarry. The chapter on Piltdown in that memoir ends with:

> Who the scholarly forger was remains one of the world's great mysteries, though, to my mind, deductions from possibility, probability, psychology, and horse sense point steadily to one figure. Before whom I bow.

He does not shed light on whom possibility, probability, psychology, and horse sense point to.

Leaving Mr. Raymond bowing, we turn to Francis Vere's conclusion to *The Piltdown Fantasy* (1955):

> Who was the hoaxer? It would be easy to write "your guess is as good as mine." But that would be unfair because I know—and you do not—the names of the many people who helped Woodward and Dawson to their fantastic discovery.

Professor A. J. E. Cave, chairman of a symposium held to honor Grafton Elliot Smith, indulged in this worthy reflection: "If motivation is wanted, in my posthumous memoirs I will leave my views as to who the nigger in the woodpile was" (summing-up following J. S. Weiner's "Grafton Elliot Smith and Piltdown," 1973; see also Daniel, 1986).

Frank Spencer continues the venerable tradition of hinting. After suggesting that the person whose skull ended up in the pit might have suffered from osteoporosis, he wrote (1984): "As far as I know this fact has not been used as a possible clue to the identification of Dawson's co-conspirator(s) in the Piltdown forgery." Professor Spencer is as of this writing editing Ian Langham's manuscript of the Piltdown hoax, and perhaps in that the connection between Cushing's disease and Dawson's conspirator(s) will be made explicit. Having met Ian Langham, having talked with him at length about Piltdown, and having benefited from his insights and from his comprehensive knowledge of the case, I anticipate finding a good deal of new data and interpretations in his book.

The irrepressible coyness of so many scholars leaves the reader with the bitter feeling that he's heard a joke without its punch-line.

Each suspect in the rogue's gallery could have fabricated the hoax, part of it or all of it, alone or collaboratively with a like-minded villain. Charles Dawson has been identified more often than any other as the hoaxer, having accomplished the feat all by himself. Or in a limited partnership with Teilhard de Chardin. Some critics have opted for Teilhard's doing it as a jonglerie to embarrass the miserable English pebble-hunters, duping Dawson in the bargain. Or maybe Dawson collaborated not with Father Teilhard but with jeweler Abbott. But, then, Abbott may have been the hoaxer and Dawson as blameless as the driven gravel. The curator of the Hastings Museum, W. R. Butterfield, has been identified as the hoaxer, wild to revenge himself upon Dawson. The British Museum's Martin A. C. Hinton did some of it, a few people have argued, to sober up his fellow paleontologists intoxicated with the fakes. No, Professor Sollas did it, to get even with Arthur Smith Woodward, claimed a tape-recording; or maybe Sollas conspired with Dawson. But then there's evidence proving that another professor, Grafton Elliot Smith of Manchester, was responsible, because he wanted advancement or was fun-loving, like Teilhard. The creator of the fictional detective Sherlock Holmes, Arthur Conan Doyle, was also the creator (Professor Winslow claims) of the fictional ape-man because he hated the materialistic evolutionists. Glyn Daniel thinks that Peter Costello's identification of Sam Woodhead as the Piltdown hoaxer (1986) is the most convincing. Sam Woodhead was a pious Presbyterian. Professor Daniel joins John Theodore Hewitt, professor of chemistry at Queen Mary College, to Sam Woodhead as collaborator, his motive to play a joke. A short paper of mine in the *Journal of Irreproducible Results* (1986) proves almost beyond the shadow of a doubt that the British Secret Service was the Piltdown hoaxer.

THE STATE OF THE ART

That the fraud required extraordinary skill and extensive knowledge is a principle advocated by the triumvirate of detectives. "The faking," Le Gros Clark affirmed in the second of the British Museum's monographs (Weiner, 1955), "obvious though it now appears, had been accomplished with extraordinary skill." He also said it was "a most elaborate fabrication," an opinion supporting Weiner's in the first (1953) monograph:

From the evidence which we have obtained, it is now clear that the distinguished palaeontologists and archaeologists who took part in the excavations at Piltdown were the victims of a most elaborate and carefully prepared hoax. Let it be said, however, in exoneration of those who have assumed the Piltdown fragments to belong to a single individual, or who, having examined the original specimens, either regarded the mandible and canine as those of a fossil ape or else assumed (tacitly or explicitly) that the problem was not capable of solution on the available evidence, that the faking of the mandible and canine is so extraordinarily skilful, and the perpetration of the hoax appears to have been so entirely unscrupulous and inexplicable, as to find no parallel in the history of palaeontological discovery.

It required "sophisticated knowledge," said *Scientific American* ("Piltdown Won't Down," 1979). Ronald Millar, in *The Piltdown Men* (1972) thinks the hoax skillful throughout. Dozens of other critics agreeing that the hoax required great skill inculpate or exculpate the suspects on the basis of whether they had it or not. The popular impression is that the hoaxer really knew his science.

While S. J. Gould finds the forger's "main skill in knowing what to leave out—discarding the chin and articulation," he thinks most of it "an indifferently designed hoax" (Gould, 1979). A few others have agreed with Gould's opinion. Richard de Mille: "This was no careful forgery" (de Mille, 1979). William Broad and Nicholas Wade, in their *Betrayers of the Truth* (1982), assert that the betrayal was "not expert—the tools were poorly carved and the teeth crudely filed." Gertrude Himmelfarb calls it a "not particularly subtle fraud" (1959). I agree with this view.

The hoaxer lived in Edwardian England. He had historical and scientific models of mistakes, hoaxes, authentic fossils available to imitate and adapt. For example, the classic blooper in the history of anthropology comes to mind—that of Dr. Johann Jacob Scheuchzer. Scheuchzer, a Swiss naturalist who began his university career (at Altdorf) in 1692, was enamored of the Deluge as God's way of wiping out a world of sinners. In addition to holding chairs in natural history and mathematics, he was a medical doctor, an editor, an assiduous collector of fossils, and the author of scores of books on natural history.

Desiring to prove the inerrancy of scriptural history, he looked for evidence of the old sinner; in 1725, in an Upper Baden quarry, he found a fossil that, to his eyes, did not merely approximate, but "corresponded completely with all the parts and proportions of a human skeleton." He named the find *Homo diluvii testis,* human witness to the flood, buried

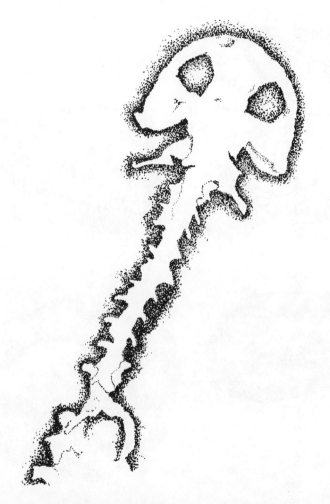

Homo diluvii testis. The skeleton of a prehistoric giant salamander misinterpreted by Professor Scheuchzer as that of a petrified sinner.

5,858 years before the exhumation. Georges Cuvier, who a hundred years later reclassified the old sinner as an old salamander, pointed out a prosaic moral: that self-deception had led Scheuchzer, who as a medical doctor should have known better, to make this egregious error.

The classic example not of a mistake but of a hoax is that of Dr. Beringer's lying stones. A contemporary of Scheuchzer, Professor Johann Beringer, was investigating fossils dug up from Mt. Eibelstadt, also in Franconia. Senior professor at the University of Wurzburg, dean of the

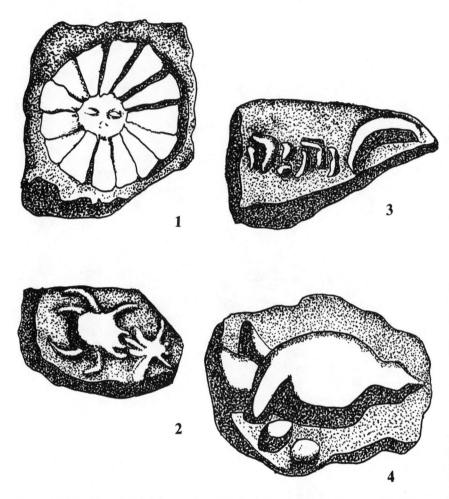

Beringer's Lying Stones. (1) The rayed face of the sun. (2) A spider catching a fly. (3) Hebrew word (*Adonai*) and crescent. (4) A bird laying eggs.

Faculty of Medicine, chief physician to the Julian Hospital and to the Prince-Bishop, Beringer dedicated his lithophilic talents to his country and to his god. Through his own digging and the efforts of students, he recovered a stony menagerie of figures raised in bas-relief on rocks—replicas of plants and animals, frogs copulating, birds laying eggs, spiders patrolling their webs; of the crescent moon, the sun with a face, comets with tails; and alphabetical letters, mostly Hebrew. After he published his report, colleagues at the university confessed that they had cooked up the fossils to discredit Beringer.

The nineteenth century offers two relevant hoaxes, America's busted miner and France's Moulin Quignon jaw. A miner excavating gold in Calaveras County, California, extracted a human skull from a ten-million-year-old stratum. The skull, that of an American Indian, may have been planted; it's of interest only insofar as Marcellin Boule thought its indices approached those of Piltdown Man and in that Bret Harte wrote a poem about it foreshadowing some of the Piltdown affair. The poem is relevant, short, and funny enough to warrant quoting:

> "Speak, O man, less recent! Fragmentary fossil!
> Primal pioneer of Pliocene formation,
> Hid in lowest drifts belong the earliest stratum
>   Of volcanic tufa!
> "Eo-Mio-Plio-whatso'er the 'cene' was
> That those vacant sockets filled with awe and wonder,—
> Whether shores Devonian or Silurian beaches,—
>   Tell us thy strange story!"
> "Speak, thou awful vestige of the Earth's creation,—
> Solitary fragment of remains organic!
> Tell the wondrous secret of thy past existence,—
>   Speak! thou oldest primate!"
> Even as I gazed, a thrill of the maxilla,
> And a lateral movement of the condyloid process,
> With post-pliocene sounds of healthy mastication,
>   Ground the teeth together.
> And, from that imperfect dental exhibition,
> Stained with expressed juices of the weed Nicotian,
> Came these hollow accents, blent with softer murmurs
>   Of expectoration;
> "Which my name is Bowers, and my crust was busted
> Falling down a shaft in Calaveras County,
> But I'd take it kindly if you'd send the pieces
>   Home to old Missouri!"

In the spring of 1863, from a gravel pit at Moulin Quignon, near Abbéville, France, came bright yellow primitive flint tools. The workmen, earning a few francs by selling such relics, brought these and a hominid tooth to Boucher de Perthes, and later showed him at the pit itself a jawbone with one tooth still in it. De Perthes concluded that the material constituted a memento of an authentic prehistoric hominid. However, English paleontologists who visited the site and examined the material came to an opposite conclusion, namely, that they were all fakes.

A small international quarrel broke out, the French believing the Moulin Quignon relics real, the English hearty in their belief that they weren't. The French invited the English not to a duel at sunrise but to a conference. The English demonstrated that the coating, seemingly an indication of the fossils' antiquity, washed off easily, that sawing the jawbone gave forth the organic odor familiar to surgeons and butchers sawing recent bone, and that both jaw and molar tooth had a high nitrogen content. Since nitrogen escapes over time from organic material, this test suggested the modernity of the jawbone. The flints, said the English, were also fakes.

Scheuchzer's and Beringer's was the time for the beginning of fossil collections. By the Victorian period, the demand for fossils was large enough to generate a forging industry. The most notorious of the forgers was Flint Jack, who after a thriving career died in 1864 while a prisoner in Bedford Gaol. A cave was named after him, in Cheddar.

One of the most informative—and funniest—passages to be found in any of the archaeological books of the time is in Worthington Smith's *Man the Primeval Savage.* He warns collectors: If you tell the workmen exactly what to look for, they may make it for you. Carpenters and plasterers, "men who knew how to use different forms of hammer and punch, speedily produced forgeries." They'd sell them to the laborers, who would resell them "often for very large sums," as much as five pounds, to the dotty collectors. Worthington Smith grows rhapsodic about these beauties:

> The best forgeries are beautifully and perfectly made, in close imitation of the best type forms. Every delicate gradation of form, shape, and thinness of point has been most successfully imitated.

If a collector wanted an implement with a polished patina, he'd get an implement with a polished patina post haste; if he wanted slightly abraded edges, he'd get that; if he had a fetish for ochre, he'd get ochre-stained tools; if he liked to see the evidence of glacial action, he'd get tools with scratches very like those etched by glaciers; he might even have an eye for tools with quicksilver-like specks, and suddenly there'd be a pushcart full of those.

Forgers were often weak on counterfeiting patina, the staining coming out a wrong color or superficial and easily spotted. Such incompetents could turn to Worthington Smith for a recipe on how to do it right: drop implements into water boiling in an iron saucepan, add old rusty nails,

Linnaean Beauty Parade. Some years after the Scheuchzer and Beringer episodes, Linnaeus published his *Systema Naturae* (1740). Linnaeus pictured four genera of (very) humanlike apes, the Anthropomorpha: from left to right: Troglodytes, Lucifer, Satyrus, and Pygmaeus. Satyrus represents a chimpanzee and Pygmaeus an orangutan.

then polish—don't polish before boiling.

Historical examples of what to do and what not to do, specimens of real Victorian cavemen, and guidance on customizing forgeries were thus all available to the Edwardian villain. So were the materials. Assiduous searching of the weald and adjacent areas like the Red Crag would have provided domestic deer, horse, beaver, rhinoceros, hippopotamus, and elephant remains. It was, says A. S. Kennard in a most informative little article of 1946, "Fifty and One Years of the Geologists' Association," a Golden Age for collectors. Hands rather than machines dug canals and quarries, and the navvies, usually thirsty souls, were glad to sell fossils for a pot of beer. "It did not matter what excavation you went in, if there were fossils the men had them safely hidden, as a rule in caches. . . ." Chalkies had available fossils from the chalk pits they mined; "Totty Jimmy," a Whitechapel rag-and-bone merchant, had early London in his storeroom; East Coast fishermen were on the lookout for fossils washed from the cliffs; at Brighton, fishermen charged 2s. 6d. for an elephant molar.

For exotic as well as domestic fossils, the hoaxer could have browsed indoors rather than tramped about outdoors. Gerrard's, in business since 1860, and Stevens, two among many such firms, sold this material, as biological supply houses sell fossils today. Auctions of fossils were held. Much trading, some of it sharp enough to cut the gullible, went on. Several of the suspects themselves had, or had easy access to, museum stocks. One of them had a comprehensive, well-stocked private museum.

Fossils came into England from all over the world, not only from Mediterranean islands and North African countries but from South America, the South Pacific, from India and other colonies of the Commonwealth, and from other nations vulnerable to the blessings of British paternalism. Sailors returning from the East Indies brought with them skulls, bones, and other curios, human and not human, for sale on the London docks. In their native land of Borneo, orangutan skulls were passed on from generation to generation in families as good-luck charms protecting against spooks. A group of these was brought to England and found permanent residence in the British Museum of Natural History as the Everett Collection. One of the jaws in the collection or a collateral collection could well have strayed from its shelf. If it had been an imperfect specimen lacking condyle and symphysis, it might have been retrieved from a rubbish bin, and from thence into a supply house or auction, into the hands of a private hobbyist, and finally into the pit in Piltdown.

Anyone wanting them could have bought the necessary supplies. Photography, the jewelry business, and chrome plating used potassium bichromate. Art supply shops sold red sienna and Vandyke brown. The hoaxer might have had such paints right at hand from his honest trade. No special tools were needed, though having at hand a variety of saws, burrs, files, abrasives, acids, and so on would have facilitated the operation. He had to have a workshop somewhere, in a museum, a shop, a cellar, an office.

What everyone could agree on is that the hoaxer was lucky. Sam Woodhead could have analyzed the jawbone for organic content, or Woodward, had he not been negligent, could have done so; such examination would have demonstrated so critical a chemical disharmony between jawbone and cranium that the fraud would have fizzled out right away. Reginald Smith and A. S. Kennard hinted that a twentieth-century artisan had whittled the elephant femur slab with a steel knife. The advocates of Piltdown Man didn't follow through on that any more than on the skeptical estimates given by Waterston, Lyne, Miller, and so many others. Testing for organic content may be a laborious procedure and extrapolating a steel knife from a cut surface a speculative one, but when the inquirer holds the fossils he finds that the skull fragments, being stone, are heavy, while the mandible, being bone, is light. Just jiggling them in the palms of one's hands should have set off an alarm. Most had to use casts, but those who had access to the originals didn't jiggle.

X-rays taken of the molar teeth should have revealed long ape roots, but showed instead short roots—they had been taken at the wrong angle. Le Gros Clark studied the original fossils back in 1913 when he was a medical student; but it wasn't until 1950, employing no superior technology, that he saw the scratches, a giveaway of tampering to mimic human occlusal flatness. Everybody had missed those scratch-marks.

Whether a genius or not, the hoaxer was skillful enough to propel many scientists into the craziest rationalizations—of reconstructions, of alibis for explaining where the canine fit, of bringing in bacteria to expand a canine cavity and inventing extinct British apes, of conversions and deceptions.

I think talking about the hoax as an entity inhibits identification of who did it. It comprised three or four distinct forgeries, each of which required a different degree of knowledge and skill: (1) anatomical; (2) chemical; (3) paleontological; and (4) lithic.

1. Anatomical. A cursory familiarity with physical anthropology indicates that the condyle and symphysis, directive diagnostic signals to the nature of the beast, could not have been modified. Miller thought that the condyle had been broken off naturally; Dawson, that it had rotted away; Pycraft, that a wretched pickax had done the damage. Though most scholars assume that the condyle had been broken off deliberately, Miller's understanding is the most credible.

The jawbone could have lacked symphyseal and condyle regions from the beginning. If it were an imperfect piece, that would account for its having been kicked out of a museum's or connoisseur's collection. That is the simplest (but I hope not simplistic) explanation. But if the structures had in fact been deliberately broken off, little more skill would have been involved than in the similar operation of breaking a chicken wishbone, though the person who did so had to have known the diagnostic values of these structures. If the forger had really known his anatomical business, he would have knocked out the temporal bone's mandibular fossa, an important feature indicating humanness, but he did not.

Contrary to Dr. Weiner's comment, what was done to the teeth shows a remarkable lack of talent for anatomical chicanery. The flatness of the Heidelberg molar occlusal surfaces served as a convenient model for the Piltdown replication. But the hoaxer was not skillful at all in filing to achieve flatness. He failed to bevel the edges to imitate natural wear, he failed to file the surfaces on the same plane, and he failed to smooth out the scratches left by his maladroit tinkering.

The canine is an even worse job. He filed the surface so roughly that he invaded its pulp cavity; he used common artist's paints to coat it; he left, as though scribbling "Kilroy was here," a tiny nugget of metal alloy on it; and, the most preposterous mistake in the whole Piltdown assemblage, he was so ignorant of anatomy that he selected a juvenile canine to go with a mature jaw. With some of the forgeries, application to the hoaxer's knowledge and skill helps identify who he might have been; with the anatomical forgery, we ought to consider someone whose weak suit was anatomy.

2. Chemical. The chemical forgery required knowledge, though not much skill. Those who wanted to transform fossils of poor color into rich earth tones or who hoped to harden fragile specimens regularly used a solution of potassium bichromate. More esoteric was the use of iron sulphates as part of the procedure to oxidize the fossils rapidly.

3. Paleontological. The paleontological tricks were more clever than the anatomical, though no prize-winners either. The hoaxer had a good recipe for the community of index fossils that would date the hominid and simian fragments. Heidelberg had been accompanied by Elephas, rhinoceros, horse, red deer, and cervus fossils. Gather those and put them into the stew with the cranial pieces. Add mastodon and hippopotamus for flavoring—the extinct Maltese hippopotamus was known to paleontologists of the time, and its bones were available. One might not, however, have at hand a cave bear fossil. Omit that. Serve to the experts hungry for just such a potpourri. The mixing in of Pliocene, Pleistocene, and Holocene specimens may have been purposeful. It led to a provocative confusion of fossils that in different times could have been brought to the pit by different vehicles. Or it may have been a mistake. It would have been useful, though by no means essential, for the hoaxer to have had some knowledge of the province, of deposition of gravel beds in the weald, of likely sites for seeding.

4. Lithic. To J. Reid Moir, the flint tools were critical in establishing the existence of pre-Paleolithic man in England. "The ill-defined cones of percussion," he wrote, "and rough heavily truncated flake-areas of the Piltdown specimens stamp them indelibly as the work of pre-Paleolithic Man." One of the Piltdown flints showed traces of chromium from its potassium bichromate dip.

The Kenward boys would have had no trouble obtaining prehistoric flint tools; they're easily obtainable today. I'm not even sure that any cunning was required in selecting the particular tools found in the pit. But

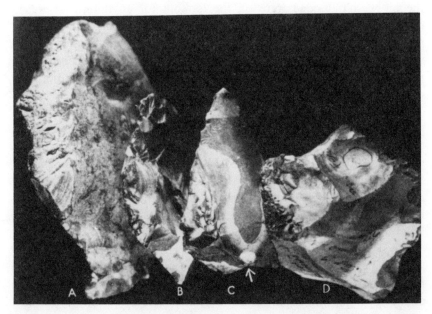

Paleolithic flint implements. A, B, and C were recorded. as having come from the Piltdown gravel; D is Morris's flint core. The arrow points to an area chipped to show pure
white cortex beneath the superficial stain. (From Weiner 1955, Plate 3.)

it is difficult to know whether the flint tools found in the pit were authentic fossils or whether they had been made to order from unworked flint or
from worked flint tools of a later industry.

In 1917, J. Reid Moir told his readers, as Lewis Abbott told everyone,
as modern paleontologists occasionally tell us, and as anyone who has
seen an expert at it will testify, making flint tools requires "an immense
amount of practice and much care in flaking." If the hoaxer made tools
from flint, he had a degree of knowledge and manual dexterity that is
most commendable; if he made old tools from late ones, he was one of a
kind.

His modus operandi obviously required that he have access to the pit
on his own or through an accomplice. I don't think it much matters
whether he visited the pit publicly or privately. After Dawson had been
given the first cranial fragment by a laborer (if that particular tale is
credible), he returned to the pit, sometimes with friends, to look for more,
but didn't find any more until 1911. The pit, one must remember, had no
more area than a tennis court. And it was being probed not only by the
pebble-hunters, but by the workmen who while taking out gravel when

the pit wasn't flooded were on the lookout for anything that wasn't gravel. The hoaxer probably seeded the pit every season, like a farmer, leaving the largest fossil, the femur implement, to be harvested last. It should be remembered that most of the fossils were retrieved, not from the pit itself, but from refuse heaps on its periphery. The hoaxer didn't have to bury many; he could have flung them.

This was an unusual kind of thievery, where the criminal brought goods to, instead of snatching them from, the scene of the crime. Maryon-Wilson, the owner of Barkham Manor, had put out the word that he would not tolerate trespassers, and he tried to renege on the permission he had given Dawson. Kenward, the renter of the farm, Dawson wrote in a letter to Woodward, hoofs off enthusiasts and the "Miss Ks are especially pugnacious against intruders" (January 1, 1912). Woodward admonished Mabel Kenward that she keep "unauthorized persons" from the site. When she was 87 years old, in 1973, she recounted to K. P. Oakley that sixty years earlier she had seen such a person in the pit, a man about 40 to 45 years old, tall, wearing a suit and boots. He refrained from saying anything to her and departed like a ghost. Hers is the only eyewitness account of the hoaxer at work—if that person were the hoaxer and not just a tourist ambling through.

Just who visited the pit and how often is a matter of conjecture. One of the oddest aspects of the case is that the diggers spent so little time digging. Woodward reports in *The Earliest Englishman* that, since he and Dawson were "well occupied with ordinary duties during the week," they could devote only their weekends and occasional holidays to the exhumation of the most important fossil in the world. After his retirement, Woodward spent more time there than he had during the feisty years of exploration. Woodhead visited more frequently than others. Occasional visitors included Dawson's friend Clarke, A. S. Kennard, Lewis Abbott, E. Ray Lankester, Reginald Smith, Davidson Black, Grafton Elliot Smith, Arthur Keith, W. P. Pycraft, and Arthur Conan Doyle. Familiarity with what these and others were writing and discussing, and with their comings and goings, would have enabled the hoaxer to keep tabs on how compliantly the pigeons gobbled up the bait.

He became more and more reckless, as though taunting his victims into conducting the exposé that took an unexpectedly long time to come. He was rash enough to attempt linking an ape's jawbone with a human being's skull. Then he planted the ridiculous bone slivers defined as a turbinal. Anthropologist William Howells sees that as an attempt to wake up Woodward and company.

The hoaxer used Woodward's plaster cast as the basis for his own deceptive replication of an ape-man's canine. That could be analyzed as a covert message that someone should call the police. Then he shaped a slab of elephant femur bone into a cricket bat. An especially sporting touch.

Finished with Piltdown, at Site II he topped off the previous sundry outrages with skull fragments that did not even belong to the same skull— the frontal came from the Piltdown skull, the occipital from some stranger's. He took a molar extracted from the original jaw and planted that at Site II.

William Krogman, who after studying the fossils in 1913 had concluded that the jawbone was an ape's, wrote that the Site II assemblage was the perpetrator's only major mistake. "In essence, what at first seemed a good thing was pushed too far, pushed over the brink of credulity" (1978). Yet it worked well enough to firm up the believers and to silence if not convert many skeptics.

Woodward's reaction to Site II is inexplicable. The first notice Dawson sent him of that was in January 1915, the second in July of the same year. Woodward appended this to the latter:

> I enclose an important postcard from the late Charles Dawson, 30th July 1915, in which he announced his discovery of the isolated lower molar tooth of Eoanthropus with the remains of the second skull in the Piltdown gravel [Site II]. I think that this should be carefully preserved, and that a reference to it should be added to the number of the specimen in the Registrar. Hrdlička (Smithsonian Miscell. Coll., vol. 83, p. 87) has already doubted my statement about Dawson's discovery, and there may be other doubters for whom Dawson's own record is needed.

Woodward himself could have been such a doubter. Doubt would explain his not publicly announcing the find until two years after Dawson told him of it and his giving only four lines to Site II in his memoir of the Piltdown case. He doesn't mention in his note that he had received a letter from Dawson in January concerning the same site. Yet doubt about Site II would have contaminated faith in Site I.

That the hoaxer got away with a canine so similar to the plaster cast one making the rounds, and unique in anatomical history, with an elephant fossilized femur slab whittled by a steel knife not in the toolkit of any prehistoric artisan, with the loot from Site II, with the whole fiction called Piltdown Man reflects, as so much else in the story does, not to the skill of the hoaxer, but to the victims' credulity. He duped them from 1912 on; but between the wars, as they negotiated Piltdown Man through the crowd of hominid australopithecines, pithecanthropines, and Neander-thals, they expeditiously duped themselves.

Another feature in drawing the profile of the hoaxer is his history. Involvement in questionable previous enterprises is no guarantee that he committed this act; and forty years of purity would not necessarily establish innocence. But one's having been a repeat offender could be given some cautious credence as a lead. Part of personal history, at least as important as opportunity, a factor as critical as it is elusive, is motive. What would the hoaxer have to gain from gulling either his close circle of friends (and, for some of them, family) or the wider circle of British and world paleontologists? And what would he have to lose? The motive had to be fairly strong to keep him going at it for the seven years from the pit's delivery of the first cranial piece to Site II's delivery of the last cranial piece, and to keep silent about what he had done for the rest of his life, which ranged from one year in Dawson's case to nearly sixty in Teilhard de Chardin's.

Patriotism could explain part of the ready acceptance of the hoax. But it's unlikely that the hoaxer's motive was to boost Mother England, especially since his being found out would be to the detriment of national prestige. The Moulin Quignon hoax, which may have been a conspiracy of the French Academy of Sciences to ridicule the idea of antediluvian man or to discredit Boucher de Perthes, or for the workmen to engage in a profitable sideline, was a small stain on French national scientific prestige, unlike Piltdown, which was a depravity. The motive may have been to enhance the glory of evolutionary theory, to prove that theory with a creature so amenable to wearing the vestments of then-current fashions; but the theory would have been debased had the hoax been exposed. Allegiance to evolutionary theory, however, may be spotted in the emphasis on the skill of the hoaxer by Oakley, Weiner, Le Gros Clark, and their peers. The more skillful the hoaxer, the less clumsy the hoaxee.

William King Gregory spoke of the possibility of a hoax, its purpose "to fool the scientists." Francis Vere also considered that possibility: to bring the evolutionists down. Winslow attributes that motive to Conan Doyle; Costello, to Woodhead. Perhaps the motive was to fool not the scientists, but a particular scientist, to get even with someone who challenged one's own authority or failed to recognize one's own genius. But there's a problem to be kept in mind about ascribing the motive of revenge—against evolutionists, against a national or local group of paleontologists, against a competitor or superior. Revenge could account for the fabrication of the hoax; but it cannot account for the subsequent failure to reveal it. The capstone of vengeance, its psychological and even aesthetic fulfillment, lies in revelation: See what a dunce he is! The canvas is incomplete, the hoax seems blunted without revelation.

Unless the hoaxer enjoyed, over a gin-and-water, laughing to himself about those fools. If we are to believe Professor Pforzheim of Angus Wilson's *Anglo-Saxon Attitudes,* there is nothing Englishmen like so much "as a joke against themselves"; the hoaxer of the novel does it as a joke against his father, who, a scholar ripe for a fall, had been in charge of the tomb's excavation. A. S. Kennard of the Geological Association and A. P. Chamberlain, Dawson's cousin, both looked back upon the Golden Age of Geology as the Age of the Practical Joke. The motive of doing it for a joke often comes up in the literature, Teilhard de Chardin, Grafton Elliot Smith, John Hewitt, M. A. C. Hinton, and Arthur Conan Doyle all having been identified as possessors of a sense of humor. Still, a seven-year joke seems a bit tedious, more a compulsive pounding home of whatever nail the hoaxer was driving than a lark in Albion.

Perhaps the hoaxer was ambitious to advance his own reputation, though that too would carry the double-edge of being found out and having whatever reputation he possessed terminated. On a profit-and-loss calculus, Arthur Conan Doyle was the only one of the lot with little to lose were he found out. He was not a professional paleontologist, but at best an amateur. All the others would have had a great deal to lose. Woodhead was a public analyst, a government official; Dawson was a solicitor, and his law-firm partner would rise to be Official Solicitor of England. Dangerous, perhaps fatal, for such people to be involved in a hoax. Though Abbott was a jeweler, his true love was paleontology. He too would have been cast out of the scientific community had he been uncovered as a forger.

The others were all professional scientists. What happens today when a scientist is found to have cooked up data would have happened to them, to Teihard de Chardin, John Hewitt, Martin A. C. Hinton, Grafton Elliot Smith, and W. J. Sollas. The theory of evolution has survived the mayhem wrought by Piltdown Man, but these professionals do not come out of the event with their good sense intact.

An insightful perspective is given about the profile of the hoaxer by Jessica North in her *Mask of the Jaguar* (1981). Two characters are discussing a fraudulent archaeological find. Ruska reminds Julia of a parallel case, a "remarkable discovery" in England that "fooled experts for years until new scientific tests unmasked the fraud." The oddest thing about this Piltdown fakery was

> the little man who must have perpetrated it—a respected, scholarly
> gentleman who had nothing—absolutely nothing!—to gain. The hoax
> brought him no money, no promotions, yet he spent months and maybe
> years perfecting his forgery. And at a terrible risk of disgrace!
>   He wanted fame, to be sure, but also to make the world agree with
> a theory he believed in. He concocted Piltdown Man because he was
> sure that somewhere, unfound, a genuine Piltdown Man *had* to exist. In
> a warped mind, fraud in the service of truth seems hardly fraud at all.

I think this is one of the best comments made on the hoaxer and would
rank it in brevity and insight with Waterston's paper on the mandible.

Although a brief is strengthened if it holds only one strong motive
rather than a bundle of weak ones, it is more in accord with human nature
to assume that what was at work here was a human being, talented,
somewhat pathetic, perhaps a bit barmy, driven by several motives.
Dennis Rosen suggests that "many scientific cheats . . . clinically are, and
most deserve to be treated as, mentally unbalanced" (Rosen, 1968).
Retreating to the irrational seems a copout, yet it could help explain
motive better than applying to an irrelevant rational. Perhaps the hoaxer
did not set up a calculus of how much he would gain by a successful hoax,
how much he would lose. People don't always act rationally.

The new direction in Piltdown research, to track down the hoaxer,
may be harmful to pursuers. The Lukases report a rumor (1983): Elihu
Progwhistle, allegedly a medium, warned Oakley after the exposé that the
spirit of Charles Dawson was threatening "extralegal action against the
Piltdown detectives unless they gave up the search."

To sum up, there are two basic points in the identification of a
criminal: opportunity and motive. The question is not who had opportunity (which would include knowledge, skill, access to supplies and the
pit), because all the suspects did; nor who had a motive, because all the
suspects had (or could easily be given) a motive; but rather who was best
placed to assemble the fossils and execute the forgeries and had the most
credible motive. All the evidence for accusation is circumstantial. It's all a
matter of footprints in the snow. The hoaxer did not confess.

But one came close.

CHAPTER SEVEN

PRIME SUSPECT: CHARLES DAWSON

Having heard the news on the radio, Sir Arthur Keith was prepared when J. S. Weiner and Kenneth Oakley dropped by late in 1954. "I know why you have come to me," Keith said, adding in a gallant understatement that it would take him "a little time to adjust to the new view." The proof that there had been a hoax saddened him less than the inescapable corollary that there had been a hoaxer. He told an interviewer from the *London Times* (January 9, 1955), "It left me in no doubt that the man I had the greatest reverence for had deliberately misled his best friend Smith Woodward and me."

A minority of Piltdown historians has acquitted Dawson (F. H. Edmunds, Ian Langham, Francis Vere, Peter Costello). But to Keith, to J. S. Weiner, Wilfred Le Gros Clark, George Gaylord Simpson, the majority of scientists and historians, to newspaper commentators, to the lay public familiar with the Piltdown case, to Piltdown residents aware of the famous site in their village (not all are), Charles Dawson was the Piltdown hoaxer.

On the Piltdown materials themselves, he stands accused of criminal negligence; on other prehistoric and antiquarian finds, of gross poofery; on issues other than his hobby, of real estate chicanery and felonious plagiarism.

He was negligent in reporting the Piltdown finds. "Several years ago," he began his 1912 report to the Geological Society, thus ensuring a scramble to decide whether he had first asked the workmen to keep a sharp lookout in 1908 or 1905 or perhaps 1898. He specifies that he visited the place "shortly afterwards," which might mean 1908, and found a piece of parietal bone—or a workman found it and handed it to him—or to Mr. Kenward. "It was not until some years later," that is, in the autumn of 1911, that he picked up a second cranial piece, a frontal bone

Searching for the Piltdown Man. A picture of Dawson and Woodward at the pit appeared in Dawson's "The Piltdown Skull" (1913); with the ovals of Dawson (left) and Woodward (right) added, it was made into a postcard. (From postcard in author's possession.)

fragment, from "a spoil heap."

The jawbone was exhumed "three or four yards" from a tree "on a warm evening in 1912." The canine—the exact date of its discovery jumping out from the usual slurred reporting as August 30, 1913—was in a "nearby" spoil heap. The elephant femur implement was under a "nearby" hedge. The same vagueness mists the reports of bones found at a site "some distance" from Piltdown and at Barcombe Mills. The reporting of Piltdown is a paragon of scientific precision compared with that of Site II.

EXHIBIT A: THE CHEMICAL FORGERY

E590, the left parietal fragment, the first fossil retrieved from the pit, might have lain there for hundreds or thousands of years. In that case, no hoax yet. The exposé revealed that this piece had been dipped in potassium bichromate and an iron ammonium sulphate solution that converted its apatite to gypsum. Dawson stained fossils. In letters of January 1911, and July and August 1913, and February 1915, he informed Woodward of his doing so to preserve them. He sometimes used the solution recommended by Woodward's assistant, Barlow, and Barlow himself gave the femur implement a bath in a hardening solution.

As we present the various exhibits, we'll call upon witnesses for comment. Two witnesses testified to J. S. Weiner (their testimonies in *The Piltdown Forgery,* a book that Professor Weiner told me in May 1981 he had written hastily, to scoop Vere) that they had caught Dawson in flagrante delicto, staining fossils. We might recall Major Marriott (of the Royal Marine Artillery), who saw Dawson staining fossils. Marriott believed Dawson was "salting the mine," that he had faked the jaw and the canine tooth. Major Marriott told this to his family. A captain—St. Barbe—well-known at Sussex soirees, corroborated the major's recollections. One day in the summer of 1913, he walked into Dawson's office unannounced. Dawson, standing by a dozen porcelain pots, in his embarrassment explained that he was experimenting on methods by which nature stained fossils and flints. St. Barbe smelled iodine, which suggests that Dawson was using some solution other than potassium bichromate and iron ammonium sulphate.

"The tale of boiling bones in Dawson's law office," said Mr. Robert Essex, "is a complete fairy tale" (Bowden, 1981). Essex, Science Master of Uckfield Grammar School, next door to Dawson's law office, and in almost daily contact with him, did not credit Dawson with sufficient knowledge of chemistry to accomplish such high-class fakery. Maybe, Essex speculated, Dawson had been trying to see if fossils could be faked.

Dawson did mention the common solution, potassium bichromate, but not the uncommon iron ammonium sulphate. This may mean that he simply neglected to mention it, or that he deliberately avoided mentioning it—or that he didn't use it. A defender of Dawson's innocence, Malcolm Bowden, claimed that there had been sufficient sulphate in the pit to effect natural conversion to gypsum, and he said that the pit still contains 3.9 mg per 100 g of sulphate. The British Museum authorities, however, were unable to detect any. Which still leaves unanswered the problem of how the occipital fragment found or "found" at Site II also happened to undergo the transformation from apatite to gypsum. That fragment was on dry ground, no natural sulphate intrusion possible.

If E590 had been retrieved unstained, in its natural condition, then some credibility has to be given to Dawson's account and honesty. He (or a workman) found the natural fossil. Later, he (perhaps with Lewis Abbott) stained that piece to harden it. Major Marriott's and Captain St. Barbe's testimonies are conjectural. The expression they interpreted as guilt at having been caught in the act might have been nothing more than annoyance at having been interrupted. If E590 had been stained (as others were to be) before burial, that proves the hoax, but not the hoaxer.

EXHIBIT B: THE ANATOMICAL FORGERY

Dawson possessed a cast of the Heidelberg jaw, which served as a model for the Piltdown fake.

He may also have possessed the Piltdown skull.

Florence Burley Pagham takes the stand. She recalled to the *Sussex Express and County Herald* ("1906 Skull Was Not the Piltdown Find") when she was sixty years old, that Mr. Dawson had visited her father in 1906, when she was thirteen. Her father gave Dawson a brown skull lacking a jawbone, with a single tooth in its upper jaw and a bruise on its forehead. Dawson said, "You'll hear more about this, Mr. Burley."

Why Dawson confided to Burley that he intended to hoax the world and waited five years to do it, if indeed that's what he said and intended, can't be known now. What can be known is that the Burley skull had come from Ashdown Forest, and skulls don't fossilize in the sands of Ashdown Forest. (L. Harrison Matthews overlooked this when he wrote in his series of *New Scientist* articles that the cranial pieces in the pit came from the skull Burley gave to Dawson.) The interview was published on January 1, 1954, six weeks after the British Museum monograph broadcast the exposé, and after Dr. Weiner's strong hint that Charles Dawson had been the culprit.

Dawson's dentist had the memorably Dickensian surname of Ditch. Dr. Ditch once shared a railroad compartment with Dawson. Dawson showed Ditch a jaw, or a cast of a jaw, and a canine tooth and asked where the canine tooth fit into the jaw. The implication of Dr. Ditch's testimony was that a man who didn't know where a canine tooth fit into a jaw could not have done the dental forgery. On the other hand, the hoaxer had before him the plaster canine tooth in the mouth of reconstructed Eoanthropus. The remodeling may have been more careless than crafty. Francis Vere, the foremost defender of Dawson's innocence, said of the mandible that it was "an utter—and not so clever fraud." An utter and not clever fraud lay within Dawson's anatomical competence.

EXHIBIT C: THE PALEONTOLOGICAL FORGERY

To deepen the mystery of the Piltdown coconut, we could use foreign intrigue. We have it in the form of a Tunisian radioactive elephant molar, a Maltese hippopotamus molar, and a Borneo sacred jawbone. We could also use some skeletons in a closet. Best of all would be a cabinet full of secret memoranda.

Mr. Pollard was executor of the estate of one Harry Morris, whom we last met scowling during a talk with Arthur Keith. Morris, another of the many amateur naturalists exploring the weald and building up a collection of its mementos, had traded a cabinet for Pollard's collection of birds' eggs. J. S. Weiner, who spins the Morris tale in *The Piltdown Forgery*, went to visit Pollard to have a look at that cabinet. He rummaged through eleven drawers and found innocuous flints and eoliths. And then he pulled out the twelfth drawer. Morris had been in the habit of writing notes to himself.

The five notes lurking in that twelfth drawer for forty years constitute Harry Morris's testimony of Charles Dawson's culpability. Here are the five notes:

Stained by C. Dawson with intent to defraud (all). H.M.

Stained with permanganate of potash and exchanged by D. for my most valued specimen!—H.M.

I challenge the S K Museum authorities to test the implements of the same patina as this stone which the impostor Dawson says were "excavated from the Pit!" They will be found [to] be *white* if hydrochlorate acid be applied. H.M.

Judging from an overheard conversation, there is every reason to believe that the "canine tooth" *found at P. Down was imported from France.*

Watch C. Dawson. Kind regards. (Emphases in original. Weiner, 1955.)

Morris did not bring his suspicions about imposture to the South Kensington (British Museum of Natural History) authorities. Considering that Barlow, Woodward, Keith, Smith, the top men in the field, all were on Dawson's side, one can sympathize with Morris's prudence. A rebuttal witness might respond that Morris's notes indicate no more than his hostility toward his famous contemporary and sour anger at having been conned in a flint trade. That is not a strong rebuttal: Morris's testimony fits in with Major Marriott's, Captain St. Barbe's, and that of the exposé.

All those who believe that Dawson was the culprit think that he had or could easily have acquired the requisite chemical and anatomical knowledge. But then, any of the suspects fit that bill. The feature of the profile best satisfied by Dawson is being at the scene of the crime. He was the only person present at every retrieval at the pit during the years 1908 to 1914. The Site II finds force Dawson's defender into making up alibis.

How could he have found the pieces in a large area? Stephen Jay Gould thought that Dawson could not have located the small fossils of Site II in a field as large as Sheffield Park (private communication, December 27, 1980).

The Neatherall farm, which is a better choice for Site II than Sheffield Park, is not as large. Anyway, Dawson may have explored not square miles, but cubic feet. Woodward said that the stones through which Dawson sifted had been brought together in heaps, which would limit the terrain considerably. Dawson said he had "a friend" with him—the friend could have been the Piltdown hoaxer. The episodes in January and June 1915 could have happened as Dawson described them in his letter and postcard to Woodward. He could also have invented Site II. There is really no way of knowing.

Others found fossils in fossiliferous places. Dawson picked them up everywhere. So did Abbott.

EXHIBIT D: A PETRIFIED TOAD

Which brings us to the question of whether there's anything in Dawson's rap-sheet, whether he put over any fast ones in the years before Piltdown. In his September 21, 1984, letter to me, George Gaylord Simpson said he thought the hoaxer was Dawson, a bit of evidence being Dawson's having perpetrated a previous hoax. Simpson did not specify which item of Dawson's career was the one he had in mind. There's a choice.

Much of what Dawson worked with has about it an odor of deception or at best inaccuracy. Although he enjoyed the prestige of being the Wizard of Sussex because he found archaeological treasures so readily, his finds prior to Piltdown were not always well recorded, well authenticated, or well received. In an 1893 excavation of Roman earthworks at the Lavant Caves in Sussex, Dawson's contribution was so disruptive as to irritate an associate into complaining that "the caves, it is to be feared, are now lost for all time and their secrets with them." (Weiner quotes this in *The Piltdown Forgery*.) After having botched that job, Dawson added insult to archaeological injury by failing to complete assigned excavations and write the requisite descriptive account. But in a 1909 dig for Neolithic skeletons near Eastbourne, Dawson participated in a careful investigation that followed the rules, including note-taking, measurements, and photographs.

Woodward's professional specialty was not human evolution, but paleoichthyology. Dawson's amateur specialty was not human evolution either. It was curiosities, discovering a cache of natural gas, experimenting with phosphorescent bullets to destroy Zeppelins, collecting medieval anvils, an oar mace, an ancient axe-head, a flint with a petrified toad squatting in it. He wrote to Woodward of a sea-serpent spotted cavorting in the English Channel, a creature as fabulous as the carp-goldfish hybrid or the horned horse he reported having seen.

Consider the Pevensey stamps—not postage stamps, but stamped inscriptions on bricks that Dawson said, in an exhibit of 1907, he had retrieved some years earlier from the Pevensey Roman wall. The bricks were supposed to be 2,000 years old. Exposing these stamps to thermoluminescence proved that they had been made somewhere around 1900 (Peacock, 1973; the conclusion is disputed by Costello, 1985). The article on the stamps said that the fossil mammal *Plagiaulax dawsoni* would "repay scrutiny"—that is, there's a question about the authenticity even of Dawson's fossil finds. Dawson may have been duped on all of these things; or may have been overeager to accept anything as a fossil or an antiquity; or may have faked it all.

EXHIBIT D: THE CASTLE LODGE CAPER

Since 1885, the Sussex Archaeological Society, of which Dawson was a member, had met in and kept a museum at the lodge of Lewes Castle. The Society expected that when the owner of Castle Lodge, the Marquess of Abergavenny, decided to sell the house, the Society would have first option on the purchase. But another owner unexpectedly appeared and evicted the group. That new owner was a member of the Sussex Archaeological Society, Charles Dawson.

Since Dawson had put in his bid for Castle Lodge on the stationery of the Sussex Archaeological Society, the vendor assumed that Dawson was representing it. Weiner asserted (in a Sunday *Times* article, January 16, 1955) that a Mr. Salzman reported that back in 1903 members of the Society had in fact asked Dawson to act as their agent; but then Dawson bought it for himself, a trick neat and nasty. Francis Vere's *The Piltdown Fantasy* (1955) says:

> The inference we are asked to draw is, I suppose, that a man who behaves like that is capable of betraying a close friend and risking his own reputation in the process. The argument is logically a *non sequitur* and offends against common sense.

Rebuttal of the accusation against Dawson would also get to Dawson's using the Society's stationery. If he were posing as the solicitor for the Society, he would have used his own law firm's stationery. In using the Society's, he may have been exercising his privilege as a member (he often used stationery from wherever he happened to be) rather than his duties as a solicitor. On January 23, 1955, a letter by Mr. Salzman informed the readers of the *London Times* that Weiner's account of the conversation the two had had was "completely untrue." The Council had not "asked Dawson to act on their behalf in negotiating the sale to them of Castle Lodge."

The Society moved to the Barcian Museum, where Piltdown never entered to take a place among other local finds. The Society did not allude to the Piltdown finds in its papers. It never invited Dawson to speak to it on the Piltdown finds. It was not represented at his funeral. But in 1928, it did exhibit a cast of the Piltdown skull, and at the memorial service in 1938, the president of the Society offered to have his group maintain the national monument.

EXHIBIT E: PLAGIARISM DAWSONI

In 1903 at Lewes and in 1909 at Hastings, Dawson exhibited a collection of iron artifacts for the Sussex Archaeological Society. In the collection was an iron statuette that he identified as having come from the Roman occupation, contemporaneous with coins from the reign of the emperor Hadrian. This cast-iron piece, it was later determined, was a Victorian reproduction of an ancient Roman statue. A contemporary antiquarian wrote of Dawson's description, "The greater part has been taken from an early writer, Topley, almost word for word without acknowledgement." Though Weiner quotes this—Weiner is a loaded source of defamatory quotes against Dawson—the paper on iron works is a small thing.

Dawson's *History of Hastings Castle,* however, was a big, two-volume exposition. A contemporary reviewer criticized it as being inaccurate, badly arranged, and plagiarized. Mr. Manwaring Baines, curator of the Hastings Museum, located the manuscript copy of a report by William Herbert, who had been in charge of the 1824 excavations of the castle. Baines wrote to Weiner on February 19, 1954, that "half the material in Dawson's volume is copied unblushingly from Herbert's manuscript. . . . The rest is gross padding." Baines also had suspicions about the authenticity of the Roman statuette and of a sixteenth-century anvil Dawson had put forward as authentic. The idea behind this part of the accusation is that if Dawson had plagiarized in writing on archaeology, he might also have plagiarized in using the Heidelberg jaw as a model for the Piltdown jaw.

Taking a lead from Vere, we as laymen do not have access to the Roman statuette or to the anvil; and, if we did, we wouldn't be able to assess their authenticity as antiquities. And we are at a severe disadvantage challenging the British Museum paleontologists when it comes to assessing the authenticity or source of a hippopotamus premolar.

But when it comes to *The History of Hastings Castle,* we are on the same footing as any of the authorities. In the preface, Dawson sets up his strategy: to present a series of records, data as given in original sources, a translation that will retain "all the vigour and beauty of the original draftmanship," that is, a compilation or anthology. He not only does not claim originality; he specifically denies that he aims to be original. He carries out his scheme of compilation through anthologizing records: registers, letters, appointments, declarations, petitions, confirmations, titles, grants, characters, decrees, and inquisitions. He alludes throughout to Willliam Herbert, noting in one place: "The author in the compilation of the present work has made free use of this magnificent record."

The accusation of plagiarism stands as not proven.

EXHIBIT F: CHARLES DAWSON

Both defenders and detractors agree in seeing Dawson as observant, imaginative, an assiduous collector, but also careless, impetuous, eclectic, all the traits that together make up the true enthusiast. Woodward described him as having "a restless mind." To discover his character, we will move outward from the circle of relatives to contemporary friends and foes to more recent commentators, in the course of which movement we may be able to discover a motive. We should be prepared to listen to and perhaps interrogate a number of witnesses.

A. P. Chamberlain, whose father was Dawson's cousin, wrote in a November 1968 letter to the *New Scientist:*

> My father never believed his cousin Charles had sufficient time free from his legal practice, or the training, to be an expert archaeologist (let alone an expert anthropologist too!), but that "finds" had been planted ready for him. It was, after all, the age of first-class practical jokes.

F. J. M. Postlethwaite was not amused by the accusations in 1953 that his stepfather, Charles Dawson, was the Piltdown hoaxer. In 1911 and 1912, Postlethwaite had been on leave from the British Camel Corps, then conducting a campaign in the Sudan. He wrote to the *London Times* (November 1953) that his stepfather had neither the knowledge nor the skill to break an ape's

> jaw bone in exactly the right place, to pare his teeth to ensure a perfect fit to the upper skull and disguise the whole in such a manner to deceive his partner, a scientist of international repute.

Charles Dawson, he exclaimed in step-filial affection, was "an unassuming, thoroughly honest gentleman . . . too honest and faithful to his research to have been accessory to any faking whatsoever."

Mr. Essex, Dr. Ditch, A. S. Kennard, Mrs. Woodhead, Miss Mabel Kenward testified in Dawson's behalf; and two others did. Dr. A. E. Wilson from Brighton Technical College acknowledged that he had guessed at a mistake in the association of jawbone with human cranium. "But Charles Dawson didn't do this. He was genuine, keen and anxious over such matters." (Millar, 1972, counters each of Weiner's incriminatory quotes with the opposite from another witness.)

One more of the witnesses who knew Dawson, Margaret Morse Boycott, said:

> Mr Dawson and I were members of the Piltdown Golf Club. Let me tell you this. He was an insignificant little fellow who wore spectacles and a bowler hat. Certainly not the sort who would put over a fast one.

Of more recent people exonerating Charles Dawson the most angry was Alvan Marston, the discoverer of Swanscombe Man. A few days after the first British Museum monograph came out (November 1953), Marston addressed a meeting of the Geological Society. He began by stating that Dawson had been accused of being the Piltdown hoaxer, at which point Professor King, the president, tried to cut him off. But he would not be cut off. He had received a letter from Barkham Manor declaring Dawson's innocence. "They should not attack this man," shouted Marston. He asked how they could

> accuse a dead man's memory and besmirch his name. How could they account for the fact a lawyer had such deep insight into dental anatomy and physiology that he could for years puzzle the greatest anatomists? Not one of the teeth was interfered with in any way by Mr. Dawson. The charges had been made to hide their own ineptitude. The syco-

phantic humility of the museum tradition had for the past 40 years been playing a hoax on public opinion. Now they made a scapegoat out of Mr. Dawson, who died in 1916 and could not answer back.

He concluded, "Let them try to tackle me." The chairman tried to shut him up again. Fisticuffs were narrowly avoided ("Piltdown Man Hoax," 1953).

What could have been Dawson's motive for conducting this hoax for so long? The one that comes quickest to mind is satisfaction of theory. The keynote of his character, as Weiner sees it, was a fascination with missing links, intermediate forms, a creature half-reptile and half-mammal, a fish half-goldfish and half-carp, a neolithic weapon half-stone and half-wood, a boat half-coracle and half-canoe, a unicorn. In a letter of 1909, Dawson wrote to Woodward that he was working on a new subject, the 13th dorsal vertebra. He thought that a skeleton at the Royal College of Surgeons was that of "a new race of man"—the chimpanzee has 13 dorsal vertebrae—and he asked Woodward to introduce the paper for him at the Royal Society. "I want to secure the priority to which I am entitled." Therefore, or of course, the construction of an anthropoid half-ape and half-human.

In the introduction to *The Earliest Englishman* (1948), Arthur Keith said of the Piltdown finds and finder:

Here, then is a record of fact which will continue to be read as long as Englishmen love the land of their birth. . . . As long as England can produce such men, her place in the Society of nations is assured.

This makes ironic reading today, but during the heyday of Piltdown, Dawson basked in such praise. His spirit would have grinned at Keith's eulogy. Dawson liked to be stroked, and sometimes expressed a frustration at nothing happening. In 1909, he was "waiting for the big discovery that never seems to come." He was irritated by neglect; declining an invitation to a banquet, he wrote to Woodward that he had "a feeling that the G.S. are treating me shabbily" (February 8, 1914). He was annoyed at the leak of the canine tooth find to a newspaper; it undermined things. He apparently wanted to be in control of broadcasting disinformation. He wanted to secure priority and nurtured an ambition to be elected Fellow of the Royal Society.

Dawson once alluded to the "secrets of the cellar," taunting some guests as though a pride of fossils lay down there ready to prowl over the countryside. The persona revealed in his essays, books, and letters does not seem to be the kind who would engage in a hoax the immediate targets of which were his closest friends, Clarke, Woodhead, Woodward, and the doyens of the study to which he had devoted so much of his life, Keith, Sollas, Smith, and others less prestigious.

Furthermore, he would have been the first one selected as hoaxer if the hoax had been exposed during his lifetime. To Millar and Krogman, that recognition alone would have prevented his getting involved in such tomfoolery; for, if he had been found out, that would have meant not only the end of his archaeological vocation. It would also have injured his professional career. An attorney found guilty of, or even suspected of, having uttered a forgery is not an attorney inspiring client confidence. His law partner in the Uckfield office (to which Dawson had moved after a time in St. Leonards, where Abbott lived) was Ernest Hart, who would become Official Solicitor of England. Dawson's reputation would have suffered even if it had been revealed only that he had fallen for a hoax perpetrated by someone else. He had no prevision that he would soon die.

His waiting three years to inform Woodward of the first find, his casual mentioning of it in the first letter, his insouciance about the Site II finds, are inconsistent with the idea that he was fashioning a hoax. If he had lusted after satisfying his theories about early man or for recognition, why wait so long for consummation? Several times during the Piltdown event, Dawson had the opportunity to clutch at someone else's find or theory to support the authenticity of Piltdown and rejected those opportunities. He could have announced the first Site II finds in the winter of 1915, but did not. In Queensland, Australia, a fossil was found and named the Talgai skull. Some favored it as another eoanthropine. Dawson, however, objected, arguing that since the lower jaw was missing it could not justly be taken as evidence of eoanthropine status. Had he been the hoaxer, he would have welcomed the Talgai skull or at least have kept cunningly quiet.

The best example of Dawson's rejection of a theory that would have boosted Eoanthropus is the position he took on the question of eoliths. Certain flints lend themselves to opposite interpretations: that they look like tools because natural agencies (being tumbled by water or subjected to pressure) shaped them or that they look like tools because people made them. Sollas and Boule and most of the paleontologists of that day (and of today) rejected the interpretation that these eoliths or dawn stones or old brownies were tools. But Harry Morris, E. Ray Lankester, Reid Moir, and Lewis Abbott preferred to consider them tools.

If he were the hoaxer, Dawson should have gone along readily with the party that looked upon Dawn Man as the maker of those dawn implements. But instead, in February 1915, Dawson began experiments to prove that natural forces could produce stones that look like artifacts. He took clumps of starch, dipped them in Barlow's spirit and shellac solution to harden them "as they are very crumbly and seemed ready to split up into other prismatic features or perhaps 'micro-eoliths'!" The next month, before an audience of the Royal Anthropological Society, he repeated the experiment. His clumps of starch, stained to simulate the mineralization color of eoliths, were put into a bag and jumbled. When he took the starch pieces out, they looked like eoliths. Therefore, analogous natural forces could produce eoliths, natural prismatic cleavages mistakenly seen as artificial flaking. Reid Moir tried to get at Dawson over these starch eoliths, but the most intemperate critic was Lewis Abbott, who seemed, as Dawson put it in a letter of March 9, 1915, "especially annoyed" and sent Dawson "abusive letters."

Postlethwaite, Chamberlain, and Francis Vere concurred that Dawson could have been duped. According to Essex, one of the diggers had come looking for Mr. Dawson, who was at the time in court. The visitor had left his bag there, and the clerk had opened it. Inside, he found "a fossil half-jaw much more human than an ape's and with three molars firmly fixed in it." The clerk called Essex, who happened to be walking by, into the office and showed him this object. The digger returned and retrieved his bag. The clerk may not have replaced the jawbone. Sometime later, Essex met Robert Kenward. Kenward was looking for the owner of the bag, who was "distractedly searching for something he had lost." Essex is cryptic about what this all portends. The owner of the bag, whom Essex names X, apparently was trafficking in jawbones.

Sometime after this incident, Essex was again in Dawson's office, this time chatting with Dawson and John Montgomery, headmaster of Uckfield Grammar School. A small group of people stood nearby. In 1955, Essex described what happened:

> When Charles Dawson said he had never seen anything like the "sixteen inch bat" found at Piltdown, Montgomery told him he had seen one in the Dordogne. Montgomery told me afterwards exactly how he saw it, but the point is that as soon as Montgomery said "Dordogne," Dawson's eyes glanced across to the nearby group of people, one of whom was the owner of the bag. Then he turned abruptly indoors. I am certain Dawson suspected something, although at the time I had no idea what he suspected.

The owner of the bag may have transported the femur slab implement from the Dordogne to Sussex. But Dawson's recorded remarks (of November 21, 1914) on the implement do not reveal his having any suspicions that Mr. X had planted it.

"It is not my business to pillory him publicly," Mr. Essex said of X. "He conceived a joke." Who was this mysterious bagman? Montgomery alluded to the Dordogne. A Morris note specified the provenance of the canine tooth as France. One of the suspects often traveled between his home in France and his seminary in England. But before we pursue the French connection and the identification of Teilhard de Chardin as Piltdown hoaxer, we have to take a brief detour to Hastings and environs, escorted part of the way by a pet goose.

CHAPTER EIGHT

A CURATOR, AN ANALYST, AND A CHEMIST

One of the major biographical fictions in the Piltdown case incriminates one of the minor characters. We first meet William Ruskin Butterfield, curator of the Hastings Museum, in the pages of J. S. Weiner's *The Piltdown Forgery* (where he receives the initials C. S.). Butterfield and Dawson, we learn, got along well together. Dawson had shown the Piltdown fossils to him, and Butterfield, recognizing their importance, had directed Dawson to consult with British Museum authorities. Dawson gave Woodward a quick image of Butterfield's intrepid explorations: Arthur Conan Doyle had spoken of a rumor that iguanadon bones were in Crowborough. There weren't any such bones, but, Dawson wrote, "Anyway, it brought the poor curator of the Hastings Museum up to Crowborough on a bicycle at a moment's notice" (May 13, 1911). Dawson mentions Butterfield again in June 1912, regarding a collection to go to the Hastings Museum. And shortly after the announcement to the Geological Society, Butterfield wrote to Woodward:

> I am venturing to ask whether a plaster-cast of the skull and jaw discovered in Sussex by Mr. Dawson could be made to the order of this Museum. The discovery has interested me very much, and I am anxious to have here, if possible, a cast of the specimen. (December 20, 1912)

On August 9, 1913, Butterfield reported, "The clubs and axes carried [in a pageant] by the Ancient Britons were made by Mr. Lewis Abbott, and all who saw them will agree, I think, that they were remarkably well done." He helped Abbott out financially. After Dawson's death, he arranged for the Hastings Museum to buy Dawson's collection from his widow. He seems a kindly sort. But, if we probe beneath the patina of avuncular philanthropy, we find, according to his accuser, a rock-hard and obsessively vengeful personality.

It was Guy van Esbroeck's secondary purpose in his *Pleine Lumière sur l'Imposture de Piltdown* (1972) to clear Dawson and Teilhard of suspicion. His primary purpose was to discover the hoaxer, an impossible task until the publication in 1965 of Teilhard's *Lettres.* "Fait Nouveau: Un incident en 1909" heads the chapter, sixth in van Esbroeck's amazing book, describing the first of two critical incidents leading to the identification of William Ruskin Butterfield as Piltdown hoaxer.

On July 1, 1909, Teilhard wrote to his parents about a meeting with Butterfield, "une aventure assez comique." Teilhard and his companion naively recounted to Butterfield that Dawson had found iguanadon bones in a quarry. It was one of Butterfield's dreams to have these for his museum. "I grow wild," said Butterfield. Butterfield, angry at Dawson (some of the anger popping off at Teilhard), decided to get even with this so-called friend who would give coveted iguanadon fossils to the British Museum rather than to the Hastings Museum, of which Dawson was himself a member.

Butterfield then selected fossils from his collection, careful to extract some of continental origin, and thus implicate Teilhard. Like a prestidigitator, he did the fakery; he then looked about for an accomplice who would, under the guise of helping Dawson, plant the fossils—Venus Hargreaves. Butterfield pretended to advise Dawson on what to make of them and where to deliver these fakes. A devilish curator, this Butterfield. A most disreputable navvie, this Venus Hargreaves, "sans doute l'unique complice du genial mystificateur." They planned a devastating supercherie.

Butterfield persuaded Dawson to search in the Piltdown neighborhood. With the fifth columnist Hargreaves at his side, Dawson had no chance of avoiding finding fossils. Butterfield continued to dissimulate friendship as the fossils were exhumed and went so far, says van Esbroeck, as to counsel Morris to exchange his flint for one of Dawson's fakes. The brief against Dawson is made airtight by another incident, that of the decoy goose.

Teilhard breakfasted at Castle Lodge one morning in August 1913 and then went off with Dawson and Woodward to the pit. In his letter to his parents, he added a pet goose to the list of diggers, the goose pestering them and acting fierce toward passersby. While the diggers were distracted by goose-antics, Venus Hargreaves surreptitiously dropped one of Butterfield's fabrications onto a rain-washed refuse heap. Teilhard was poking about and he found the canine of the jawbone of the famous man of Piltdown.

Workers at pit with goose. Left to right: Teilhard, Dawson, workman, ferocious goose, and Woodward. (From archives of the British Museum [Natural History].)

Manwaring Baines had never met Butterfield, his predecessor as curator of the Hastings Museum, but he had been advised that Butterfield was bizarre. Butterfield had founded the *Hastings and East Sussex Naturalist*. He had a history not quite clean: between 1892 and 1930, 542 of his identifications of birds were rejected. Birdwatchers had been delighted by a flurry of rare specimens over Sussex. Butterfield had imported rare specimens from overseas. He and Dawson patched up their differences, and were reconciled, their British pride preventing them from showing their rivalry to a stranger, particularly to the alien Jesuit Teilhard de Chardin. Butterfield finally received what he desired: when Dawson died, part of the fossil collection, or what remained of the remains, went to the Hastings Museum.

Van Esbroeck, professor emeritus of the University of Gand, detests his fellow Catholic and professional colleague, Father Teilhard. He is offended at Teilhard's believing in the theory of evolution and censorious about Teilhard's placing man as judge of God. Teilhard's philosophy he finds thoroughly heretical. Teilhard was an apostate, not quite sane, "dans la lune," a theological troublemaker, though probably not quite bright enough to conceive of such a hoax.

Van Esbroeck's thesis has not been given the slightest attention by other Piltdown scholars, which might mean that he hit on the truth about Butterfield as the Piltdown hoaxer or that his *Pleine Lumière* is itself an *aventure assez comique*. The only person to pick up on his book was A. P. Chamberlain, who, perhaps flailing about for some target other than his cousin Dawson, reminded Dawson's accusers "of recent press articles on suspected ornithological frauds on the Sussex coast about the same period."

If it were not for the prestige of the authorities I will now rely on, I would not invite you to visit the next two suspects. However, Peter Costello, a biographer of James Joyce and one of a handful of Piltdown scholars, and Glyn Daniel, a world-famous archaeologist, editor of *Antiquity*, and student of Piltdown for decades, cannot be disregarded in any inquest into the Piltdown case. There is (at the time of this writing, June 1986) very little upholding the incriminations posed by Costello and Daniel—in chronological order, an article by Peter Costello in *Antiquity* (1985), a BBC program (November 22, 1985) on that article, and another article in *Antiquity* by Glyn Daniel (March 1986).

Lionel Woodhead, son of Samuel Allison Woodhead, wrote a letter (dated in Costello's article as January 10, 1954) to Kenneth Oakley. In this, the son says that Dawson brought the skull to analyst Woodhead; both returned to the pit to look for other parts; "Dad himself found the eye tooth"; but Dad was not party to any hoax. A reply from Oakley elicited a further comment (January 16, 1954): Sam Woodhead and Dawson found the jaw a few days (not months) after Dawson had brought the skull. A day or so after Sam Woodhead found the jaw, he found the tooth. A year later, Teilhard found some other tooth.

In another letter (undated) to Glyn Daniel, Lionel said that his father refused to talk about Piltdown. Mrs. Woodhead remembered that Dawson had brought the bones in to find out how "one would treat bones to make them appear older than they were and my father told him how it could be done." Then Dawson "found" (the quotation marks are in Lionel Woodhead's letter) bones and so did Sam Woodhead. He continues: "Unknown to Dawson my father took some back to his lab where he became very suspicious. Before he could ask Dawson what he was trying to do the 'find' had been publicized. Unfortunately for what happened later my father was an extremely loyal friend and did not give the secret away."

These letters by Lionel Woodhead, written to exculpate his father, pointed Costello precisely to the opposite conclusion. According to Lionel Woodhead, his father had known of fraudulence as early as 1911; but

Woodhead continued to dig as late as October 1913. Since (a) he knew it was a hoax and (b) he continued to help out, then (c) he was in on it. It could be that he collaborated with Dawson, but Costello is firmly persuaded that Dawson was innocent, hence (d) Samuel Allinson Woodhead was the Piltdown hoaxer.

Lionel did not find that logic persuasive. On the BBC "Newsnight" program of November 22, 1985, Lionel Woodhead and Peter Costello had a go at it. Lionel said that Sam Woodhead accused Dawson of doing "something funny" and "there was a terrible row." His father kept quiet out of "misplaced loyalty."

Peter, however, returned to the point that if Sam Woodhead had continued digging at the pit after knowing "something funny" was going on, he was at least part of the funny business. Furthermore, Sam Woodhead used potassium bichromate in his chemical analyses. That clinches it.

Why did Sam Woodhead do it? Because, Costello said on the program, as a "devout Presbyterian," he hoped that exposure of the hoax would destroy evolutionary theory. (Sam Woodhead died in 1943; Costello did not discuss why Sam Woodhead had not revealed the hoax in the thirty years between its initation and his death.)

Lionel Woodhead countered that his father, as a public analyst, would not fake anything. The narrator said that Samuel Allinson Woodhead was a "model of Edwardian respectabity."

Glyn Daniel, who had rejected every prior identification of a culprit, approved of Costello's. In a heading to Costello's article, Daniel said that Piltdown scholars had wondered whether they would "ever know the truth. Now we think we do." In his own article on the subject, that of March 1986, he offered up John Theodore Hewitt (1868-1954), professor of chemistry at Queen Mary College in London, as a collaborator. Hewitt had read a paper on the natural gas that Dawson discovered at Heathfield; Sam Woodhead, like Hewitt a member of the council of the Society of Analysts, analyzed that gas.

The day after the BBC interview was broadcast, a Mrs. Elizabeth Pryce wrote to Daniel. She said that in 1952 she had been a neighbor of Professor Hewitt in Hurst. At a Sunday luncheon, "he told my parents and me that he and a friend had made the Piltdown Man as a joke." She didn't remember who that friend was "or if in fact it is true." She and her mother had discussed Professor Hewitt's confession. In another letter to Glyn Daniel, she elaborated: she and her mother had "talked about the time when Dr. Hewitt, as we knew him, spoke about the making of the skull. How he laughed when he said, 'One day they will find out it was made by man.' My mum says she can close her eyes and see this."

Dr. Daniel went to visit Mrs. Pryce and her mum, Mrs. Hawkins, who remembered clearly the conversation that had taken place with Dr. Hewitt 34 years before. Daniel is impressed by the fact that in the entire field (he comes to a total count of 21 suspects), Hewitt was the only one who said he did it—with a friend who may have been Samuel Woodhead.

The case brought against Woodhead (I don't know whether Costello accepts Hewitt as Woodhead's accomplice) is more reasonable than that brought against Butterfield, and shorter. If the accusation hinges on Woodhead's having access to potassium bichromate and his being a devout Presbyterian, it's shaky. But final judgment awaits Costello's book.

CHAPTER NINE

THE FRENCH CONNECTION: TEILHARD DE CHARDIN

In late July 1980, Bostonians reading their *Boston Globe* were quizzed, "Did This Joke Work Too Well?" The *Herald American* asked "Did Theologian Have a Hand in Great Missing Link Hoax?" and the *Washington Post* answered: "Piltdown Hoax Said to Involve Jesuit Scholar." *Time* burst into capitals: "HOLY HOAXER?"

The accusation that provoked these headlines, titillating the public imagination more than any before or since, was entitled "The Piltdown Conspiracy." Both author and suspect were famous people: the author, Stephen Jay Gould, a professor at Harvard University, was (and is) one of the world's foremost authorities on evolution and the history of biology and of world-rank as a popularizer of science. The suspect was Teilhard de Chardin, Jesuit theologian, paleontologist, philosopher, and best-selling mystic. Gould had caught a fallen star of great eminence.

Teilhard's posthumous reputation arouses strong emotions. As a priest, he has been a target for evolutionists who laugh at his mysticism; as a paleontologist, for mystics who despise his evolutionism. Others believe that his synthesis of Roman Catholicism and evolution deserves the highest respect. His best contribution to paleontology was his participation in excavating the Choukoutien caves; his most dramatic, that at Piltdown.

Suspicion about Teilhard's role had been running underground for at least 25, perhaps 55, years before it surfaced in Gould's articles. Essex in 1955 claimed that back in 1913 he and Dawson had suspected Teilhard of deception. The thesis that Dawson was innocent and Teilhard guilty impressed Francis Vere and Malcolm Bowden.

Louis Leakey also seemed to have thought Teilhard guilty. I say "seemed" because his comments were not straightforward, and sometimes became insinuations. His *Adam's Ancestor* gave no hint that Piltdown Man is anything other than a reality (Leakey, 1935). After the exposé, in *Unveiling Man's Origin* (Leakey and Goodall, 1969), he designed a profile of the hoaxer that differs substantially from that of this inquest's Chapter 6.

> The last word on the subject has not yet been written. There can be no doubt at all that at least one of the persons involved in making the forgeries must have had considerable knowledge of chemistry as well as some training in geology and human anatomy. The perpetrators also must have had access to fossil bones from outside Great Britain, since some of the animal fossils "planted" with the skull and jaws, at the site, came from places like Malta and North Africa.

Teilhard de Chardin is the shadow being boxed at in this passage.

In his autobiography (Leakey, 1974), he restated the critical criterion of knowledge of chemistry. A reporter from the *Sunday Times* called him to pin down whether he really did have Teilhard in mind. Leakey shrugged off the question with, "I don't say so in so many words, do I?" (Bowden, 1981). Mary Leakey prevented her husband's publishing a manuscript in which he did say so in so many words. She feared that its publication would hurt her husband's more than Teilhard's reputation. Glyn Daniel, who reports this story, often opposed Leakey on the Teilhard incrimination (Daniel, 1981).

Others who didn't think him guilty still felt that Teilhard had done something. Ronald Millar, in *The Piltdown Men*: "The evidence against the priest is as black, if not blacker, than that against Dawson." L. B. Halstead wrote that Teilhard's finding the canine is a clue to his guilt (Halstead, 1979). As early as September 1975, four years before Gould's first article appeared, Glyn Daniel, while feeling that Teilhard certainly had nothing to do with the beginning of the hoax, "just could have been curiously involved in the affair of the canine. . . . The whole incident of the canine stinks." In the last of his series on the Piltdown hoax, Harrison Matthews, who included Teilhard as one of the quartet of hoaxers, alluded to rumors that in some bank vault lies Teilhard's confession, not to be read until all those concerned with the original case have died.

They have all died, as have the chief investigators who produced the exposé, but the confession has not appeared. Until it does, the inquest will rely upon available evidence in attempting to ascertain whether Teilhard was the sole Piltdown hoaxer, or a collaborator, or a dupe, or a bystander as innocent as his accusers. Accusations against him are based on his activities before and during the Piltdown episode and his responses afterward both to the growing fame of Piltdown Man and to the exposé. This chapter will examine these specific clues: his expertise in the techniques of the four forgeries, his access to the fossils and to the pit, his errors in relating what happened when, his reticence to talk about Piltdown, his ambiguous language when he did, and his sense of humor.

A warning might be of use here. General statements won't suffice in this investigation any more than in an investigation of an ape's jaw. We will be getting into lamentably fine details about dates, the Fifth Amendment, and a garbage dump. The inquest moves from the psychology of the hoaxer to the reasoning of the judges, from canine to rules of evidence, from the meaning of a fossil to the meaning of a phrase, and from propositions to a misunderstanding of a preposition.

CHIEF PASSION

Charge #1: The hoaxer had to have special expertise in chemistry, anatomy, and paleontology. Teilhard had it.

As a child, Pierre followed his father's footsteps over mountains, collecting beetles, minerals, fossils. Juvenile interest in naturalism led straight to Cairo, where from 1905 to 1908 he taught physics and chemistry at a Catholic school and went exploring. The hoaxer knew his chemistry. Teilhard was the only one among the suspects to teach that subject.

Leakey's emphasis on this criterion of hoaxery was paraphrased by Malcolm Bowden, who with customarily extravagant use of italics wrote that "Teilhard's knowledge of chemistry was considerable, *for he had been a lecturer in this very subject whilst at Cairo University.*" This is a little misleading: Teilhard lectured not at a university, but at a secondary school—the College of the Holy Family—where he was reader in elementary chemistry. Still, ignorance of advanced chemistry can no more exonerate Teilhard than knowledge of elementary chemistry incriminates him.

Dawson, said Bowden, couldn't handle the technology for a hoax. Teilhard, however, was "a keen student of paleontology" who

> went on to obtain international recognition as an expert, writing numerous papers and assisting at the excavation of Pekin Man. He would have had more than sufficient knowledge to know which animal fossils should be implanted in the grave, to give it the correct age for dating the finds. . . . He would be aware that the atmosphere in scientific circles was ripe for the finding of an ape-man link.

Teilhard told a different story about himself. He wrote to Oakley (March 1, 1954; the letters exchanged by Teilhard and Oakley are reproduced in Teilhard de Chardin, *L'oeuvre Scientifique*, 1971):

> You know, at that time, I was a young student in theology,—not allowed often to leave much his cell of Ore Place (Hastings),—and I did not know anything about anthropology (or even pre-history): my chief passion was the Wealdian bone-beds and their fossil teeth content.

His achieving recognition later as a scientist, such as his rising to the post of professor of geology at the Institut Catholique in Paris after World War I and his field work in China, Africa, and elsewhere, does not relate to his expertise before 1912. One way of finding out something about his alleged expertise is to zoom in on his publication record. To 1912, this record shows that he was interested in the Tertiary period and the natural history of Fayum, physical laws, the miracles of Lourdes, volcanic rock, religious ethnology, and a cricket.

Comment on charge #1: In 1909, Teilhard had sufficient expertise in chemistry, anatomy, and paleontology to execute the hoax. So did the others. I should express my own bias here at the beginning of the inquest on Teilhard de Chardin, since it will affect the commentaries on the charges as it affects my views on which of the Piltdown suspects best fits the profile of Chapter 6: I think that we ought to believe what Teilhard says unless there's strong proof that he's lying.

Charge #2: The hoaxer had to have easy access to exotic fossils and to the pit. Teilhard's history shows that he could easily have obtained the fossils and deposited them in the pit.

Essex reported that John Montgomery had discerned a resemblance between the elephant femur slab and one found in the Dordogne, site of the Cro-Magnon Les Eyzies culture and about a hundred miles from Teilhard's home. J. O. Head, who knew Robert Essex, described the femur slab implement as "a tool used in the alpine regions of France as an aid to thatching roofs" (Head, 1971). Experts of the Geological Society of London examining that fossil disagreed. They thought it resembled a fossil from an Egyptian deposit of Elephas. But switching from France to Egypt, far from getting Teilhard off the hook, impales him more firmly. He had, after all, lived in Egypt. The Elephas molar tooth fragments could have come only from Ichkeul, near Bizerta in northern Tunisia. Ichkeul is 1,400 miles from Cairo. As for the Maltese hippopotamus tooth, Malta is about 1,100 miles from Cairo, and Teilhard could have stopped off there for that curio.

Bowden, Leakey, and Le Gros Clark found geographical proximity (if 1,000+ miles is proximate) an opportunity for Teilhard to obtain the mammalian molar fragments. But, as Gould pointed out, while Teilhard could have stopped off at Tunisia and Malta, he didn't have to. North African collectors, like their counterparts elsewhere, traded fossils. Teilhard was friendly with Ines Bey, a dedicated fossil-hunter of the region who could have come up with anything wanted.

There is no anecdotal evidence that Teilhard had a habit of secreting fossils in his habit, but if he were the hoaxer, certain fossils that would later appear in the Sussex pit accompanied him as cargo on the voyage from Egypt to Europe. He stopped off to visit his family and friends in France, crossed the channel, arrived at Ore Place in Hastings, began the life of a seminary student, and participated in or initiated the series of events that make him a candidate for Piltdown hoaxer.

"HOLY HOAXER?" *Time* asked in 1980. "Geologist?" Dawson had asked when he and Teilhard met in a quarry in 1909. Perhaps a year after that encounter among iguanadon fossils, Dawson told Teilhard of the Piltdown pit. Being well into his digs at Ore Place, Teilhard then joined Dawson in the digs at the pit, Dawson having settled Woodward's anxiety by saying that the 27-year-old priest was "quite safe." Although some historians maintain that Teilhard often visited the pit, the record evidences three or four visits. On one occasion, when Charlie called to him to come out and play in the pit, Pierre said that he'd like to, "Mais, je n'ai plus guere le temps par cela."

Whether one thinks the seminary, forty miles from Piltdown, providentially close to the pit or far away doesn't much matter. Nor does it matter whether Teilhard had a lot of time to go hiking about the weald or very little. Those who think he did not have much time emphasize the tight control of a Jesuit education, with its strict schedule of mandatory activity, classes five days a week; study, prayer, and exercise periods. An excursion once a month would have been more than enough time to do the planting.

It is unlikely that Teilhard could have used the seminary's facilities for renovating the fossils. The forger boiled chemicals whose aroma would have alarmed fellow scholastics and worse, superiors who could have barged in on Teilhard anytime they wanted to and caught the precocious novitiate fiddling away. If Teilhard worked with Dawson, then he would have had access to Dawson's cellar or office.

Comment on Charge #2: Proximity to the sites where the exotic fossils came from has no bearing on availability of those fossils in England. Access to the pit is more important, and Teilhard, whether he had a good deal of free time or not, whether he had always been in the company of a compère or had been able to escape now and then, had that. He lacked a convenient alchemical laboratory in which to work the miraculous transubstantiation of a couple of handsful of fossils into the apparition *Eoanthropus dawsoni.*

A GRAND EXCITEMENT

Charge #3: Teilhard was too successful at finding fossils to have found them by sheer luck.

In April 1912, Dawson showed Teilhard some fossils from the pit and invited him to dig, to which Teilhard responded that he didn't have time. His first recorded visit to the pit was on May 31. About that he wrote to his parents on June 3 from Bramber, where he was chaplain, that he had found a fossil. "This find considerably enhanced my reputation with Woodward. . . . This first tooth of an elephant impressed me the way another man is impressed by bringing down his first snipe." He might also have found a flint implement on that dig. He refers to "the famous human skull."

During the following months, he went about his clerical and paleontological businesses, including (in July) a return to France for graduate training in paleontology under Marcellin Boule and (in January 1913) duties as priest to glassworkers. After returning from France to Lewes on August 8, 1913, Teilhard visited the pit a second time and then, on August 30, found the canine. Harry Morris said afterward that that canine had originated in France. Teilhard wrote home, in the letter referring to the pet goose, "It was a moment of grand excitement. Remember that it was the last dig of the season." That last dig of the season would be the last time Dawson and Teilhard would meet.

From Vere (1959):

What a lucky man was Teilhard! A flint *in situ* and a *stegodon* fragment within two days of beginning inspection in 1912, and the invaluable canine within a few hours of his arrival in 1913. . . . Is it not "inherently possible"—to use one of Weiner's phrases—that some one other than Dawson had "planted" it and Teilhard by sheer good luck had found it? Or even that the latter had brought it?

In a letter to Oakley, Teilhard wrote that the canine was so inconspicuous, it seemed "quite unlikely" that it could have been planted (November 23, 1953).

Comment on Charge #3: Dawson was even luckier. Woodward found a flint. Davidson Black and E. Ray Lankester, both of whom just dropped in, picked up fossils. Teilhard found an inconspicuous darkly stained canine in a mound of darkly stained gravel of the same size. The leaner explanation, namely that he had sharp eyes, is more presentable than the padded speculation that he didn't find it, but took it out of his pocket.

THE SOUND OF SILENCE

Charge #4. Teilhard did not comment often enough about the finds before the exposé or about the hoax afterward. He was silent because he was guilty.

When Teilhard recalled the Piltdown excavation, he spoke of his good luck at having been invited to participate in it, one of his "brightest and earliest" paleontological memories. He praised Hastings as the Cannes d'Angleterre. But he shied away, or so the brief against him goes, from talking much about Piltdown Man. In 23 volumes of Teilhard's collected works, Gould states (1980), there are not half a dozen references to Piltdown Man. Yet certain events clamored for his reference to that hominid, such as the finds at Choukoutien, which Grafton Elliot Smith seized on as another opportunity to discuss the finds at Piltdown.

His reticence would be even more suspicious if Piltdown Man were a good example of Teilhard's philosophy of evolution. He sometimes did speak (as in an early paper, 1920) as though that were the case: Eoanthropus "admirably resumes life's previous effort," journeying along the human line while Neanderthal Man rode a rail destined for extinction. But, according to a Teilhard partisan, the sequence of Piltdown skull followed by smaller skulls argued precisely for what Teilhard rejected in his philosophy: "the domination of matter over spirit" (King, 1983). His mature judgment is in one of his last published statements on human evolution (1953). In this late paper, "The Idea of Fossil Man," he escorts Eoanthropus out of the human lineage. Eoanthropus was only "sapientoid," a "para-hominian" like Neanderthal Man rather than a "pre-hominian." Though he rejects Piltdown Man as an ancestor, he does accept it as "a paleontological reality." Whatever gambit one tries to open an understanding of whether Piltdown Man did or did not exemplify Teilhard's cosmic philosophy, the game ends in stalemate.

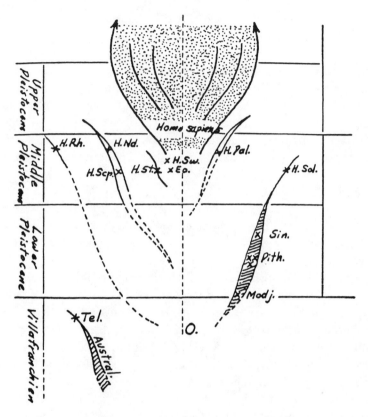

Hypothetical structure of the human phylum, as suggested by the Australopithecines and the Pithecanthropines. Key: *H.Rh.*, Rhodesian Man; *H.Nd.*, Neanderthal Man; *H.St.*, Steinheim Man; *H.Sw.*, Swanscombe Man; *H.Pal.*, Palestine Man; *H.Sc.*, Saccopastore Man; *Eo.*, *Eoanthropus*; *H.Sol.*, Solo Man; *Sin.*, Sinanthropus; *Pith.*, *Pithecanthropus* group (and *Meganthropus*); *Modj.*, Modjokerto Man; *Tel.*, *Telanthropus*; *Austral.*, Australopithecines. *O* is the presumed point of human origin. In *H. sapiens*, the originally diverging elements composing the human phylum are decidedly converging under the pressure of forces of socialization. (Teilhard, 1952)

When he was told about the hoax, he shied away from entering into conversation about it. When Oakley tried to engage him in a conversation, the priest, in Gould's words, "always changed the subject." Oakley, Gould continues—Gould hearing significance in Teilhard's silence—guided Teilhard through the British Museum exhibit of the hoax.

> Teilhard glumly walked through as fast as he could, eyes averted, saying nothing. . . . Finally Teilhard's secretary took Oakley aside and explained that Piltdown was a sensitive subject with Father Teilhard. (1980)

This embarrassed silence, Gould concludes, "arose from guilt."

Comment on Charge #4. I shouldn't doubt that Gould's account is entirely correct. (Gould reports in "The Piltdown Conspiracy" that A. S. Romer witnessed the same reticence from Teilhard; Leakey said he did too.) But I would not extrapolate guilt from silence. Taking the Fifth does not mean that the taker by doing so thereby incriminates himself. Silence does not signify culpability, nor even knowledge.

If Teilhard were silent not because of guilt, the interesting question is why he did not write about Eoanthropus in that fable's heyday or speak about the exposure of the hoax as much as we would wish. One reason might be that he was more impressed by the excitement of the digging than by the significance of the find. Of 158 letters he wrote from 1908 to 1914, only 12 relate to Dawson; and only half of those to Piltdown, which converts into 1/13th of the total epistolary collection. His attitude toward Piltdown Man in these letters to friends and family is like Dawson's own in his letters to Woodward. We might feel that he should have been more interested; but he wasn't.

Although there isn't an abundance of references to Piltdown Man in Teilhard's letters and articles before the exposé, the references are significant. From as early as 1913, he urged upon others his thesis that Eoanthropus should be applied only to the skull; the Eoanthropus we all know and some loved, that is, skull and jaw, he repeatedly severed.

1. On New Year's Day 1913, he wrote to his companion Fr. Pelletier:

The last news from Dawson is a postcard giving me information on the skull he found at Lewes, *Eoanthropus dawsoni,* which was presented to the Geological Society on December 18. To know the importance of the discovery, one must wait some time for publication of the paper and for the critical evaluation that will follow. . . . Anatomically it seems that the form of the skull, and especially of the jaw (which I have not seen) is very remarkable. I am in a special position to hear the opinions of Boule and Obermeier who are not easily taken in—especially if the findings are English. (Ore Place records are now in the Jesuit archives at Chantilly, France; this letter is quoted in Schmitz-Moorman, 1981.)

Boule's opinion (as of that time; he wavered after Site II's finds were made public) was that the mandible and its molars were ape.

2. In 1920, Teilhard wrote an article entitled "Le Cas de l'Homme Piltdown." This opened with an apology: others, including Marcellin Boule, had already explicated Piltdown. But the author's having been a friend of Dawson and a participant in the hunt might make his testimony

of interest. He proceeded to give an account of the excavation. One reads along, familiar stuff, and comes to the section subheaded "Restes d'animaux" (Animal remains).

But the section on human remains is headed "Restes presumés humains" (*Presumed* human remains). The skepticism indicated in that heading is bolstered by Teilhard's references to Waterston, Boule, and Miller, the three major opponents of Piltdown Man's being a single being. He elaborated upon their criticism—that the mandibular (or glenoid) fossa, typically human, could not have accepted the articular condyle of a chimpanzee's jawbone and that the cranium belonged to a human being, the jaw to an ape. It is clear from this paper that he belonged to the skeptics. In this article, describing Eoanthropus as "human skull, ape jaw," Teilhard explicitly came out in favor of dissociating the two. Piltdown Man was a geological accident: a prehistoric human skull (Eoanthropus) neighbor to a prehistoric ape-jaw (*Pan vetus* or *Troglodytes dawsoni*).

3. On February 23, 1952, in an address to the Anthropology Section of the New York Academy of Sciences, he designated Piltdown Man only by the skull.

4. He again defined Piltdown Man only by the skull in the 1953 "The Idea of Fossil Man."

5. Then the exposé broke. He wrote to Oakley (November 28, 1953, in *L'oeuvre Scientifique,* 1971) that anatomically Piltdown Man had constituted a kind of anatomical monster and paleontological aberration. Because he had early (back in 1920) realized that, he was "fundamentally pleased" by the solution despite its spoiling a bright memory.

6. A collection of Teilhard's paleontological essays, *L'Apparition de l'Homme,* came out posthumously, in 1956. The editor, N. M. Wildiers, wrote that Teilhard had requested that references to Piltdown Man be deleted. Teilhard explained he was happy that he no longer had to refer to Eoanthropus, which had always posed, with reason, an insoluble classification problem. The exposé had settled the matter.

Another reason for someone choosing to be silent is a reluctance to snitch on friends. Maybe Teilhard had known all along about the hoax. Von Koenigwald said that Teilhard, knowing that Europe had not been the habitation of any Pleistocene ape, must have realized that something was in the works, and must therefore have felt "deceived and cheated" (1981).

I doubt that Teilhard had any suspicion before the exposé that there had been a hoax. Others, people who knew him, also doubt that. Sherwood Washburn remembered that Ashley Montagu had brought the bad news to Teilhard about the results of the British Museum investigation. The occasion was a meeting of the Wenner-Gren Foundation. Montagu said that Teilhard, reeling backward and raising his hands, was "either the best actor in the world or the thought of forgery came as a complete surprise" (Private communication, August 18, 1981). Washburn referred to a letter he had received from Teilhard, who said "at once that he could not believe that any of the people with whom he had been associated was guilty and that he was sure some other explanation would be found" (Washburn, 1981). Teilhard said much the same thing to a *New York Times* reporter on November 25, 1953.

To Washburn's and Montagu's accounts, I'd like to add that of George Gaylord Simpson. Simpson wrote that Gould's thesis was unacceptable. One day after the exposé, Simpson met Teilhard at the American Museum of Natural History. "Teilhard told me that he had never before known and that it had never occurred to him as possible that '*Eoanthropus*' was a hoax" (Private communication, September 21, 1984).

FREUDIAN AND FATAL SLIPS

Charge #5 with comments. Teilhard left ambiguous clues scattered around, as if on purpose to tantalize Piltdown historians. In the letter of June 3, 1912, he referred to "the famous human skull." In his article "Le Cas de l'homme Piltdown," he inadvertently used an expression that clues us in to his knowledge of the hoax. After he had been told of the exposé, he created a false chronology about when he had met Dawson and then he built a garbage dump.

1. *The famous human skull.* In his letter to his parents of June 3, 1912, the day after he had joined the diggers and before the skull had become famous, or even a skull, Teilhard referred to it as "the famous human skull." Bowden wrote that this slip means that Teilhard not only participated in the fraud but anticipated its reception. The phrase is "du fameux crâne." I think that Teilhard meant by "fameux" not "famous," but something more akin to "wonderful" or maybe even merely "interesting." In the same letter of June 3, 1912, he refers to "la trop fameuse miss Peter," who was the author of a book on George Tyrrell.

2. *As if on purpose.* By using a phrase "stunning in its directness," Teilhard clued us in to his complicity in the plot. This is the relevant passage from Teilhard's 1920 "Le Cas de l'Homme Piltdown":

It is curious to note that we lack a direct and basic measure to decide between the two contending parties. Since the glenoid fossa exists on the temporal in perfect condition, it would have been possible, had *the mandible kept its condyle,* to attempt an articulation: we could have seen, without any doubt, whether the one and the other fit.

As if on purpose, the condyle happens to be missing! (Comme par exprès, le condyle s'est trouve manquer!)

And now, Gould's analysis:

Comme par exprès. I couldn't get those words out of my mind for two days. Yes, it could be a literary line, a permissible metaphor for emphasis. But I think that Teilhard was trying to tell us something he didn't dare reveal directly. (Gould, 1980)

A kind of security prevails with empirical solutions—tracing where fossils originated or how they were made presentable for their debut through being dressed up and cosmetized. But when it comes to "comme par exprès" and other phrases we have to examine, the inquiry slows, gets waylaid by the inaccuracy of translation, the imprecision of memory, the subtleties of authorial intention, and the vagaries of critics' psychohistories.

Gould interprets the phrase to mean that Teilhard knew Piltdown Man was fraudulent, "as if on purpose" a code for "on purpose." Edward O. Dodson (1981) thinks that Teilhard was expressing "his disappointment that the defects of the fossils prevent a critical test," not that the fossils had been deliberately altered to prevent a critical test.

There is, alas, another option. In the article, Teilhard refers favorably to Gerrit Miller's theory that the cranium was that of a human being, the jawbone that of an extinct ape. Miller had written, in a passage already quoted, but important enough to quote again:

Deliberate malice could hardly have been more successful than the hazards of deposition in so breaking the fossils as to give free scope to individual judgement in fitting the parts together.

Miller had no cognition in 1915 of any fraud. By "deliberate malice," he was venting his aggravation that the fossil jawbone had been (accidentally) broken or had, in Dawson's phrase, "rotted off." Teilhard's "comme par exprès" may be nothing more than a rendition or even translation of Miller's "deliberate malice." More likely, Teilhard simply observed that the condyle looked as though it had been broken off deliberately, without any messages underneath that he thought it had been or that he had broken off the structures. We might recall that there is no evidence anyone broke off the condyle or symphysis.

3. *A decoy chronology.* On March 1, 1954, Teilhard informed Kenneth Oakley that he had not known Dawson in 1908, which is true, but, as Gould points out, misleading—he had met Dawson in 1909. At another time, he recollected that he had met Dawson in 1911. If the plot had begun in 1909, and Teilhard had not been on the scene, then this false dating would remove him from involvement.

I think he just forgot when he had first met Dawson. What's important about this is that if he were forgetful about the year of his first meeting with Dawson, which he enjoyed, found profitable, and reminisced about pleasantly, we ought not to be surprised if he was forgetful about other, less important occasions.

4. *A garbage dump.* Teilhard invented a story to justify how the pit could have received its fossils without anyone's planting them. The pit, flooded during the winter with water that iron-stains remarkably fast, was available as a "perfect dumping place" for Barkham Manor. Suppose some collector had thrown a discarded ape jaw into it? That would have been stained as was a fresh-sawed bone Teilhard had seen in a Hastings stream, a butcher's bone "stained almost as deep brown as the human remains from Piltdown." He admitted to Oakley that this was a fantastic hypothesis, but held to the opinion that it was "no more fantastic than to make Dawson the perpetrator of a hoax."

Guy van Esbroeck sneered at the rationalization that the pit was a dump as an "ideé bien farfelue." Bowden reminded us that butchers don't dispose of their bones in streams: Teilhard was probably testing the staining property of stream water. Oakley in his November 19, 1953, letter wrote that he would send *The Solution of the Piltdown Problem* "almost immediately"; it's unlikely that Teilhard received the monograph by the 23rd and therefore unlikely that he knew just how the staining had been accomplished.

I suppose he built the garbage dump to get the reputations of his friends—not his own—out of the net.

WHAT DID TEILHARD DE CHARDIN KNOW?
WHEN DID HE KNOW IT?

Charge #6. After being informed that Piltdown Man was a hoax, Teilhard wrote letters full of all kinds of errors and strange interpretations that seem deliberately contrived as alibis for Dawson and for himself. The most important of these, the fatal error, was not deliberate—the truth slipped out: he had participated in the Site II hokum.

From the November 28, 1953, letter to Kenneth Oakley:

> As far as the fragments of Piltdown Location 2 are concerned, it must be observed that Dawson never tried to emphasize them particularly, although (if I am correct) these specimens were announced *after* the finds in Locality 1 were complete. He just brought me to the site of Locality 2 and explained [to] me that he had found the isolated molar and the small pieces of skull in the heaps of rubble and pebbles raked at the surface of the field.

When could Dawson have brought Teilhard to Site II to show him the heaps of rubble and pebbles? It had to be before late 1913 because Teilhard left England for France then or early in 1914. Oakley wrote to Teilhard for a clarification. Teilhard responded on January 29, 1954:

> Concerning the point of "history" you ask me, my "souvenirs" are a little vague. Yet, by elimination (and since Dawson died *during* the first war, if I am correct) my visit with Dawson to the *second* site (where the two small fragments of skull and the isolated molar were supposedly found in the rubble) must have been in late July 1913, certainly not in 1914. . . .
>
> P. S. When I visited the site no. 2 (in 1913?) the two small fragments of skull and the tooth *had* already been found, I believe. But your very question makes me doubtful! . . . Yes, I think definitely they *had* been already found: and that is the reason why Dawson pointed [out] to me the little heaps of raked pebbles as the place of the "discovery." . . .

According to this clarification, Dawson found the Site II fossils in July 1913, and told Teilhard of them, even taking him to the place. Woodward, we know, didn't find out until January 1915. Teilhard visited with Woodward in September 1913. He would certainly have told Woodward of this choice find, and then the game would have been up for Dawson. Certainly Teilhard would have told Woodward—unless Teilhard were in on the hoax.

In another letter, on March 2, 1954, Teilhard wrote to Mabel Kenward: "Dawson showed me the field where the second skull (fragments) were found. But, as I wrote to Oakley, I cannot remember whether it was before or after the find" (quoted in Mary Lukas and Ellen Lukas, 1983). One resolution is that Teilhard was guilty all by himself. Bowden maintained that Teilhard planted the fossils in Site II "for discovery by Dawson long after Teilhard had left for France." How Teilhard could have hoped Dawson would come upon a few small fossils in a field raises a mystery that we needn't pause to solve.

An alternative resolution is that Dawson and Teilhard were collaborative culprits. Gould defines Teilhard's "fatal error": Teilhard "could not have seen the remains of Piltdown 2 with Dawson, unless they had manufactured them together before he left"; and again, in reply to a critic, "If Teilhard saw the Piltdown 2 material, he probably helped Dawson to manufacture it before he left."

Comment on Charge #6. If we review Teilhard's letters, we find that he never said he saw the remains of Piltdown 2. He said that he had seen the site, and that Dawson had told him fossils had been retrieved from the heaps. In 1920, Teilhard returned to England. Cuénot tells us that he was "excited being shown the new fragments of cranium and the new fossil tooth" of Site II. Apparently, he hadn't seen them before; it's possible he hadn't heard of them. I've found no mention by Teilhard of the Site II fossils before 1920 or after, until Oakley's inquiry.

Two economical explanations are available. The first is that Dawson was the Piltdown hoaxer. Teilhard's letters confirmed Oakley's impression, as Oakley wrote on February 9, 1954, that Dawson "withheld information from Woodward. Thus according to the records we have here [at the British Museum] he said nothing to Woodward about having found the specimens at the second site until 1915!" Dawson fabricated the Site II finds, told Teilhard about them, even most diabolically showed Teilhard the pebble-heaps, and somehow persuaded Teilhard to keep it quiet. That explanation has its difficulties. (Why would Dawson have wanted to keep it quiet until 1915? What could have persuaded Teilhard to go along?)

An even more economical explanation is that both Dawson and Teilhard were innocent. Dawson, having discerned a similarity between flints in the pit and flints in a ploughed field, imagined that since the former had been accompanied by fossils the latter would be too. He and Teilhard toured Site II in 1913, seeing nothing but grass and flowers and trees. In the spring and autumn of 1914, Dawson returned to that site, this time with Woodward. They also found nothing. He returned again in the winter of 1914-1915, this time accompanied by someone else.

But if Teilhard hadn't seen the heaps of pebbles, how come he had such a clear picture of them? I think he got his picture from this:

When, however, in the course of farming, the stones had been raked off the ground and brought together into heaps, Mr. Dawson was able to search the material more satisfactorily; and early in 1915 he was so fortunate as to find here two well-fossilized pieces of human skull and a molar tooth, which he immediately recognized as belonging to at least one more individual of Eoanthropus dawsoni. Shortly afterwards, in the same gravel, a friend met with part of the lower molar of an indeterminable species of rhinoceros, as highly mineralized as the specimens previously found at Piltdown itself.

This passage comes from Arthur Smith Woodward's 1917 paper on Site II. Teilhard's only detail of the site—"in the heaps of rubble and pebbles raked at the surface of the field"—is very like the detail in Woodward's paper—"the stones had been raked off the ground and brought together into heaps."

TEILHARD ON THE HOAXER

Teilhard's opinion about the possibility that Dawson was the Piltdown hoaxer changed over the post-exposé years. In the letter to Oakley, he entirely discredits the idea that Dawson (or anyone) committed the hoax. In a letter to Abbé Breuil, reproduced in Mary Lukas's biography, he is more hospitable to the interpretation of fraud, though still not to the identification of Dawson as hoaxer:

I still have trouble believing that Dawson himself perpetrated the fraud. Fantastic though it seems, I would prefer to think that someone else innocently threw the bone fragments from a neighboring cottage into the ditch. . . . Nevertheless, I must admit to you that this new discovery, splendid though it is, spoils one of the happiest memories of my early scientific career.

Shortly before his death, Teilhard moved to accepting Dawson as hoaxer. A very close friend of his, Comte Henry de Bégouën, whom Teilhard had known for forty years, submitted a statement to *Antiquity* (March 1981) relating two meetings, one during World War II, the other after 1953, with Teilhard. One evening, on the Belgian front by the village of Killem, Bégouën greeted Teilhard with "C'est donc vous l'homme de la dent de Piltdown," which might have brought back memories of Dawson's "Geologist?" Asked to do so, Teilhard recounted the story of Piltdown: he was conducted by Dawson to the pit, found the canine. "C'est tout."

Bégouën visited Teilhard after the scandal broke. Teilhard said that, if he had had doubts on the authenticity of the find back in the Piltdown days, he would have expressed them, but that he lacked experience of the terrain and he was blinded by friendship. He claimed that he still had difficulty admitting that Dawson had deceived him, yet a "deception cruelle" had been practiced on him by this friend in whom he had had full confidence; and he felt the mortification of having been duped. In any case, it was comfortable to know that Science had attained a degree of finesse such that it was now immune to the most elaborate frauds. Bégouën adds his persuasion that, above all, Teilhard tried to safeguard the reputation of his old friend. He was of too high a "valeur morale" to take vengeance.

Teilhard progressed from believing that Piltdown was the remains of two authentic fossils (monstrous if they were jammed together) to defending it as a mistake, to accepting it as a hoax, and finally, to accepting Dawson as hoaxer.

FUN-LOVING TEILHARD

Charge #7. Teilhard's motive was to play a joke on Dawson. Or Dawson and Teilhard together decided to have some boyish fun. Maybe they came to that decision over a couple of mugs of stout or a more lethal brew, Teilhard favoring snails in whisky. Many paleontologists Gould consulted suspected Teilhard—A. S. Romer, Bryan Patterson, Louis Leakey, even K. P. Oakley, who said to Gould in April 1980, "I think it's right that Teilhard was in it." That quick clue, which can scurry under a sentence in a blink, has to be brought forward: "I think it's right that Teilhard was *in it*."

It was only a joke on Teilhard's part, the motive to embarrass Dawson. The first person to come up with that explanation of Teilhard's motive was Robert Essex, Dawson's schoolmaster friend, who linked Teilhard (Mr. X) to the elephant femur piece and jawbone. In 1961, Essex, then an old man, met Mr. J. O. Head, who reported, ten years later ("Piltdown Mystery," 1971):

> One of Essex's points lay in his estimation of the personalities of the two men: Dawson being pompous, self-opinionated and unimaginative, far more likely to be the victim than perpetrator of such a hoax, whereas Teilhard was, as Leakey states, well known as a practical joker. One has only to read Dawson's patronizing references to Teilhard to find a motive.

Leakey rewrote the story by having Teilhard not a sole hoaxer duping Dawson, but a co-conspirator duping everybody except Dawson. Gould embroiders Leakey's bland prose, imagining "Dawson and Teilhard, over long hours in field and pub, hatching a plot . . . to expose the gullibility of pompous professionals; Teilhard to rub English noses once again with the taunt that their nation had no legitimate human fossils." (Gould gets carried away: we soon have a Teilhard who hides "passion, mystery, and good humor behind a garb of piety," a "fun-loving" Teilhard who "strove to experience the world in all its pleasures and pains.") At any rate, after the thing was done, the two planned to tell everybody and have a good laugh.

But two unfortunate things happened. First, Dawson died. Second, anybody who counted for anything went for it with unexpected ferocity. Teilhard was scared to confess. Maybe he thought his friends and colleagues would stone him. So he kept quiet about it for the rest of his life. The unexpected roaring success accounts for Teilhard's willingness to surrender Dawson to the critics—according to Bowden; and for his sulky silence, evasive tactics, irritation when pressed—according to other accusers. In the traditional fashion of golem-makers, having animated the monster, he couldn't stop it from smashing its way into the human party.

This portrait of a prankster, a young Jesuit who strove to experience the world in all its pleasures and pains (all?) isn't what Teilhard's partisans draw. Marcellin Boule, Cuénot, the Lukases, Schmitz-Moorman, Thomas J. King, S.J., Winifred McCulloch, and others who have studied Teilhard's life, found him not a double-crosser, but an honest, authentic person, industrious, observant, keen in analysis, talented at synthesis. His career, wrote Boule (as quoted in Cuénot), "though just begun, already gives promise of being among the most brilliant."

The biographers and friends of Teilhard have a vested interest in protecting their hero. But it is not only from that direction that a personality opposite to the accuser's comes through. We have seen that the defenders of Teilhard's innocence include evolutionists—Washburn, von Koenigswald, and Simpson. J. S. Weiner wrote to me that he had done his best to counter the theory that Teilhard was the—or a—Piltdown hoaxer (May 14, 1981).

One more authority has to be heard from. K. P. Oakley told Gould (in April 1980) that Teilhard had been "in it" and wrote to Gould (in June of the same year) of Gould's accusatory paper that he could not find "anything (of importance) which I would wish you to alter." But Oakley seems to have altered his own opinion, moving from support of the accusation against Teilhard to uncertainty and to a position close to exoneration. I wrote to him to find out what he thought of it all. He answered in a long letter.

The letter begins with Oakley exclaiming that more than some writers on Piltdown had put their words into his mouth. He recalls that Gould, however, took care in transcribing their conversation. He guesses that Gould was impressed by Oakley's having held the view that a letter he received from Teilhard (January 1954) "might be taken as circumstantial evidence that Teilhard had been working in collusion with Dawson on a joke." On Site II, Oakley felt that there was some confusion in Teilhard's report: how could Teilhard have rendered so "vivid" a description of the heaps of pebbles if he had not been at Site II with Dawson and seen them there? Oakley does not rule out the possibility that "Teilhard was visualising the site as a result of reading" its published description.

He quotes his own letter to the *London Times* (July 23, 1980):

> Teilhard's letter about his recollections of 1913 suggested that he and Dawson were working in collusion. The evidence for this is circumstantial and consequently I strongly maintain that until *positive* support for Teilhard's involvement with the forgery has been brought forward, he should be given the benefit of the doubt.

In his letter to me, Oakley added to this that imagining Teilhard as the hoaxer "seems contrary to all we know about [his] transparent honesty." The confusion seems to rest on the iota of what Oakley meant by telling Gould that he thought Teilhard was "in it." Gould took that to mean support for the identification of Teilhard as a collaborative hoaxer. But Oakley meant only that Teilhard, having found three specimens in the pit, was more "in" the Piltdown scenario than Keith, Smith, or Sollas.

In a letter to the *New Scientist*, Oakley alluded to three long meetings he had with Teilhard in 1954 at the British Museum of Natural History, at his home, and at the Swanscombe site. Teilhard talked freely on topics other than the Piltdown forgery, which he termed "so very sad." Max Bégouën's having explained the reasons behind that remark, Oakley said we can no longer regard Teilhard as having felt guilty about Piltdown. Oakley described Teilhard as "the ideal fall-guy to find the fraudulent canine tooth": an "eagle-eyed collector," he would have spotted it. Impressed by Teilhard's dedication "to what he saw as truth," Oakley could not believe that Teilhard would have placed a fraudulent Eoanthropus on the tree of human evolution that he displayed to the February 23, 1952, meeting of the New York Academy of Sciences. Oakley's letter was published on November 12, 1981. He had died on November 2.

Comment on Charge #7: The motive attributed to Teilhard—that he wanted to play a joke on or with Dawson has no support. Designing a motive for any of the suspects challenges the imagination; designing one for Teilhard de Chardin exhausts it. Twitting the tail of the English lion hardly justifies seven years of hoaxing and forty of evasive action.

The Piltdown finds would have ended up as curios on some collector's shelf had it not been for the support given it by top authorities. The accusation against Teilhard is flimsy and had it remained with Essex, Bowden, Vere, or L. S. B. Leakey, no one would be much concerned with it now. But though the argument is flimsy, Stephen Jay Gould is not. The esteem in which Stephen Jay Gould is held by those who admire him elevated it to importance. Yet Gould's procedure in conducting the argument is not as careful as his arguments about hen's teeth, horse's toes, panda's thumbs, or any of the other subjects that make his monthly column in *Natural History* and his books worth reading and deserving of the awards they have received. His concluding moral to the four papers on Teilhard as hoaxer tends to minimize the seriousness of the hoax, and that may conduce to minimizing the quality of proof needed for indictment. The moral is that, if Teilhard had been the hoaxer, it wouldn't be very important to our sense of him.

I don't think that there's any more evidence that Teilhard suffered pain for having collaborated on the hoax or that he paid his debt than there is that he committed it in the first place. I do wonder about what kind of a Teilhard he would have been to do it. It's not just that he would have had to fool the priest who trotted with him from bone to bone over the weald, and Woodward and all his friends from Cannes d'Angleterre, but also Marcellin Boule and, worst of all, his parents. He wrote to them faithfully, enthusiastically, warmly about the great happenings at the pit, Dawson's unearthing cranial fragments, his own discovery of a tooth fragment. It's hard to imagine anyone, much less this devoted son, filing a canine tooth, planting it, retrieving it, and then exclaiming to his mother and father about how happy he was to be part of that fraudulent excavation.

The Piltdown hoax was far from one of the greatest crimes of the twentieth century. But it did injure that evolutionary science to which Teilhard contributed proudly. So much time spent by so many scientists for so little in trying to make sense of Eoanthropus. The hoax gave, and still gives, aid and comfort to the enemies of evolutionary theory. Not much of a joke. "The evidence," Sherwood Washburn pointed out, "suggests a serious attempt at fraud, not a joke or minor hoax."

We may have to wait for the withdrawal from its bank vault of that letter Harrison Matthews mentions as the final word of Teilhard de Chardin on his friend and foe, Piltdown Man. Unless the rumor of that letter is also a hoax.

CHAPTER TEN

THE BRITISH MUSEUM: M. A. C. HINTON ET AL.

L. B. Halstead, a geologist; Malcolm Bowden, a creationist; and L. Harrison Matthews, a former director of the London Zoo, each put forward a startling thesis: that the sanctum sanctorum itself, the British Museum of Natural History, harbored a nest of hoaxers. Each advocate's brief contains a cast of characters; L. Harrison Matthews's, a central plot with subplots weaving through it, rich dialogue and inner thoughts, conflicts, disguises, a doublecross, and a complex and farcical denouement. The British Museum of Natural History is so incredible a suspect that the accusation succeeded in convincing other scholars.

The briefs differ in their cast of characters, but agree on the hoaxers' target: Arthur Smith Woodward, curator of geology during the Piltdown fiasco. Woodward has not been accorded much of the interest, and has missed the infamy, of others associated with the hoax. There is good reason for his rarely being given even a passing glance as the Piltdown hoaxer. Rumor has it that he was too uncoordinated to fabricate the hoax (he broke an arm in one mishap, a leg in another) and lacked manual dexterity and, worse, a sense of humor. More important than such silliness is that Woodward had no motive to do it and was brought in years after recovery of the first piece. He was himself thoroughly duped. The picture of him in his old age wistfully revisiting the pit and reliving the adventure as he prepared the manuscript on the earliest Englishman solicits compassion rather than suspicion.

The British Museum held in its stores enough fossils to equip a multitude of hoaxes and a staff among which were several people competent to do the Piltdown hoax. That staff was divided between those who affirmed the authenticity of Piltdown Man, Woodward and Pycraft, and those who were disposed to dismiss it as a mistake, if not a fraud. In the latter party were Reginald Smith and Martin A. C. Hinton. Reginald Smith, of the Museum's Department of Antiquity, appears briefly in the history of the Piltdown case with a single skeptical remark delivered during the discussion of Woodward's 1914 paper: that the bone implement might have been "found and whittled in recent times."

That appraisal of the pit's most extraordinary artifact was shared by A. S. Kennard. Though in the construction rather than the museum business, Kennard was a productive paleontologist. He participated in field work with Reginald Smith and M. A. C. Hinton, amassing a productive bibliography of 250 papers, his specialty fossil mollusks. Friendly with W. J. L. Abbott, under whom he had studied at the City of London School, and with Captain St. Barbe and Major Marriott, Kennard could have been privy to the military men's stories about Dawson's secretly staining flints and to the gossip that the mine had been salted. He knew in 1926 of the resurvey of the River Ouse that showed the pit to be more recent than assumed; he was a member of and eventually president of the Geological Association. He claimed that he knew there had been a hoax, and knew who the hoaxer was, though he never came through with a public identification, except for stating—and coming from Kennard, it's an important statement—that it wasn't Charles Dawson.

In his presidential address to the Geological Association, in March 1946, Kennard lamented a change in attitude: "There has been a marked decline in humour." This view of the Edwardian period as a humorous age recalls Chamberlain's remark in defense of his cousin Dawson that the Edwardian period was the time of "first-class practical jokes."

The British Museum group associated with Piltdown Man consisted of Woodward; his assistant, F. O. Barlow; W. P. Pycraft, the ornithologist curator of the Department of Anthropology; Reginald Smith, curator of the Department of Antiquities; and Martin A. C. Hinton, in 1910 a volunteer worker at the Museum who would rise to assistant (1921), deputy (1927), and keeper of zoology (1936-1945). Hinton wrote many articles on Pleistocene geology, some with A. S. Kennard, and on his specialty, voles. In 1908, he described a rare find from the Norfolk Forest Bed, a part of a fossilized humerus like that in the macaque. Many people before the revelation of the hoax assumed that an authentic simian jaw had arrived naturally into the pit (Gerrit Miller, Boule, Teilhard, Montagu) and they were happy with the scraps of evidence that England had been host to monkeys and apes in prehistoric times. Hinton's find was therefore something to hang onto.

He also studied hoaxes, including Nessie of Loch Ness.

In a 1926 article ("The Pleistocene Mammals of the British Isles and Their Bearing upon the Date of the Glacial Period"), Hinton found a consistency between the relics from the pit and those from other English sites, such as Ingress Vale, Kent, and the Cromer Forest Bed, which the geologist James Geikie described as the stratum for Heidelberg Man and which W. J. Lewis Abbott described. Thirteen years after its discovery, Hinton wrote of the pit's assemblage thus:

> At Piltdown, in my opinion, we see dim indications of what the fauna of the South of England was in the earliest part of the High Terrace stage. . . . Eoanthropus himself is surely as primitive a mammal as one could wish to find in a post-glacial deposit; too primitive probably to be associated with Chellean implements, but possibly responsible for the Eoliths. (Hinton, 1926)

It seems as though M. A. C. Hinton had fallen for the hoax.

In 1953, after the exposé, in a letter to the *London Times,* Hinton, the tone of his criticism reminiscent of Gerrit Miller's, chastised Woodward and the others for bad methodology: "Eoanthropus is the result of departing from one of the great principles of palaeontology: each specimen must be regarded as a separate document and have its character read" (quoted in Vere, 1959). He said that, had he been able to investigate the actual fossils themselves, instead of Barlow's casts, he would have spotted the jaw as simian right away. W. D. Lang responded privately:

> I saw Hinton's letter and it read as if he thought that if he had had the material handed to him, he would have detected the fraud. But perhaps he didn't mean that. In any case, I think S. Woodward was right in letting only Anthropological specialists and men like [Jones?] see the stuff for detailed handling, and Hinton was not one to be included, for all his eminent work on Voles! I should say that his letter cuts very little ice. . . . (British Museum Archives)

If in fact Hinton was skeptical back then, that skepticism would have been invigorated not only by Kennard and Reginald Smith, but also by Captain St. Barbe, whom Hinton met while spelunking and with whom he became friendly. There's a rumor about Hinton's legacy comparable to that about Teilhard's hidden letter—that just before his death, he "virtually confessed" to being one of the Piltdown hoaxers.

There doesn't seem much in this history to incriminate M. A. C. Hinton as Piltdown hoaxer. However, we have often seen that the talented historian can make a case out of shreds. The really creative historian can make up the shreds themselves.

Public accusation of the British Museum of Natural History began in November 1978. In a letter to the *London Times*, Dr. L. B. Halstead said that the orangutan jaw had been taken from the British Museum by the volunteer M. A. C. Hinton. Halstead sketched a cast that included not only members of the British Museum, but also a professor from Oxford (W. S. Sollas) and Teilhard de Chardin. He expanded on this in a BBC External Service broadcast (November 14, 1978). In a letter to *Nature* a few months later (Halstead, 1979), he alluded to the rumor that Hinton had "virtually confessed" to the hoax. Bowden, who reproduced Halstead's letter and quoted Halstead's comments on the BBC program, approved of incriminating the British Museum of Natural History, the motive of the several villains to embarrass Arthur Smith Woodward (Bowden, 1981).

L. Harrison Matthews changed the casts set up by Halstead and Bowden. While deleting Sollas, he kept Hinton and Teilhard, and added Dawson and Abbott. His approach to the hoax was refreshingly different from that of all other historians: he invited us to enter not only into the private doings but into the private thoughts of the various suspects. It's a story as fascinating as it's fantastic.

The original fakes were made and planted by the co-conspirators Dawson and Abbott. Then M. A. C. Hinton came into the act. He visited the pit in June 1912; he was the one whom Mabel Kenward saw, the 40-to-45-year-old tall man who said nothing and flitted away like a ghost. (Hinton was 28 at the time.) His exploration of the pit and study of the casts convinced him that Piltdown Man was not merely a mistake in interpretation but a deliberate, and stupid, fraud. He thought about the way in which his colleagues had been gulled and decided to pull a leg by planting a tooth. Sometime after his visit to the pit, he plucked an ape's canine from the Everett collection of orangutan skulls.

Meanwhile, Teilhard de Chardin was sorely perplexed about what to do with his suspicion that Dawson was faking the fossils. He couldn't very well tell anyone, and thus get his ami into trouble; nor could he justifiably keep his mouth shut and allow the hoax to continue.

During a reflective lunch hour, the volunteer Hinton took the canine to Barlow's workroom and, using Woodward's cast as his model, filed away industriously, going too deep, through the surface of the tooth, and having to plug the hole. Rummaging about in a box of paints, he was caught by C. P. Chatwin, whom Harrison Matthews identifies as "the boy attendant." As embarrassed as Dawson had been when he was caught by Captain St. Barbe, Hinton alibied, "Just looking for a bit of colour to tint this specimen. But don't let-on to Barlow that I've been in here—or anyone else."

Nothing in any recorded conversation, letter, or other memorabilia gives any evidence backing up this story of a young man on the lowest rung of the professional ladder engaging in such shenanigans to embarrass Woodward. But Harrison Matthews is on a roll:

> Chatwin thought nothing of the episode at the time; he was used to Hinton's way of carrying a specimen or two in his waistcoat pocket. It was not until months later, when Teilhard found the canine tooth at Piltdown, that he guessed the truth and when he saw Barlow making casts of it he recognised it for what it was. He had the sense to say nothing, not even to Hinton, for he could see what trouble he would land them both in if he mentioned what he knew. Besides, Hinton was his friend and he could not let him down—and loyally he never did. (Harrison Matthews, June 11, 1981)

There's no evidence that Chatwin said anything to anyone, ever. That fact makes it hard to know what he saw.

Gleeful over the prospect of fooling his dim-witted boss, Hinton had drawn Teilhard into his confidence, showing him the fake canine and asking him to plant it. Teilhard at first virtuously refused, but then, reflecting on this being an excellent way to expose the hoax without having to expose the hoaxer, he gave the proposition some thought. He traveled to Paris, met with Marcellin Boule, a good man severely tried by doubts about Piltdown, and returned to England, his mind made up to do it.

On August 30, 1913, while Dawson and Woodward were probing the pit, Teilhard reached into his cassock. He removed a canine tooth—the one slipped to him by M. A. C. Hinton, or maybe a different one, smuggled in from France—in any case, the canine hadn't been part of that orangutan jaw found earlier, the one Dawson had manufactured. He bent down, put his fist on the spoil heap, stood up, opened his fist and shouted—Harrison Matthews doesn't tell us just what Teilhard shouted, but it must have been something like "Hé, look what I found!" At Woodward's excited exclamation of pleasure, Teilhard—Harrison Matthews does tell us this—"chuckled inwardly." What Dawson experienced inwardly when Teilhard rose with a fossil not of Dawson's manufacture can be easily imagined.

Then somewhat more than a year later Teilhard left to join the 4th

Zouaves in the French Army. Hinton remained at home, more amazed than ever at the turn of the screw. Broad and Wade, present experts on the subject of scientific fraud, pick up the story at this point:

> Hinton was astonished that his scientific colleagues could be so taken in by so transparent a fake, and he suffered the additional mortification of seeing Charles Dawson, whom he suspected to be the culprit, acquiring kudos for his handiwork. He decided to try again. Only this time with something so outrageous that the whole country would laugh the discoverers to scorn.

Hinton required something that had never been found before, anywhere, by anyone, one of a kind. He rummaged some more in the treasure house of the British Museum, coming up with many possibilities, but none quite right—until there it was, maybe under a table amidst a melange of prehistoric debris. A 16-inch-long fossil fragment of an elephant thigh bone. That alone would have been a good enough joke, but he provided a neat punch-line: he whittled it to resemble a cricket bat. Teilhard being off to war, he would have to plant this one himself. That shouldn't be too hard. He took the underground.

Harrison Matthews again:

Fossilized cricket bat. The femur slab having been shaped to look like a cricket bat testifies to Kennard's thesis that in Edwardian days geologists had a sense of humor. (From Weiner [1955], Plate 29.)

When he left the museum at mid-day he took the Inner Circle train from South Kensington to Victoria and caught the next train to Brighton via Lewes and got out at Uckfield. He knew the way to Piltdown, only three miles away, because he had been there the year before with Teilhard, when Miss Kenward had caught him in the pit.

Harrison Matthews's omniscience is infectious. The imaginary details are so fine that one can hardly resist going even further than he does, seeing Martin A. C. Hinton on that train, dozing off as it hummed over the tracks, cradling in his arms a femur slab wrapped in swaddling clothes.

He walked to the pit. His hat may have been drawn over his forehead. One hand clutched a garden trowel. At the pit, he began to dig a hole in an outcropping of yellow clay in which to bury the bone. But he was caught again, this time not by Mabel Kenward, "that wretched young woman sticking her oar in again," but by a farm laborer, the very farm laborer who had been hired by Dawson and Woodward in earlier exploits. Venus Hargreaves warned Hinton to leave that be; Hinton was glad to do so, and escape; Venus was glad to see a brand-new fossil poking up, for the toffs might give him a shilling for this one, it was big enough. God knew what it was. It looked for all the world like a cricket bat.

Harrison Matthews knew Hinton and often dined with him; but, sad to say, they never got around to sharing Hinton's confession, though Hinton did remark, the metaphor pregnant with meaning, "one canine doesn't make a dog's dinner." The boy attendant, C. P. Chatwin, grew up to become M.Sc., a member of the Geological Survey (and therefore colleague of one F. H. Edmunds, whom we will meet later), and a professional paleontologist. Sometime in 1953 or early 1954, K. P. Oakley, walking along Cromwell Road, saw Chatwin and asked him directly about the hoax.

Chatwin went red in the face and with an embarrassed giggle said, "No. I am not talking about that," and hurried off. Oakley never had a chance to speak on the matter to him again, although Chatwin lived until 1971.

It is most regrettable. Harrison Matthews, a neighbor of Hinton for six years, often having dinner with him, often talking about Piltdown, yet never getting around to resolving that question so much on their minds: Who did it? Then K. P. Oakley, also much concerned to arrive at the answer to that interesting question, meeting Chatwin and just as unaccountably failing to follow through with him for the remaining seventeen years of Chatwin's life.

It is also regrettable that there are several problems with Harrison Matthews's account besides the noteworthy one that it's all fiction. We cannot willingly suspend our disbelief because the story is inconsistent in itself—one part of the episode about the femur has it covered with yellow clay from outcropping, another part with that clay from a different place, the bottom layer of the pit; the canine is said to have come from the Everett Collection in the British Museum, Hinton painting it there with Vandyke brown, but then quite unexpectedly its origin shifts to France. We can quickly enough agree that Venus Hargreaves may have caught someone planting a fossil, but it's difficult to go along with the notion that he refrained from telling his patrons about the visitor who left the gift.

Harrison Matthews's story does, however, have a redeeming value: it's comical. Readers can delight in imagining Teilhard slowly twisting in the wind, deeply perplexed by the responsibility to expose the hoax without exposing the hoaxer, and finding such a nice resolution in helping to stop the crime by becoming a criminal. And the change of complexion on Dawson's ruddy, good-natured face as he witnessed the appearance of the canine tooth and of the femur, both not from his factory. Best of all is that maddening frustration Hinton must have felt, his surprise at the swallowing of the canine tooth, and then his trying a larger object that they also swallowed. He must have been tempting apoplexy brought on by their insatiable gullibility. It is all so comical one wishes it were true.

Conspiracy has its problems. Having someone else competent to talk about what was done increases the risk of disclosure, and the more conspirators, the more that risk is increased. Since any one of the suspects could have done the deed all by himself (even Butterfield), there is no prima facie reason for him to have brought in another. Yet several historians of the case think conspiracy is the answer—Leakey and Gould accuse Dawson/Teilhard; for van Esbroeck, the deadly duo is Butterfield/Hargreaves; Halstead and Bowden like the trio Hinton/Sollas/Teilhard; Harrison Matthews (followed by Broad and Wade) expand that to the quadruplicate Dawson/Abbott/Teilhard/Hinton. Dodson ("Piltdown in Letters," Gould 1981) tells us not to "overlook the possibility that there may have been three or more conspirators at Piltdown."

Still, the British Museum staff, Hinton himself or Hinton with others, is attractive as a suspect. This identification, in addressing well the larger questions of opportunity and motive, provides solutions to specific problems, such as the concordance between the real canine tooth and its plaster-cast model, Barlow's staining the femur slab in solution, the possibility that other fossils may also have been immaculate in the pit but stained in the Museum, Kennard's and Reginald Smith's hint that the femur slab had been whittled recently, Kennard's disavowal of Dawson as the hoaxer, and Marston's complaint that the British Museum jokers were making a scapegoat out of Dawson.

Most of the suspects and observers who would after the exposé congratulate themselves on having suspected a hoax knew one another. Some were together in the same institutions and organizations: for example, Woodward, Barlow, Pycraft, Hinton, and Chatwin on the staff of the British Museum; F. H. Edmunds and Chatwin, when he grew up, on the Geological Survey; Dawson, Butterfield, and Abbott in the Sussex Archaeological Society; Dawson, Woodhead, and Hewitt in the Society of Analysts; A. S. Kennard, Sollas, Elliot Smith, and most of the others members of the Geological Association. Networks can be drawn that would include these and Major Marriott, Captain St. Barbe, and Henry Morris. These people rubbing against each other generated a good deal of smoky rumor.

I don't believe Harrison Matthews's tale any more than I do van Esbroeck's, but I like it much better. And I particularly like Bowden's "Probably some members of the Museum staff could reveal a great deal more, but are prevented by their signing of the Official Secrets Act." What I find seriously deficient in the imaginations of Halstead, Bowden, and Harrison Matthews is their failure to go the whole hog. It would have been simple to throw in the inventor of Sherlock Holmes, Arthur Conan Doyle, whom we will now meet.

CHAPTER ELEVEN

THE ADVENTURE OF QUEER STREET: ARTHUR CONAN DOYLE

It was with a sense of no small surprise that, upon retrieving the envelope from the letter box and opening it, I found a note within from Sherlock Holmes, written in his characteristic fine hand, each letter as precisely wrought as a musical note, and in his characteristic laconic style:

Come see me, Watson.

I shared this with my wife, who queried, "Are you starting that up again?" In the taxi-cab, I reflected upon this sudden but valued summons. I had not seen Holmes for years, and I had, I confess, studiously avoided our former bachelors' quarters, for the nostalgia that overcame me felt like an old wound awakening. I still retained my latch key to #—b, having kept it more for the incitement of reminiscence than for any utilitarian purpose. As I ambled up the stairs, I heard the familiar strains of a violin concerto. As I raised my fist to knock on the familiar door, it opened. From a thickly woven wall of smoke emerged the classical features constituting the countenance of Sherlock Holmes—the aquiline nose, the high forehead, the defiant chin. "Dear boy," Holmes smiled.

"My dear Holmes," I responded, unable to say more because of a moderate coughing fit which rattled the words in my throat. The familiar room had hardly changed, except that the stacks of case histories were even more monumental. On an end-table stood a porcelain hookah, its serpentine smoking tube emitting a light puff of what I instantly sensed as the unfamiliar odor of hashish.

For five or six minutes, we brought ourselves up-to-date on the events of the preceding five or six decades, and then Holmes, his eyes flashing in impatience, asked, "You have heard of Arthur Conan Doyle?"

At times, Holmes exaggerates my ignorance. Of course I had heard of Sir Arthur Conan Doyle, an honourable member of my own profession,

Arthur Conan Doyle

and a writer of considerable stature. He authored a history of the Boer War, *The British Campaigns in Europe, 1914-1918, The British Campaign in France and Flanders,* historical novels, novels of chivalry, and, I believe, penny dreadfuls. He had taken a most active interest in the political affairs of the country, had run twice for Parliament, and had been knighted. "Of course, I have heard of Sir Arthur Conan Doyle," I protested.

"This morning I received a letter from him. I should like to know what you make of it." He handed an envelope to me.

> I would be appreciative if you would grant me a minute of your time to discuss a matter of minimal importance to myself but of major importance to you and Dr. James Watson, whose attendance would be gratifying. His peculiar talents will stand us all in good stead. Would 7:30 this evening be satisfactory?

I could make neither head nor tails of it. What connection could there conceivably be between Sir Arthur and us? And which of my peculiar talents were to be of use? It distressed me, but only for a passing moment, that this famous man was uncertain of my given name. Imitating what Holmes had done in our investigation of a scandal in Bohemia, I held the paper up to the lamp's light, but found nothing in its texture to indicate its national origin.

"You have no idea of what Doyle wishes to consult us on?"

"None whatsoever."

"Look at the envelope."

In its upper left hand corner was the return address, below and to the right of that, Holmes's name and address. It seemed entirely normal. A 16-pence stamp in the upper right hand corner where, it occurred to me, the stamp was usually placed.

Holmes was leaning against two large cushions of oriental brocade, his silk dressing gown emblazoned with an oriental dragon. He put aside the hookah coil, from which he had been drawing smoke which fogged the place. "Ah, Watson, the years have not improved your perspicacity. You see, but you do not observe. Notice the return address, Crowborough."

"It is a village in Sussex, Holmes."

"And has not Sussex been in the news of late?"

"Not to my knowledge." My schoolboy excitement was rapidly being replaced by schoolboy anxiety at this impromptu examination.

"In Sussex, some time ago, there occurred a forgery that shook the scientific world to its heels," he coughed. "The site was a gravel pit called Piltdown."

"And who was the forger?"

"That has never been determined, Watson. It was and remains a slur on British science."

The light that suffused my mind at this information clarified the forthcoming visit of Sir Arthur. "Ah, then he wishes us to discover the culprit and thus redeem national prestige. Sir Arthur was ever concerned with the honor of the nation."

Holmes extracted a cigarette from a crumpled pack of Benson and Hedges and ignited it. "Is there anything that strikes you as unusual in receiving a letter from Doyle?"

"I don't know what you mean." The familiar odor of cigarette smoke assailed my nostrils.

"He's dead, Watson. He died in 1930."

"Ah," I countered. Holmes's ability to drive to the important clue never ceased to amaze me.

Over our early takeaway of Moo Goo Gai Pan rung up from a local establishment, Holmes filled me in on the Piltdown story. As we cracked open cookies of fortune, Holmes announced, "He's here." I had heard nothing, not even the doorbell.

Arthur Conan Doyle was of Holmes's height, but moustachioed and of a build far sturdier than Holmes's. But opposed to his imposing bulk was the equally impressive sinewy strength of my friend. I would not have known on whom to wager in a pugilistic confrontation. We shook hands all round and I served Holmes a glass of port, Sir Arthur a glass of burgundy.

"I will come right to the point, gentlemen," began Sir Arthur. I observed him carefully. When he raised his glass to his lips, I thought I could see not only through the glass, but through his hand. There was also, if I might take the metaphoric license, a remarkable translucency to his voice—a tremulous quality rather than the boom one would anticipate from so stout a source. He looked as though he weighed seventeen stone, but his movements were as delicate as a ghost's. These clues confirmed Holmes's hypothesis of Sir Arthur's state.

"Up to fairly recent times, I was associated with the Piltdown forgery only tangentially. Charles Dawson wrote to Arthur Smith Woodward that I was excited about the cranium and that I offered to drive him anywhere. Once Mr. Dawson found and gave me this." He took an arrowhead from his pocket. "It is one thing having my name associated with the Piltdown finds. It is quite another seeing myself accused of being the Piltdown forger."

"You!" I submitted.

"Yes, James, I."

"John."

"John. This identification occurred first in an article which Mary Lukas wrote defending the French priest Teilhard de Chardin. She wrote that Sir Arthur Conan Doyle is among those who 'have stood as possible suspects.' That article appeared in 1981, I being mentioned only in that single statement. However, in 1983, while I was mulling over the implications of the Argentinian challenge to our sovereignty of the Falkland Islands, I was startled by a headline in the *New York Times:*

Arthur Conan Doyle Is Piltdown Suspect

A Dr. John Hathaway Winslow moved me, in the frenzied words of the reporter, 'out of the mists of literary legend into the uncomfortable position of suspect,' and the following month an article entitled 'The Perpetrator of Piltdown,' co-authored by Professor Winslow and Alfred Meyer, enlarged on this allegation."

Holmes put down his cheroot at the corner of a high stack of memoranda.

"And you are applying to us, Sir Arthur," I reasoned, "to clear your name?"

"No."

"No?" I smelled the familiar odour of paper burning, but could not ascertain its etiology. "Surely, this is a libel, traducing a good man's name for the purpose of titillating a public always hungry for new sensation. Were I you, I should bring these slanderers in on a charge of malicious libel."

"That is not my way. What I should like you two gentlemen to do is to conduct an investigation the goal of which will be to determine whether Arthur Conan Doyle was or was not the Piltdown hoaxer. What I have revealed is the only intelligence I will reveal. Planning the general line of attack to arrive at a conclusion free from prejudice will be entirely up to you."

This was an extraordinary assignment. It made the hound of the Baskervilles look like a puppy in comparison. "I can recall no precedence for this," I reminded Holmes, who was engaged in stamping out a small conflagration with his Persian slipper, "wherein a suspect has come to us willing to have us prove him guilty, should the facts so necessitate. Holmes, do you remember the man with the twisted lip and a case of identity? In both those, the criminals did apply to us in the guise of victims. But this is quite different. Quite. Very interesting. Hm."

"Shall we send a report to you?" puffed Holmes, depositing ashes from his meerschaum into an adjacent carafe, a twinkle in his eye. It was a courteous way of settling the question of where Sir Arthur lived, still at Crowborough or in airier environs.

But Sir Arthur was a deal too sharp for us. "No," he explained, and the twinkle in his eye could have stood cousin to that in Holmes's. My own eyes were, I verified by first wiping them and then gazing into a wall-mirror, more luminous than all of theirs combined, a consequence of exposure to the stimulants of burning paper, tobacco, and Cannabis sativa, more commonly known as bhang. "I'll return at the same hour a fortnight hence." And he vanished.

"I can make neither head nor tails of this, Holmes," I apologized. "And further, I'm quite famished."

"When a doctor does so wrong he is the first of criminals," Holmes mused, as he had in our adventure of the speckled band.

"We do not yet know if he had done wrong."

"I was only musing, Watson," he flashed.

The assignment he entrusted me with was of a sedentary nature, that is, reading Sir Arthur's memoirs, biographies of him, and, of especial importance, *The Lost World.* What Holmes would do he did not deign to enlighten me with. He had always been loath to communicate his plans. We were to meet a fortnight hence at the British Museum of Natural History on Cromwell Road.

"Where?" I inquired.

"Eryops," he burped.

"God bless you," I intoned. I couldn't blame him, what with all the smoking, drinking, and consumption of evanescent oriental dainties.

"No, Watson, you foolish fellow, we'll meet by the display of Eryops, a prehistoric salamander, in the hall."

* * *

The Natural History Museum rose behind an iron fence like a cathedral, a grand building, twin towers flanking the entrance. I passed two large earth-brown structures, one vertical, about 15 feet high, the other a smaller horizontal chunk. They seemed much like the dismembered torso of an antediluvian giant, or I may have thought that from the lasting impression Sir Arthur's *The Lost World* had upon my imagination. Actually, they were flora.

> Fossilized tree trunks. These are parts of the trunk of a primitive tree. They were excavated at Craigleith Quarry, Edinburgh from rocks of Lower Carboniferous ages and are about 200 million years old.

As I approached closer, I observed that the building was ornamented with gargoyles of prehistoric animals and with plump masonry lizards slithering under Romanesque windows. I fed to pigeons bits of the roll from a native American dish called a hot-dog. It was not hot, though it could well have been made from dog.

Inside the Museum, I was received by a large skeleton of a Diplodocus dinosaur, and on the reception committee were also a horned Triceratops and pterodactyls winging out as though from a Fuseli nightmare. In a case lay a skeletal head of *Tyrannosaurus rex*, its mouth big enough to chomp on all four tykes gawking at it. And then I spotted the display case of Eryops, a 10-million-year-old amphibian from Wichita Basin, Texas.

Holmes appeared behind a nest of dinosaur eggs, one baby Protoceratops fossilized in the very act of hatching. "Holmes, look here!" In a display case were the Piltdown fossils.

"Those are fake fakes, Watson. The real fakes are not on public display." He pushed a buzzer by the door to the Palaeontology Department. Allowed in after a short wait of forty minutes, we entered our names and addresses into the visitors' book and were then led through a room full of white cabinets, rank upon rank of them, all holding, I assumed, old bones. Our guide turned us over to a young man of lanky appearance, who directed us to a smaller room, sat us at a table, and withdrew from a wall of cabinets a tray laden with fossils. Fragments of teeth and cranium, flints. These were the real fakes. The familiar smell of the grave rose from these relics.

Holmes extracted a magnification glass from his pocket and began examining the fossils closely, occasionally nodding, even whistling the familiar tune of a violin concerto.

"As for Sir Arthur's alleged involvement," I commenced.

"It is a capital mistake, my dear fellow, to theorise before one has the data," he reprimanded. "Let us take up these cranial pieces first."

During my medical practice, I had had absolutely nothing to do with ape specimens, and even less with those of other mammals, outside of Londoners, but I was familiar with the human cranium. These fragments were of a particularly thick-skulled person. I shared with Holmes information on Sir Arthur's interest in skulls and phrenology, his acquaintance with one Jessie Fowler, an American phrenologist whose office was in London. She sold human skulls. "Sir Arthur could have obtained one from her."

"To be sure. And from other sources as well." He transferred half a jaw to me. It fit lightly and easily into the palm of my hand. "A featherweight," I commented. I picked up one of the cranial fragments. That was much heavier.

"This is so apparent, Watson, that the jaw is bone and light and the cranial pieces on the way to full mineralization and heavy, it is wonderful that so few have deduced what you have."

I confess I was so well occupied dandling the two fossils that I didn't hear a word of what Holmes said. "The articular condyle has been broken off," I lectured. "And so has the symphyseal region. Two implanted molar teeth. Broad ramus."

"You are unjustified in saying that those two structures have been 'broken off.' We can only go so far as to claim that they are lacking."

"At any rate, it is not a human jaw," I reassured myself.

"An orangutan's. Now, Watson, is Doyle said to have had any particular access to an orangutan's jaw?"

I ransacked my memory.

"He had never visited the East Indies?" Holmes prodded.

"No. Ah. But a friend of his, a neighbour, back in 1906 had been in Malay. This man, Cecil Wray, a member of the Royal Anthropological Society, could have obtained such a jaw from his brother, who was director of a Malay museum that had just obtained orangutan specimens."

"Then the orangutan jawbone could have come from Doyle's friend Wray's brother's Malay museum's Borneo collection?"

"Precisely."

"And this fragment of hippopotamus tooth? Had Doyle visited Malta?"

"In 1907 he was, with his second wife, in the Mediterranean. They may have gone ashore in Malta. Professor Winslow pointed out that—let me look at my notes. Ah. 'Coincidentally, the *Daily Malta Chronicle* announced on November 16 the discovery of the fossilized remains of a hippopotamus by workmen excavating a limestone fissure on the island.'

"In all probability, Professor Winslow says, they went ashore at

Malta. Sir Arthur had lived in Egypt with his first wife for six months in 1896."

Holmes said nothing for so long I feared he had fallen asleep at my lengthy recital. When I observed him closely, I saw that he had. To enliven him, I picked up a small fossil and asked him what it was, loudly.

"Elephantine, my dear Watson," he murmured. "The tooth of Elephas. It's radioactive, you know."

I hastily put the thing back.

"Then Doyle lived in Egypt. You recall, Watson, you and I were in South Africa then, in 1896, July it was. As the *Cape Town Times* so cleverly discovered. We know that this Elephas tooth fragment came from Ichkeul. Did Doyle stop off at Tunisia?"

"He visited Algeria in 1909, on another Mediterranean tour. Professor Winslow says he 'almost certainly' visited Tunisia. He even wrote a story about Carthage, which is near Tunisia."

"And these other fossils—such as this Pleistocene beaver incisor, which comes from England. Did Doyle have a collection of domestic fossils?"

"Ah, yes, Holmes, there too! On his various golfing expeditions, he could have picked up all kinds of domestic fossils. It begins to look black for Sir Arthur."

"Let us recall, Watson, what Goethe always used to say."

"By all means!"

"*Thätige skepsis.* Have an open mind, a healthy skepticism, until all the facts have come home to roost. So, then, Doyle on his foreign and domestic adventures did have access to all the fossils of living things. How about the flint implements?" He pointed to them in the tray.

"No lighting up here, mate," the attendant informed us. Holmes ground out his cigarillo. I daren't say where.

"Professor Winslow says that most came from a British palaeolithic factory, most of the larger ones being rejects; some were smoothed by weathering, and some had sharp edges."

Holmes took a calculator manufactured in Japan out of his pocket and began punching in numbers as he surveyed the tray. "I cannot understand this, Watson. You spoke of 'most' and 'some.' But I find only four flints here."

I counted them without the aid of the machine. There were only four.

Holmes applied his glass to one of the flints and invited me to look at it. I saw a tiny roundish object the size of a button, but more wrinkled. "What is that, Holmes?"

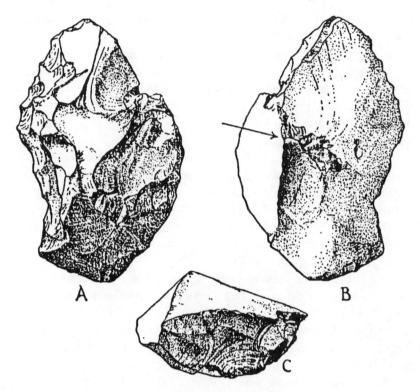

Inoceramus in a flint. Three views of paleolithic handax from the Piltdown gravel:
A = Front, B = Back, C = Lower. The arrow indicates presence of *Inoceramus inconstans*
fossil shell remarked on in the Dawson and Woodward paper of 1914. (From Woodward
[1948], Figure 7.)

"You have heard of Inoceramus?"

"Of course I have! Professor Winslow talks of this. It is often found
in flint implements from Gafsa, a town in Tunisia, 'site of the largest
palaeolithic flint factory in North Africa.' The circle is complete," I
apostrophized. "Sir Arthur transported this very flint implement from
Tunisia to Crowborough to Piltdown."

Holmes leaned back, his lengthy legs extending under the table.
"Inoceramus is a pelagic pelecypod, Watson, much like our familiar
mussels. It had a widespread range in time, from the Jurassic to the
Cretaceous. It also had a widespread range in space, its eggs being carried
far and wide by ocean currents. Dawson, in his 'Supplementary Note on
the Discovery of a Palaeolithic Human Skull and Mandible,' mentions

this very fossil, *Inoceramus inconstans,* in this very flint tool."

"Ah," I summarized.

"Fossils of *Inoceramus inconstans* lie not infrequently in the chalk beds of England and in gravel pits, such as those in the Piltdown region. For my authority I refer to H. J. Osborne White, who speaks of Inoceramus as a common fossil near Lewes, and writes, 'flint casts of Chalk fossils found in this or other parts of the gravel include *Echinocorys scutatus* Leske, of a shape indicative of the Cortestudinarium Zone, and *Inoceramus inconstans* Woods.' Osborne White, H. J., *The Geology of the Country near Lewes,* London: H. M. Stationery Office, p. 65. The flint is Anglican, Watson, not Tunisian."

"Douse the fag," the attendant recommended.

"Twerp," cursed Holmes, but did so again, reluctantly. "You recognize this, Watson?" He showed me two pieces of rock.

"No."

He put them together to form one implement.

"Ah! This is the famous cricket bat, Holmes. Sir Arthur was an expert cricketeer. His fabricating this is just as good as his putting his signature on it."

"We can now summarize all this information on the fossils. 'In all probability' Doyle went ashore at Malta. He 'almost certainly' visited Tunisia. He may have obtained the orangutan jaw from Cecil Wray. He may have obtained this flint tool from Tunisia. I do not find any of this convincing evidence, Watson."

"The evidence is circumstantial, Holmes. And as you have always said yourself, in, for example, our adventure of the noble bookseller, circumstantial evidence is occasionally very convincing. Sir Arthur knew his chemistry, his human pathology; he had an abiding interest in anthropology and archaeology."

"I believe we have exhausted whatever clues this tray has to offer."

"What about the cricket bat?" I nudged.

The telephone rang. The attendant, who had been watching us for further signs of malfeasance, went to answer it, leaving the fossils to our discretion. Had we been of larcenous intent, we could have nipped a few of them. The picture of Inspector Lastrade pursuing us through London was so exhilarating, I almost did cop the canine. But Holmes was rising. We retraced our steps to the Palaeontology Department office, but instead of leaving the Museum, detoured to an elevator. This took us to the fourth floor, to a door which automatically swung open outwards, causing us both to jump away, yet another door was unlocked and we were in the Palaeontology Library.

* * *

Holmes filled out a slip and a small woman brought us, in far less than an hour, several volumes. Holmes and I sat together at a desk. He opened a volume inscribed

DEPARTMENT OF GEOLOGY
LETTERS, 1911 A-L

He riffled through letters. "Perhaps," Holmes opined, pausing at a letter, "we shall find here some evidence of whether Sir Arthur is qualified to be the Piltdown hoaxer."

"He was highly qualified. Interested in everything from skulls to chemical experimentation. Did you know, Holmes, that he had a financial interest in a Kent coal mine? And was very excited at dinosaur fossils which came from it. As a medical man, he would, of course, be expected to have deep and comprehensive knowledge of all sciences. What are you looking at?"

The first of the letters that Holmes handed me, from Mr. Dawson to Professor Woodward, had been written in April of 1911. In it, Dawson reports that Doyle had thought a whole iguanadon had been discovered at Crowborough; but it was only a rock. In late November of that year, the Dawsons lunched with the Conan Doyles. On 11 November 1911, Dawson wrote about another fossil that had greatly excited Sir Arthur. I should like to quote this because it is relevant to our quest and because it has not, to my knowledge, appeared in print:

I regret to say it was a mere concretion of oxide of iron and sand. Sir Conan and the ladies pointed out several "striking resemblances" to the "carcases" of various animals, all mutually destructive!

But the visit was not altogether lost for as I was trying to draw Sir Conan away from the hope of finding much in the Sandstone and directing his attention to the drift deposits above I espied a beautiful flint arrowhead embedded, and in view of us all.

Subsequently we found worked flints; and so I started him off on a new and I hope more fruitful enterprise.

I was so sorry at his disappointment—he is such a good fellow—but the new find revived him a lot. Of course, I have given him the arrowhead and a little flint saw I found at Crowborough (a mile away) some years ago. They are both late neolithic and no use to us, but being found so near to him he is very interested.

"It does not seem that Doyle was held in high regard as a palaeontologist, to Dawson at any rate." Holmes unearthed a small tin of tobacco and inserted a pinch of snuff into each aquiline nasal passage. "Ah," he commenced. "Chew!" he concluded.

"No sneezing in here, sir," scolded the plump young librarian.

"You are being premature, Holmes," I ejaculated.

"The next letter, Watson, might resolve the issue."

In that epistolary document, Mr. Dawson, apparently in response to a request from Professor Woodward, wrote:

Yes, C. D'oyle is writing a sort of Jules Verne book on some wonderful plateau in S. America with a lake, which somehow got isolated from Oolitic times, and contained old [?] fauna and flora of that period; and was visited by the usual "Professor." I hope someone has sorted out his fossils for him!

People do find in the outer world what accords with their thoughts in the inner world. I found this letter important because it alluded to *The Lost World* and it was dated 14 February 1912. Holmes, however, snickered, "You see, Watson, again: Dawson hopes that someone has sorted out Doyle's fossils for him."

"He may have been feigning ignorance, the better to mislead Dawson. Look here, this letter dated 29 November 1912, Dawson wrote that Sir Arthur was excited about the skull and offered to drive him in his motor-car. Well, Sir Arthur had access to the pit."

"I myself drove to Crowborough and then walked to the Piltdown pit. A distance of 17 kilometers, on a day so delicious, it quite brought the strains of the Pastoral Symphony to mind."

"Only 17 kilometers," I interjected. "Sir Arthur was a great walker. He could easily have attained the pit to dig in and to plant the fossils in."

"He needn't have done much digging. Only a few fossils were found below the surface. The hoaxer could have dropped them on the spoil heaps easily enough. How often did he go to the pit?"

"Professor Winslow writes 'there can be little doubt' he often visited the site."

"What does the record indicate?"

"Once."

"Other suspects might have been able to sneak in and out without anyone paying much notice. But Doyle's appearance there would have drawn much attention. I'm afraid that we must discount this part of the accusation. That Doyle lived in Crowborough signifies no more than that he had lived in Egypt. Professor Winslow's 'there can be little doubt' is appropriately tentative. Whenever anyone says there can be little doubt, you can be assured there is much doubt. The rhetorical technique is called begging the question."

"Incidentally, interviewed about the identification of Sir Arthur, an American professor, one—let me see—." I had recourse to my notebook. "Stephen Jay Gould. Yes. He says, in a letter to *Science 83,*

> You can't implicate somebody just because there is a motive. It seems silly when you have concrete evidence against other people, not just circumstantial evidence. You can't just throw bones on the ground at a large site and expect somebody will find then. You have to be led to a bogus discovery.

And Professor Ian Langham—here—Winslow's is 'the flimsiest of recent attempts to identify the hoaxer.' But we may approach the subject of Sir Arthur's motive by talking about *The Lost World.* Now—"

"Concrete evidence? I didn't know there was any against anyone. However, when I walked to the pit and, with a garden trowel, did a bit of digging on my own, I saw no one."

"Which does not mean that no one saw you."

"True, Watson," Holmes gasped.

In the 1913 volume, another letter referring to Sir Arthur. Dawson remarked that he had heard from C. Doyle about the "separates," which I understood to refer to reprints of the forthcoming joint paper to the Geological Society. I was eager to discuss the date of that letter mentioning Sir Arthur's Jules Verne novel, *The Lost World.* Holmes removed a small camera from his jacket pocket and snapped a photo of the drawing of the arrowhead Dawson had given to Sir Arthur.

"No picture-taking here, sir."

"Good God!" Holmes sermonized.

"No blasphemy here, sir."

"Let's go, Watson." He returned the volumes. We walked the greensward to the subway leading to the South Kensington station, and bought our tickets to Baker Street.

* * *

We sat side by side on the train platform bench, behind us planters tropical with ivy and laurel, in front of us tracks, a fence, and behind that an ancient gray wall. Holmes borrowed 20p from me, walked to a confectionary machine, and returned with a Cadbury fruit and nut bar.

"*The Lost World*," I reiterated.

Holmes lit a cheroot and puffed away contentedly. I observed the yellow stains on his fingers. I had always attributed those to his chemical experiments, but now, my insight, sharpened by the Piltdown grind, suggested that the stains were due to some other cause.

"All right, Watson," he conceded. "But you had better first relate why *The Lost World* is important to a determination of Doyle's guilt or innocence as the Piltdown hoaxer."

"Well, Holmes, first of all, it contains many references to forgery and even to what the forger was going to do. One character says that the exposure of a fraud would be a journalistic coup bringing romance into the world; another is afraid that people will think the loss of photographs a fakery; a third speaks of coming upon 'a practical joker, which I should think would be one of the elementary developments of man.' Holmes, are you falling asleep again?"

"Very curious, very curious," he murmured somnolently.

"What is?"

"That a train has not yet arrived."

"But you said very curious twice."

"Caverns generate echoes. Do you think Doyle suspected a hoax?"

When I asked Holmes a question, I did not, so to speak, have the answer in my pocket. But I often felt that Holmes did have the answer as he searched me looking for it. "My thesis, Holmes, is that Sir Arthur did not suspect, but committed, the hoax."

"Go on."

"Another character says"—I had my notebook open again—" 'Even professors might be misled by the desire for notoriety.' And of a photograph of bones, not fossils, of an animal long thought extinct: bones can be 'vamped up for the occasion.' Is there any better description of the Piltdown hoax than that?"

"Excellent details, Watson."

"I cannot resist one more quote. 'If you are clever and know your business you can fake a bone as easily as you can a photograph.' Isn't that astonishing, Holmes? Sir Arthur confessed to the crime before he had even committed it!"

"Watson, you are not merely seeing, you are observing." Our train finally arrived. I headed for a no-smoking, but Holmes elbowed me into a smoking car. The door slid shut. Holmes lit up a stogy.

Recovering from his praise, I continued, "Additional evidence not

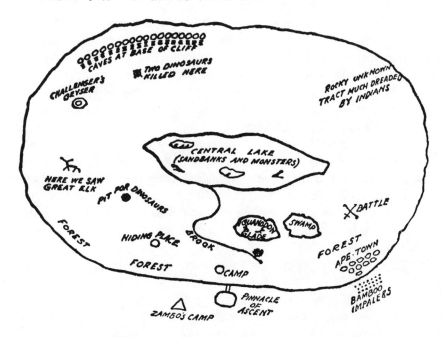

Map of Maple White Land

only that Sir Arthur was the hoaxer, but that he foretold what he was going to do, is this." I handed him two maps I had xeroxed, one of the Sussex weald and the other of Maple White Land, the terrain in *The Lost World*.

With Professor Winslow's analysis as our guide, I pointed out resemblances between sites in the novel and sites in the weald—such as the explorer's camp being located where Lewes was, Lewes the town where Dawson had lived. The brook of Maple White Land corresponded to the River Ouse, and so on.

Holmes scrutinized the maps until the train pulled into Gloucester Road. "*The Lost World,* Watson, is a roman à clef?"

"Doubtless, though I fail to see the significance of that."

"Indulge me, my dear fellow. Like the fox-hound you have often compared me to, I do have to sniff about here and there before snatching the prey. Which real people are the characters modelled on?"

"Professor Challenger is modelled upon William Rutherford, a physiologist of the Edinburgh Medical Faculty. It has been proposed that Lord Roxton, another character, is based upon Roger Casement, in that both the fictional Roxton and the real and pitiable Casement vigorously opposed the slave trade. There's even a comment on the staff of the British Museum being unable to identify some fossils."

"Then Doyle fashioned certain of his characters upon real people?"

"To be sure. The ape-men in the novel are red-haired. I believe that orangutans are red-haired apes. Sir Arthur even indicated in the book that he would plant an orangutan jawbone."

"Then suppose as Doyle fashioned his characters upon real people, he fashioned the terrain of Maple White Land upon Sussex."

"That's apparent." I was beginning to feel like one of Socrates's students being gently guided to a precipice.

"This map of the lost world can, by adroit selection, be shown to be modelled upon Piccadilly Circus. But I'll concede that its model is the weald."

I shrugged my compliance. I could not speak. I was being asphyxiated by a barrage of smoke, Holmes having switched to an exquisitely odoriferous tobacco for his pipe, something quaintly tinged with the familiar odour of Afghanistan mountain goat dung. It occurred to me that he may have taken unfair advantage throughout the years of our concourse in depriving me of oxygen. The rumble of switching tracks announced our imminent arrival at High Street, Kensington.

"I wonder, Watson, if in the interests of justice you would be so kind as to specify whether Doyle tells us that he was in fact using the Sussex weald as his model for the book."

"I must admit, Holmes, you do ask deucedly clever questions. Yes, the plateau is explicitly said to be as large as Sussex; footprints are compared to those in the wealden clay; iguanadon footprints are said to have been found in Sussex as well as in Kent. Other terrains are also referred to—the basaltic upheavals are compared to the Salisbury Crags at Edinburgh and a stream is said to be like a West Country trout stream. The lake, why that's compared to the basin of Trafalgar Square. Deucedly clever, I must admit. But what are the heads and tails of it?"

"Then, Watson," he shouted, "of what bloody value is all this talk of the map in the book being like the map of the weald? Of course it is. Doyle used the weald as his geographic model, and said so. Just as he used real people as models for his characters. Your Professor Winslow has violated the science of deduction by committing a causal fallacy. Here, let me show you, Watson." He stubbed out a madura of such mephitic stink it could have melted the ball-point pen he took from his pocket. He turned the photocopy over, and drew:

A. The Weald > Model for Maple White Land > Piltdown

B. The Weald
/ Model for Maple White Land
\
Site of Piltdown planting

"I submit to you, Watson, that B is more congruent with the facts than is A. The weald has been ever favored as a place for prehistoric man; Doyle knew that, as anyone even with a dilettante interest in natural history would have known that. The reputation of the weald was the source of its being chosen both for the novel and for the forgery."

"But, Holmes, *The Lost World* was written before the Piltdown hoax began. Professor Winslow says: 'The timing is crucial, for the seeds of *The Lost World* appear to have been planted in Doyle's mind long before Piltdown was a site of recognized significance in anyone's mind.' Sir Arthur began the manuscript at least as early as August 5, 1910. The Geological Society announcement was on December 28, 1912. *The Lost World* was published in April 1912, eight months before that announcement. How could Doyle have known the details of what was discovered in the pit? Why, the jawbone itself was not discovered until June 1912!"

Holmes withdrew his calculator and punched its buttons. "The orangutan's jawbone then was discovered two months after the publication of *The Lost World,* which novel features orangutans." Holmes here merely aped my own words. "What does that signify?"

I was embarrassed by my friend's lack of perspicacity. "It signifies that Sir Arthur had planted the orangutan jawbone."

"Really?" he drawled. "But it is at least as likely that the orangutan inhabitants of *The Lost World* were modelled upon Edgar Allan Poe's 'Murders in the Rue Morgue,' which features an orangutan as its villain. Ha, ha," he emitted.

"What are you laughing at, Holmes?"

"Your Sir Arthur and the savage orangutans. Conan and the barbarians."

My poor friend's execrable sense of humour appalled me.

"May I ask you, Watson, why Doyle is supposed to have committed the Piltdown hoax?"

"Why?"

"What was his motive? We have here a man who has no reputation as a jokester. Though that scene comparing the Ape-Man King's hairy chest with Professor Challenger's—" Holmes permitted himself a giggle.

"What? I didn't mention the detail of hairy chest. Why, Holmes, you scoundrel, you've read the book!"

"I didn't say I hadn't," he huffed. "I didn't spend all my time traipsing from Crowborough to Piltdown. Now, Doyle appears to me as precisely the sort of man who would not pull a prank like this. He was ever eager for justice, not just for national honour, but for the honour of persons, even the most insignificant. His defense of Roger Casement is a point, Casement a traitor no less. And of Oscar Slater, of the Hindu George Edalji. He was passionate for justice and for legality."

"Holmes, you double scoundrel! You've read the biographies!" We were now at Nottinghill Gate.

"Passionate for justice, Watson. Think of what he was involved with at the time of the Piltdown hoax. Lecturing around the country on the Belgian atrocities in the Congo. At Liverpool, 2,500 people attended. He represented the Congo Association, and wrote *The Crime of the Congo*. Involvement in a forgery, and Professor Winslow says that he pushed the thing so as to have it exposed as a forgery, would have tainted his crusade on matters of far greater importance than what came from a Sussex pit. Doyle was a man of affairs, one of the most famous citizens of the time." He went on itemizing Sir Arthur's achievements as the train whistled into Bayswater Road. "What kind of a man was he, then?"

"I suspect, Holmes, that he knows us better than we can possibly know him."

"A good point, Watson. But if character has anything to do with crime, then Sir Arthur's character perfectly prevents him from having been the hoaxer."

"Still," I insisted, "Sir Arthur could have done it. You ask about motive. Sir Arthur's motive was to embarrass arrogant and narrow-minded materialistic evolutionists such as Sir E. Ray Lankester. Sir Ray apparently believed that spiritualism is a symptom of cerebral disease."

"And so it may be, Watson."

"You see, Holmes, Sir Ray also anticipated that a certain kind of ape-man would be found. He would have a brain cultivated enough to manufacture flint implements. Thus, he set himself up. In Professor

Winslow's words, 'He provided a list of objects to be discovered or verified as being man-made, and the hoaxer obliged him on every count.' Sir
Arthur's motive, then, was to use Sir Ray's own predictions as a way of
embarrassing him and the other materialistic evolutionists who, by falling
for Piltdown, demonstrated an ineptitude that denied their pronounce-
ments on spiritualism."

"I didn't understand a word of what you just said, Watson."

"Sir Arthur wanted to show the world that evolutionary science was
as fallible as spiritualism."

"Excuse me." Holmes rose and begged a long, thin cigarette from a
child with green hair. "Now Watson, we both know something of Doyle's
attitude towards Lankester."

"Yes. In the novel, Professor Challenger, to prove the authenticity of
the photograph he had taken, shows Malone pictures from one of Sir
Ray's books, a stegosaurus, a pterodactyl and a diagram of its wing. Ray
Lankester is called by Challenger his 'gifted friend.' *The Lost World* may
be, though I'm no literary critic, as you well know—."

Holmes agreed, much too eagerly.

"It could be an animated cartoon of Lankester's book."

"Very nicely put. Challenger is a humourous character, eccentric,
physically kin to an orangutan. Yet he is the instrument to show up the
bias of his colleagues, and I detect an affection for him. There was one
line, Watson, you recall? 'Summerlee and Challenger possessed the highest
type of bravery, the bravery of the scientific mind.' That doesn't sound
much of an attack on the scientific mind."

"Sir Arthur was being ironical."

"Irony is the last refuge of the literary critic probing authorial intention." Holmes went into a diatribe against those critics who look so deeply
into things that they miss what is right in front of their eyes. First, he
pontificated, we ought to consider that a person means what he says, we
ought to look for the least costly hypothesis; if that makes no sense, we
can then probe deeper. The train had stalled, though Holmes had not.
"Now, Challenger, whom Doyle likes, likes Lankester, a pattern we may
describe as guiltless by association."

Paddington Station was crowded with commuters from rail facilities.
"What was Lankester's position on Piltdown, Holmes?"

"Very much of a mixed bag. Sometimes, as in an article on the
missing link, he claimed unity between cranium and jawbone. On the
other hand—"

I began to fear that Piltdown Man had as many hands as Siva.

"On the other hand, at the Geological Society meeting, Lankester said that the jaw and cranium may not belong to the same individual. And after the Site II finds, he thought that perhaps some of that had come from the Piltdown pit. Even in his article, he adds a cautionary footnote. Lankester surmised that the skull was only 1,000 years old and that the mixture of fossils is to be accounted for by their having been carried by streams from different places into the one pit. I believe that his view was most clearly stated in a letter he wrote to H. G. Wells, 'I think we are stumped and baffled.' The most prudent way is to keep the jaw and the cranium apart in all argument about them.' "

The appearance of Edgeware Road coerced us to talk fast.

"I am obliged to admit, Holmes, that Sir Arthur was a proponent of evolutionary theory. The synopsis of evolution provided by a minor character, Professor Murray, was quite attractive as it is related in the novel, from the initial flaming gaseous globe to solidification, the forming of mountains and streams, the beginnings of organic life, up the rungs from mollusks to reptiles to early mammals to the creation of an obnoxious heckler in a red tie. Evolution, Professor Murray says, 'was not a spent force, but one still working, and even greater achievements were in store.' That does not show an animosity towards evolutionary theory."

"We are strolling down Queer Street to be sure, Watson. Here is an anti-evolutionist who defends the theory of evolution and an anti-Lankesterian who corresponds with Lankester and uses his book as a guide to the fantasy of *The Lost World*. If we remove Lankester as a target of Doyle's, we remove Professor Winslow's motive for Doyle to be the Piltdown hoaxer."

Something rankled in me.

"John Lamond," Holmes postscripted, "Doyle's first biographer, has shown that to Sir Arthur evolution will continue beyond material development into spiritual, which may remind us of the Omega theory of Teilhard de Chardin. And in an interview published in the *Buenos Aires Standard,* 4 August 1929, Doyle said: 'But spiritualism is developing. It is undergoing a process of evolution, as our world itself did, according to Darwin. And just as we are told that man has descended from the monkey, so from the visible phenomena of early days, when spiritualists commenced table-lifting and other like experiments, we are now changing to something higher, something more intelligent.' "

What was it? Something quite wrong about Holmes's position.

"Holmes, what are you doing?"

He had removed a tin from his pocket and was stuffing debris into his mouth. "This is the latest thing, Watson. Chewing tobacco." Holmes was ever up on technological advance.

"It's not quite that simple, Holmes. I have some references from the autobiography that are pertinent to our inquiry as to whether Sir Arthur's attitude towards evolutionary theory justifies his being the Piltdown hoaxer. Have we time for me to read them?"

He chewed his approval.

"As a child at Stonyhurst School, Arthur objected to the priestly threats of hell, which objection he gives as reason for abandoning ortho- dox Catholicism."

Holmes mouthed something, which I translate as, "He substituted unorthodox spiritualism for orthodox Catholicism, hooked deeply by the barb of immortality."

"He says that his years of medical training were also the years 'when Huxley, Tyndall, Darwin, Herbert Spencer and John Stuart Mill were our chief philosophers, and that even the man in the street felt the strong seeping current of their thought, while to the young student, eager and impressionable, it was overwhelming. I know now that their negative attitude was even more mistaken, and very much more dangerous, than the positive positions which they attacked with such destructive criticism.' In fact, Holmes, he thought that every materialist was a case of arrested development. So you see, he was intensely hostile towards the materialists, and could well have designed the hoax to ridicule them."

Again, a garbled response, translated as: "On the other hand, Doyle said that the worst enemies of religion are not the materialists, but 'those who clamour against all revision or modification of that strange mass of superbly good and questionable matter which we all lump together' and he places Darwin's *Descent of Man* on a pedestal."

My mind scrambled for the point I wanted to make, but I could not locate it.

* * *

On the street, Holmes deposited the recycled rubbish in his mouth into a bin. I observed two shafts of sunlight, two beacons sweeping the pave- ment. Two rays. Edwin Ray Lankester. John M'Alister Ray. "Ah ha!" I contended. "The Captain of the 'Pole-Star.' "

"John M'Alister Ray's journal."

"John M'Alister Ray is Edwin Ray Lankester."

"To be sure."

"In that short story, Sir Arthur directly attacks Edwin Ray Lankester as a materialist. Holmes, you are in trouble."

"Why is that, Watson?" His infernal coolness was a disgrace. The caporal he was smoking despatched several pedestrians unfortunate enough to have chosen the subway to avoid the automotive bedlam of Marylebone Road.

"Because M'Alister Ray is the object of Sir Arthur's satire! He is the one who talks about superstition being absurd and puerile, about the supernatural as a delusion. Here." It was awkward, walking and reviewing my notes at the same time, but this would demolish Holmes's defense of Sir Arthur. "When Captain Craigie speaks of modern spiritualism, M'Alister Ray 'made some joking allusion to the impostures of Slade, upon which, to my surprise,' Ray reports, 'he warned me most impressively against confusing the innocent with the guilty, and argued that it would be as logical to brand Christianity as an error because Judas, who professed that religion, was a villain.' Sir Arthur was outraged by Lankester's exposure of the medium Slade. That is motive enough for the Piltdown hoax, better motive than those ascribed to any of the other suspects. Lankester and the evolutionists were attempting to destroy Sir Arthur's very religion, to which he held with the tenacity of a convert, and that is the best reason for his being the Piltdown hoaxer."

Holmes had fallen fast asleep. He was truly a genius, not the least of his superb talents the ability to sleep and walk simultaneously. My argument had no effect upon him, but my thumping him on the head did.

"When was 'The Captain of the Pole-Star' written, Watson?"

I was sure he knew the answer, but I will give it for your edification. "1883."

"Then Doyle had his revenge in 1883. More wish-fulfillment than revenge. M'Alister Ray learns in the course of that silly story never to ridicule any man's opinion, even if the opinion is a belief in ghosts. I assume your premise—or is it your conclusion?—is that Lankester's exposure of the medium Slade boiled in our friend from 1883 to 1911, when he lanced it by committing the Piltdown hoax. You know, St. John's Road, two kilometers from here, was the home of T. H. Huxley?"

Holmes would have beaten anyone at trivia. "I am no literary critic," I reminded him, "but that metaphor—"

"Come, Watson, in direct opposition to your thesis, I would suggest rather that Doyle in 1883 disliked Lankester sufficiently to satirize him in the short story, but by 1910 had grown to like him, to use his works and his personality favorably in *The Lost World*, and to become friends with

Nondescript. A prototype for Eoanthropus? (From Waterton [1828].)

him. For your thesis to be credible, Doyle should have executed the hoax in 1883, not 27 years later," Holmes grunted.

We were seated, not comfortably, and sharing a repast of Egg Foo Yung. The house mustard brought tears to my eyes. One last charge in the accusation against Sir Arthur lingered. "How do you account for Nondescript?" I wept.

"You'd better describe that hoax, Watson. People reading this now never heard of Nondescript."

"A book by Charles Waterton, *Wanderings in South America*, published in 1828, a new edition in 1880. After describing the prehensile monkeys of South America, how they transport themselves through the trees, what their flesh tastes like, Waterton talks about a certain specimen, he calls it Nondescript, too heavy to take back, so he cut off its head and took that alone back to England. An artist sketched it. Waterton describes it as having features of a Grecian type."

Holmes contributed, " '. . . a placidity of countenance which shows that things went well with him when in life.' "

"Exactly. Then he wonders whether it's a new species or whether the original features had been destroyed and a set of new ones given to it. He welcomes someone to go and make great and innumerable discoveries in the remote wilds. He says that renovation could be performed on monkey heads. Here." I hurriedly put aside the chopsticks and read from my notes: " 'We could make the forehead and eyes serene in youthful beauty, and shape the mouth and jaws to the features of a malicious old ape. Here is a new field opened to the adventurous and experimental naturalist.' Now, Holmes, Sir Arthur had long been thinking of revenge on Edwin Lankester. He decided to fabricate a second Nondescript, forehead human but mouth and jaws that of an ape. Dawson had found a cranial piece in the Piltdown pit. Sir Arthur planted the rest. Charles Waterton was the most famous alumnus of the Jesuit school of Stoneyhurst, the very school which Arthur Conan Doyle attended as a child."

"On the other hand, you see, Waterton's book could well have been the inspiration for *The Lost World* without any contribution whatsoever from the Piltdown pit. Have you ever read *When It Was Dark?*"

"No." I always feel outre when people ask me if I've read a book of which I have never heard.

"It's all about a hoax. I don't recommend it, Watson, it's a sanctimoniously dreary tale. But of relevance. May I tell you about it? Have a slice of pineapple. A wealthy industrialist named Schaube conceives a plan to destroy Christianity. He blackmails an archaeologist, Llewellyn, to fake the sepulchre of Jesus. The hoax works, just about everyone thinks that Jesus had died and been buried, no divinity there, no resurrection, no redemption. The effect on the world is, as you might well imagine, dreadful. Riots, rapes, murders, desertions, Sepoy mutinies, a return to slavery, dynasties tremble, civil wars break out, Jews, Unitarians, and atheists are delighted. Then a clergyman named Gortre discovers and publicizes the hoax. Christianity lives. One of the archaeologists dies of a broken heart, another just dies, and Schaube ends up an idiot in a kook farm."

"Some more tea, Holmes?"

"The parallels to the Piltdown hoax are numerous, as many as in the Doyle stories you've mentioned. And this penny dreadful was published in 1905, three years before Dawson came up with the first cranial piece. Perhaps the hoaxer read the novel and was inspired to attempt a similar archaeological stunt."

I poured a cup of tea for Sir Arthur, who had joined us.

"What have you discovered?" he demanded.

Holmes took the lead. "The evidence against you is weak. We should be laughed out of court if we came with such a story and such evidence."

"And your opinion, John?"

Arthur Conan Doyle had been a proponent of spiritualism back in 1883. Irritated by the attacks on spiritualism by the materialists, especially Edwin Ray Lankester, he composed the story "The Captain of the 'Pole-Star,'" in which Lankester is dramatized in the character of M'Alister Ray. Sir Arthur, I realised in ruminating over a slice of tart pineapple, was not an opponent of evolution then or later; but he disliked those who would not see what he thought clear evidence for the existence of ghosts and fairies. Lankester still made known his view that spiritualism was ridiculous. His *Kingdom of Man,* published in 1907, was the immediate impulse for Sir Arthur to attack him once again. Sir Arthur was familiar with Waterton's Nondescript, and he used one aspect of that source, its adventure, for the plot of *The Lost World.* But the book also gave him another idea, that of showing that some materialists were as credulous as some spiritualists. In *The Lost World,* he informed the real world that he intended to perpetrate a hoax. References are made to a prehistoric practical joker and to bones "vamped" for the occasion. I recalled that critical line, "If you are clever and know your business you can fake a bone as easily as you can a photograph." Sir Arthur knew his business—anatomy, geology, palaeontology. He even told everyone where he would plant his home-grown Nondescript, right in the Sussex weald, and he generously provided a map. He had travelled widely, and could easily have collected the exotic as well as domestic fossils, and the skull. True, he was occupied with important affairs of state, but planting the fossils would not have taken much time away from them. He was a great walker.

Two questions have always remained unanswered in the Piltdown quest. How could any of the suspects have placed his own career at such risk should the hoax be exposed and he be identified as the hoaxer? For the amateurs, moderate injury would have followed that revelation; for the professionals, serious loss of standing. The only one who was not placed at any risk, who could have walked away scot-free, was Sir Arthur. As a literary man, he was not subject to the rules of civilized behavior. Had it been found out that he was the hoaxer, those interested would have laughed with him, not at him.

The other question is why the hoaxer did not reveal what he had done. Vengeance could only have been satisfied if people were told. The reason why Sir Arthur did not reveal it is that the hoax backfired on him. The object of the enterprise, Sir Edwin Ray Lankester, had not been hoaxed: he did not believe in Sir Arthur's resurrected Nondescript, he questioned the combining of human skull and ape jaw and the Site II finds. It would have been ludicrous for Sir Arthur to claim credit, for intead of proving that the exposer of the medium Slade was as gullible as Slade's clients, he had proved the very opposite. His autobiography does not even mention Piltdown (as hoaxer, he did not want to have the hoax associated with him). Best to forget all about it. I felt that Professor Winslow's brief was even stronger than he has so far indicated, and that Sherlock Holmes was wrong. I felt, to speak personally, that the adventure of Queer Street had emancipated me from Sherlock Holmes. Having thought out all this, I began, "You were a proponent—"

"You needn't repeat it, John. It is just for such thoughts that I was desirous of your participating in this investigation."

I handed him a glass of burgundy, which he sipped as he sat lightly for a man of his stature upon an unsteady pile of yellowing case histories. "Gentlemen," he toasted, "I express my whole-hearted agreement with you." He upended the glass, and there was nothing left of him but a trickle of red wine in the smoky air and an echo of a bubbly laugh.

Though Sir Arthur had read my mind, Holmes had not, and so I explained to him what I had concluded, emphasizing the three points of Sir Arthur's having alerted the world to the forthcoming hoax, of its having been relatively risk-free for him, and of its failure, thus the subsequent suppression. Holmes disagreed with each of my arguments. To the first, he responded that the hoaxing talked about in *The Last World* referred to the past episode of Nondescript and not to the future episode of Piltdown; to the second, that there was indeed risk to Sir Arthur's reputation not as a writer but as a statesman; and, to the third, that it was my most creative effort since he had known me, but that Lankester's attitude was sufficiently ambiguous that Sir Arthur could have claimed victory.

Well into the night we discussed the possibility that Sir Arthur had suspected a hoax at Piltdown—which explained more the more I thought of it. Brush-strokes of dawn painted the sky azure and chimneys a rusty red. Finally, in exasperation, I urged Holmes, "Well then, who do you think was the perpetrator of the Piltdown hoax?" If anyone in this world could crack this awful coconut of a case, it had to be Holmes, his keen mind applied to exhaustive research being an irresistible combination.

"It is obvious, my dear fellow." He lit up a joint.

I nodded my head. "Yes, it is, I see that, but, Holmes, who?"

"So obvious. Staring us right in the face all this time."

"Who? Who?"

"Would you care to perch somewhere, Watson?"

"Holmes!"

"All right. It was none other than, the Piltdown perpetrator, the man who so confused the world of science and seduced generations of scholars into unseemly occupation, was none other than—Professor Moriarty!"

"You must be joking, Holmes," I cried. "It is absurd. Professor Moriarty died at Reichenbach Falls fifteen years before the first Piltdown cranial fragment was found!"

"I was never more serious in my life. I survived the fall into the chasm. You yourself long thought me dead. It is reasonable to deduce that, if I survived, Professor Moriarty also survived, and has enjoyed the most cunning, the most diabolical, and the most malicious revenge in the entire history of fiction."

"The motive, Holmes, the motive!"

"To frame Sir Arthur Conan Doyle."

I saw. "I see," I said.

I now understand why Sir Arthur had warned us that the resolution of the Piltdown case would be important to Sherlock Holmes and myself.

CHAPTER TWELVE

HUNTER OF ANCIENTS: W. J. SOLLAS

This ghastly story is of one dead man accusing another dead man of having been the hoaxer. It convinced a number of historians.

As they took their seats, members of the Society of Comparative Anatomy and Palaeontology meeting at Reading, England, in 1978 had much to chat about—those in the know whispering urgently to the ignorant about that report in the journal about—but the tape recording had started its round.

The voice that crackled over the loudspeaker was from the dead. Professor J. A. Douglas, holder of the Chair of Geology at Oxford University from 1937 to 1950, began by saying that Dawson remains a strong suspect, but that the solicitor would have needed a collaborator who knew more than he about anatomy, paleontology, and anthropology, someone who had access to fossils, who knew the staining properties of certain chemicals.

> As I am no longer able to see, to write, or to read, I was determined to make a tape record of my ideas, hence the following notes.
>
> A grudge against one of the principals. Obviously Smith Woodward would suffer and did suffer most. Did they ever try to find out if Smith Woodward had any particular enemies who might do such a thing? No. They did not. And if they had done, they would, I am sure, have come face to face with my predecessor at Oxford, namely Professor Sollas. (Quoted in Halstead, November 2, 1978)

W. J. Sollas was a former student of T. H. Huxley, a professor of geology at Oxford after previous appointments at Bristol and Dublin, the recipient of many awards, among them the Royal Society's gold medal, author of books on minerology, crystallography, invertebrate and vertebrate fossils, and an excavator of the Paviland Cave in South Wales (and correct in identifying the Red Lady as Cro-Magnon and the Galley Hill skeleton as recent). Although he agreed with Smith that human beings early achieved intellectual powers, that theory was not as important to him as it was to Smith. He shared with most of the other Piltdown researchers the theory that the earliest hominids would have manifested features of both human being and ape. He had seen them in the Neanderthal specimens and would see them again in the Piltdown specimen. In 1915, the second edition of his *Ancient Hunters* appeared, *Eoanthropus dawsoni* put forward as a rival to Heidelberg as the oldest known European. He praised Woodward for having guessed at just the kind of canine Teilhard found: in the tooth's agreeing "in a remarkable manner with the tooth inserted in the restoration," it vindicated the Woodward-Barlow method. Nobody has wrung out a hypothesis that Sollas was the Piltdown hoaxer because he wanted to support a theory. Several have given him another motive.

Douglas had worked with Sollas for 30 years. In the Piltdown case, there are few accounts by people closely associated with the suspects, knowing their daily activities and their ways of thinking. Professor Douglas was such a person. Regarding Sollas's opportunity to perpetrate the hoax, those who accuse him, the foremost among them L. B. Halstead of the Reading University Department of Geology, list these points (I offer my own quick replies to each):

1. In 1910, 26-year-old Douglas sent Sollas some fossils from Bolivia, among them a mastodon lower jaw.

No Bolivian fossils were exhumed from the pit.

2. Sollas borrowed ape teeth from the university's Department of Human Anatomy collection.

These objects were available elsewhere to others.

3. Douglas once opened a package addressed to Sollas and found in it potassium bichromate, used in photography. Sollas was not the department's photographer. The photographer himself, C. J. Bayzand, had not ordered the crystals.

Potassium bichromate was available at any druggist's. "The truth of the matter is," wrote K. P. Oakley in a 1980 letter to *Nature,* "that after the passage of some 70 years, there is nothing to be gained by speculating on the purpose for which Sollas ordered the packet of bichromate crystals."

4. A query by L. B. Halstead: "Does it not strike one that Sollas, who was one of the leading anthropologists of the day, is conspicuous by his absence from the picture in Burlington House with Smith Woodward

and his colleagues examining the Piltdown skull?"

No.

J. S. Weiner, like K. P. Oakley, also wrote to *Nature* (January 4, 1979) dismissing each of these data, and affirming his conviction that Dawson was the sole hoaxer. Ian Langham, of the University of Sydney, joined in attacking Halstead, writing (*Nature,* January 18, 1979) that we would have to know when the alleged incidents of the borrowing of ape teeth and receipt of potassium bichromate took place. If they took place after 1912, they are irrelevant. (If they took place before 1912, they might be equally irrelevant.) When Halstead returned to the fray, in the expected rebuttal of these rebuttals (Halstead, February 22, 1979), he implicated Grafton Elliot Smith, Teilhard de Chardin, M. A. C. Hinton, and, or so his statement implies, Arthur Smith Woodward: "Everything that Smith Woodward wanted, turned up and, moreover, in the order in which he wanted it."

As with almost all of the other suspects, getting caught would have injured Sollas's career; success would have injured his profession. He must have had a strong motive to engage in such a fraud. Professor Douglas's voice intoned the motive: a grudge against Smith Woodward. Sollas so disliked Woodward that he refused to lend Woodward an assistant to help him with ichthyosaur fossils. Halstead tells us why Sollas was so mean:

> Sollas was Britain's leading expert on fossil man, who had just given his Presidential Address to the Geological Society on fossil man and had recently published *Ancient Hunters* (1911). Here was a man who had pioneered over many years the technique of serial sectioning which enabled palaeontologists to examine the internal structure of fossils that otherwise would never have been accessible for study, a technique which Smith Woodward contemptuously dismissed as a "mere toy." And here was Smith Woodward with pretensions, but no expertise, announcing his ambition to discover the earliest man and, moreover, in Britain. Was this not as close to an invitation as one could imagine?

It started as a joke that then "got out of hand." But it didn't end with the pit.

As one traces out the portrait of each of the suspects in the Piltdown tapestry, filaments that seemed at first unimportant grow dramatically. Tracing the portrait of W. J. Sollas leads to a horse's head. The incident is supposed to prove that Sollas hated Woodward so much that even the success of the Piltdown hoax was insufficient to sate that passion. Sollas developed another stinger. Here's the plot of this playlet:

In September 1911, two freshmen of the Sherborne School, A. S. Cortesi and P. C. Grove, found a piece of bone about five inches long, similar to the anterior rib of the Mongolian wild horse, in a dry valley in Dorset. An outline-drawing of the head and forequarters of a horse illustrated the smooth convex face of the bone. The artifact commanded interest because it had been found in a Pleistocene deposit of debris from a quarry and because only one comparable object had ever been found in England, at the Robin Hood Cave, Creswell Crags. The Geological Society heard the first public announcement of this find at its March 11, 1914, meeting. A. S. Kennard, in the ensuing discussion, emphasized the rarity of the specimen. Other people thought it certainly of some Paleolithic industry. Smith Woodward described it.

There the matter rested for years. Sollas does not mention the find in his second edition of *Ancient Hunters* (1915), but in the third edition (1924) he does, and in a way designed to pique Smith Woodward. After discussing Cro-Magnon mural art engravings of horses of Magdalene and Aurignacian industries, tools and other productions of prehistoric cultures, Sollas provides, in his Figure 299, drawings of five implements from caves, the last one a rib-bone on which is a sketch of a horse with a crew-cut, from Robin Hood Cave. A footnote to this is first friendly and then insultingly specific:

> There is a singular absence of any attempt at art in all the Palaeolithic stations of England. The horse figured here is, I am assured, a forgery introduced into the cave by a mischievous person; the horse described by Dr. Smith Woodward is a forgery perpetrated by some schoolboys.

This dart traveled for a couple of years before it struck a bull's eye— Arthur Smith Woodward. In the January 16, 1926, issue of *Nature,* Woodward quotes the last clause of Sollas's footnote, refers to the Geological Society's having accepted the artifact as genuine back in 1914, and reports that he communicated with Arnaldo Cortesi, one of the two schoolboys (the other had died in the war). Cortesi reminded Woodward that he had been only 15 at the time, and asserted that he had not taken part in any trick.

Sollas did not let two years go by to answer Woodward on this forgery within the larger tapestry of the Piltdown forgery. In a letter written on February 13, 1926, Sollas said that "it is with great regret" that he found himself obliged to repeat that the Sherborne bone-drawing was a clumsy forgery, a practical joke by schoolboys who had at the school an

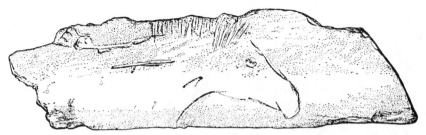

Sherborne horse's head. Drawing of head and forequarters of a horse on a fragment of rib; from a dry valley north of Sherborne (Dorset). (From *QJGS* 70, April 1914.)

illustration of the Creswell Crag horse they used as a model. Sollas's assistant, Mr. Bayzand, analyzed the two artifacts, the one from Creswell Crag and the one said to have come from a quarry deposit near the school, and concluded that the latter was a mere copy of the former. The letter by Sollas was followed by one from C. J. Bayzand, who adds that he had been at the Sherborne School arranging its museum collections when he learned of the find, a trick played on the school's science master, R. Elliot Steel. Bayzand took responsibility for having informed Sollas of the trick and thus for Sollas's footnote in the third edition of *Ancient Hunters*. That was enough to arouse R. Elliot Steel. As soon as he read the letters by Sollas and Bayzand, he submitted his story. It was, he recalled, in September 1911 that A. Cortesi found the bone; back at school, the boy was about to throw it into the fire when E. A. Ross Jefferson, an older student, stopped him and brought the bone to Steel. The boys felt that the bone had to be authentic since Cortesi could not draw "for nuts." A note from E. A. Ross Jefferson followed Steel's letter, to the effect that when Cortesi was about to throw the bone into the fire, Jefferson told him not to be "such an ass; as I had been reading about the Palaeolithic Period, and saw at once that it was a real find." Steel showed the bone to Woodward, who showed it to the Geological Society. "The idea of the bone not being genuine," wrote Jefferson, "was a rumour started by that arch-humourist, Mr. X." The thing we can be sure of in this story is that Jefferson's Mr. X is not Essex's Mr. X—unless that arch-humorist Teilhard de Chardin had decided on one of his days off to pay a visit to Dorset.

Half a century after this exchange of pleasantries, which itself took place more than a decade after the initial event, Professor Douglas re-animated the issue in his taped memoirs, and Halstead picked it up as an example of Sollas's lifelong hatred of Woodward. Sollas's reputation as an honest man hangs on the slim thread of whether he had deliberately drawn a picture of a horse's head on a horse's rib and planted it in a cave to be found by two schoolboys, the whole elaborate business to show the world what a fool Woodward was.

R. A. H. Farrar, of the Royal Commission on Historical Monuments, reported in *Nature* (January 25, 1979) that Oakley had demonstrated back in 1957 that the bone itself was a semi-fossilized Pleistocene production and that the engraving may have been authentic, quite beyond the power of adolescent ingenuity. In his retaliation, Halstead ignored Farrar, insisting that "the incident of the Sherborne Horse's head, if nothing else, was a successful and deliberate demonstration by Sollas of Woodward's incompetence." In the exchange on this issue, the question about the authenticity of the Sherborne horse's head overshadowed the more important question: whether Sollas faked it to avenge himself on his presumptuous colleague.

In *Ancient Hunters* Sollas came out for Piltdown Man as an authentic hominid, insisting that coincidence could not explain how an ape jaw and a human cranium fell together. Such an explanation is "unworthy of serious consideration." He devoted twelve pages to Eoanthropus, an increase of three over the 1915 edition's section. The combination of human skull and ape jaw at Piltdown is like that of the Heidelberg find: ape jaw and human teeth. He called the femur, illustrated, a remarkable implement, sui generis, "fashioned in all probability by Eoanthropus himself." He took sides with those who defended Eoanthropus, such as Osborn and Pycraft, and against the skeptics, such as Miller.

Weiner asked why, if Sollas wanted to do Woodward dirt, he should "have so firmly supported the new *Eoanthropus dawsoni* in the first place." And, one may add, why so long afterward? On the surface, by defending Smith Woodward's production, Sollas seems to have been defending Smith Woodward. But in the Piltdown saga, things are not always what they appear to be. Sometimes, they are the opposite of what they appear to be.

On the surface, Sollas seems again and again to praise Smith Woodward. Woodward's account was "full and admirable"; his reconstruction of the skull "accompanied with great success"; his method unexpectedly and "triumphantly" vindicated by the discovery of the canine tooth. In the preface to the third edition, Sollas includes Woodward in a list of the friends to whom he was indebted (along with Professor Grafton Elliot Smith).

A naive explanation of all this is that Sollas meant just what he said and accepted contributions attesting the authenticity of Eoanthropus from whatever source they came, even from fish-men and from bird-men, that he felt no animosity toward Woodward or Pycraft.

We know now, thanks to the exposé, that Woodward's account was not "full and admirable," but often vague and incomplete; that his reconstruction was accompanied with considerable debate; and that the canine tooth was not a vindication of his method. A student of the case may then assume that, since we know these things, Sollas knew them too, and in saying the opposite of what he knew was practicing the ancient and devious art of irony. Traipsing down that path, we'll come to the conclusion that the more he praised Woodward overtly, the more he was damning Woodward covertly.

Stephen Jay Gould thinks that Sollas was completely innocent, but recognizes that Sollas's "obsequiously glowing" praise of Woodward "Could be read as subtle sarcasm" (Gould, 1980). Gould's comment illuminates what one critic did with Sollas on Pycraft. Sollas had said that Pycraft's rebuttal of Miller was "masterly." Halstead reads "masterly" as subtle sarcasm. "This is a telling phrase," wrote Halstead, "since Pycraft was the Museum's bird expert and was known to have had less knowledge and understanding of human and ape anatomy than even Smith Woodward." Thus, if he had supported Piltdown Man and praised Woodward even more than he did, we could be even more certain that he had faked the former and hated the latter.

On the side of those who think Sollas innocent are Weiner, Oakley, *Scientific American* (1979), and Sherwood Washburn, who expressed his belief "that what Sollas wrote is a far better guide to what he thought than the recently disclosed suspicions." On the other side are Douglas, Halstead, Bowden, Curtis Fuller, and *Brewer's Dictionary of Phrase and Fable:* "The hoax, which took in most of the experts, was apparently planned by William Sollas, Professor of Geology at Oxford (1897-1937), through his dislike of Sir Arthur Smith Woodward." James K. Page, Jr, in the *Smithsonian* (also 1979, the year for pummeling Sollas) wrote, "Thus, it seems that Dawson, the solicitor, may have been talked into trying to make a fool of Smith Woodward by his bitter rival, Sollas, who supplied Dawson with the material for the hoax." The most recent accuser of Sollas is Donald Johanson, the discoverer of the famous australopithecine Lucy, who agrees with the alleged motive: Sollas simply "detested Woodward." Johanson is not only the most recent of those accusing Sollas, but, I suspect, also the last.

CHAPTER THIRTEEN

A COUNTERFEITER: LEWIS ABBOTT

I believe that of all the suspects Lewis Abbott has the best credentials to
be the Piltdown hoaxer.

"NOT A VERY STRONG CASE": CRITICAL OPINION

Most Piltdown historians have passed over Abbott as a suspect or have
explicitly acquitted him. A few have hinted that the accusation has merit.

A hunt through published literature on Piltdown will turn up very
little on the possible complicity of Louis Abbott as Piltdown hoaxer. Vere
and Dodson toyed with that in a few sentences. L. Harrison Matthews
allows Abbott a role in his quartet of hoaxers. J. S. Weiner, in *The
Piltdown Forgery*, locates Abbott as "a likely source" for the jawbone.
Gould views Abbott "as a quite plausible suspect" (Private communication, August 6, 1986).

Searching through the Piltdown archives uncovers passages that hum
with a leitmotif of suspicion. Kenneth Oakley seems to have been tracking
Abbott. He asked Teilhard whether the Site II finds could have been
before 1914, and then unexpectedly exclaimed: "Do you remember a man
named Lewis Abbott? He was a believer in eoliths!" (Teilhard replied that,
though he had heard of Abbott, he had not met him.) In a letter requesting information about amulets from Abbott's gem collection, Oakley
tempts the reply he wanted: "They may, of course, be forgeries" (February
3, 1954, BMNH). Years after the exposé, Oakley continued inquiring
about Abbott. He asked J. de Heinzelin de Braucour, of the Institut
Royal des Sciences Naturelles de Belgique, about Abbott's correspondence
with A. Rutot; de Heinzelin believed that Abbott had "played his part in
the plot." Oakley wrote back asking whether de Heinzelin knew the name
of Abbott's assistant. "If his principal assistant was young in 1914, he
may still be alive to tell the tale!"

William James Lewis Abbott. Taken in London by Maull & Fox, Piccadilly, probably upon Abbott's election to FGS in 1888. (From archives, Geological Society of London.)

Oakley also corresponded with F. H. Edmunds of the Geological Survey and Museum, whose lengthy reply is informative and a good clue.

> While I was in the district I made the acquaintance of a jeweller who owned a shop in Hastings, one W. J. Lewis-Abbott, whose name is not unknown in the geological world of 40 years ago. He himself told me that he had worked with Dawson on the Piltdown skull and that the skull had been in his possession in his house six months before Smith Woodward saw it; and I gathered from him that he soaked it in bichromate to harden it. I have every reason to believe that these statements were matters of fact.
>
> This has some bearing on the view as to who was the author of the forgeries you have detected. It seems to be unlikely that Dawson, a solicitor, would either have the knowledge or the ability to make skilful forgeries; although that is only an opinion as I never met Dawson. Abbott certainly had the knowledge, skill, tools, and opportunity to do so. He certainly tried to pull a fast one over me, by offering me erratics of various types of rock, plus photograph of section, to show a boulder clay at 150 ft. O.D. just outside Hastings! Unfortunately I could not make the photograph fit the countryside.
>
> As to motive, I also have my opinions, but they don't matter. (November 24, 1953, BMNH)

I wrote to Weiner and others requesting their views on Abbott as hoaxer. Weiner replied:

> Although I left this matter a little open, there can be no doubt that Dawson was the sole perpetrator. The little army [of people trying to solve the Piltdown problem] includes people who are keen on Abbott as the perpetrator or accomplice and this is entirely because I rather titillated people's interest in Abbott's direction. But I have material about Abbott which I think makes it difficult to incriminate him. (May 14, 1981)

Mrs. A. B. Milligan, archivist of the Wellcome Institute for the History of Medicine, thought that Abbott took himself too seriously to be the hoaxer and that, if he were, he would have taken credit for the discovery. Glyn Daniel wrote me that Miles Burkitt, his teacher in prehistory at Cambridge, used to lean toward Abbott as hoaxer, but realized that "it was not a very strong case." Peter Costello wrote that the BMNH staff leaned toward Abbott at the time of the exposé, "and if one were suspicious Abbott has some bad points against him," but also thought the case against him weak.

"A RECKLESS ENTHUSIAST": BIOGRAPHY OF A HOAXER

A biographical survey of Abbott, including his view of himself, suggests that his personality and career fit the profile of the Piltdown hoaxer better than do those of his fellow suspects.

Born six years before the *Origin of Species,* William James Lewis Abbott grew up during the Darwinian excitement about human ancestry. The most complete account (two paragraphs) of Abbott is given in A. S. Kennard's "Fifty and One Years of the Geologists Association" (1947).

> He was a short, stocky man with a ferocious moustache, nearly always wore a boater in the field and came from a remote part of Essex, the Dengie Hundred. Abbott at first was a frequent speaker at outdoor meetings, defending orthodox religious views, but at one meeting a working man asked some awkward question based on geology, of which Abbott knew nothing; so he made up his mind to learn.

Abbott early developed an interest in gemology, teaching at the Polytechnic Institute on Regents Street. That early interest broaded out in two directions, into his profession as jeweler and into his avocation of bone-grubber. Wanting to be close to the land that hid the prehistory he felt himself uniquely qualified to discover, he moved to Hastings and there opened a shop in 1898. Fossils eventually replaced customers. Over the years, his business declined. He made bad investments, buying gold when it was high and selling it when prices fell, building up inventories for Christmas sales that didn't materialize, borrowing money that he had difficulty repaying. His wife's and his own health failed.

"In his own estimation," Weiner wrote in *The Piltdown Forgery,* "he was an ignored genius." In others' estimations, he was eccentric. Harrison draws a temperamental and troublesome Abbott, a person verging on mental unbalance. Joyce Emerson, who with Weiner wrote two popular accounts of the exposé for the *London Times,* described him as bombastic, a "reckless enthusiast, championing Piltdown Man without reserve" (Emerson, 1955). The persona emerging from Abbott's letters is opinionated, frustrated by the persistence of false theories, by the tardiness of others to understand and act on his advice, and then impatient at them for taking the credit and reaping the rewards of his novel insights. Were the theory of humors medically respectable, Dawson, open and cheerful, would be a specimen of the sanguinary character; Abbott, impatient and quick to take umbrage, shadowy and choleric.

He condemned the British Museum because of its failure to make

Kent's Cavern fossils available to him, and during one of his arguments sent Dawson, in the latter's phrase, "abusive letters." Sharp in attacking enemies, he was passionate in his affection to "wiffey" (who had been a music hall actress) and to his heroes, the English archaeologist Benjamin Harrison and the French archaeologist Boucher de Perthes.

Immune to modesty, he expressed an outstanding loyalty to himself. In 1914, he wrote to his friend Yates, "I have made a few more very important discoveries, new races and new things in flint. I wonder if the world will have to rediscover them all." Frustrated by the Geological Society's delay in publishing a paper of his, he boasted to Woodward that his foreign friends had said this paper

> will prove a blessing on the continent, where definitions appear about as muddled as they are here; they maintain that this is just what was wanted, and that it will put not only prehistoric archaeology on a new basis, but many other branches of science also. (January 26, 1916, BMNH)

Looking back upon his life, he wrote of the professionals:

> Upon various occasions they have refused papers of mine upon New discoveries, then in perhaps five or ten years they have been discovered by other Countries, and published with a flourish of trumpets, and now for ever in the literature of the Science, the various Countries will get the Honours that really belong to this Country. Upon one occasion I appealed to a celebrated past President, he said, The fact is you are a generation before your time, and like all pioneers you are suffering the consequences. (June 6, 1932, WIHM)

His articles and letters overflow with such claims, "the first discovered example of a British palaeoglyph," a Roman bronze statuette the finest ever found in England; Hastings kitchen middens, the best artifacts ever found from the people who left the rubbish; a coconut pearl, the only one in the country; his anthropological collection, the most complete of any known; from the frozen gravel of the Yaniesei, unique things; cat's-eye opals, wonderful specimens unknown to the British Museum; and so on.

Arthur Keith took the occasion of writing an obituary (Abbott died in 1933) to reflect on this egoism:

> He was bold and resolute in formulating scientific explanations of past events, and perhaps more occupied with the contributions he himself had made to his favourite subjects of study than those made by his

fellow-workers. Making all allowances on this score, a long series of
discoveries must be placed to his credit. (Keith, 1933)

As his business declined, his reputation as an excellent observer and
provocative theorizer improved over the years. Just about everyone consulted him in the game of seeking what was hidden, not only the amateurs
cruising the landscape but the professionals as well. On the Hastings
Museum Committee with Butterfield and Dawson, he was, at least before
December 1912, more famous than either of them. Abbott is cited for his
work on the geology and fossils of the weald by W. J. Sollas, G. F. Scott
Elliot, J. Reid Moir, Arthur Keith, Miles Burkitt, A. S. Kennard. Keith
turned to Abbott's ideas on prehistoric geology, on flint industries, on the
age of the Piltdown pit. Agreeing with Abbott on prehistoric man's symmetrical brain and on the antiquity of the Galley Hill skeleton, Keith summarized the evaluation of other professionals: Abbott was "an explorer
whose opinion in all that pertains to the geology of the Weald deserves
serious consideration," particularly his opinion on flint industries. Keith
commended Abbott's theory that "each generation of Palaeolithic men we
now know copied and modified the flint tools of an older generation."

And yet, in so many references to him, an uneasiness about Abbott's
having misinterpreted what he found colors the commentary. J. Reid
Moir noted that Abbott had found flints in the Cromer Forest Bed that
"he claimed" were humanly flaked. Miles Burkitt, Daniel's professor at
Cambridge who once suspected Abbott as hoaxer, wrote that Abbott's
claim about finding these tools was invalid—the "tools" were natural
creations (Burkitt, 1921). John Ray, a solicitor at Hastings, advised
Woodward that Hastings should not buy the part of Abbott's collection
offered to them because Abbott's conclusions and theories were suspect.
Woodward replied that some things should be bought by the Town
Council, though long ago he had found Abbott's prices too high and his
good work "spoiled by the use of his many speculations, and perhaps too
much enthusiasm."

Today's opinion on Abbott's many speculations is exemplified by this
passage from John Wymer's *Lower Palaeolithic Archaeology in Britain*
(1968). The context is that of finds that "must be regarded cautiously":

There is a flake in the Reading Museum, acquired from the old Wembley
Museum, marked as coming from the boulder clay at Finchley, and with
the finder's name W. J. Lewis Abbott. Lewis Abbott was a remarkable
man and his name is connected with many of the palaeolithic discoveries

made about fifty years ago. . . . His observations must, in view of his imagination, be accepted with reserve.

Well, then, Abbott made mistakes in interpreting some finds. But the coloration in the commentaries darkens as we come upon the hints that he did not merely make mistakes, he salted sites and forged artifacts.

F. H. Edmunds's complaint comes to mind—that Abbott tried to pull a fast one on him. A. S. Kennard, in his 1947 article, afraid that Abbott's newspaper articles, though amusing, "must be classed under fiction," noted that Abbott's claim to have discovered a certain fossil "is not correct"; that he had taken specimens from an excavation "without permission"; that his discovery of "a nearly complete skeleton of a mammoth" consisted of "a few foot-bones"; that another skeleton, of an arctic fox, "included many bones of the Hare"; and, most significantly, that fossil ivory Abbott claimed to have found "never was there." Responding to Oakley's inquiry about the amulets, a curator at the BMNH wrote of the amulets:

I have never seen anything quite like these objects and they certainly look to me pretty good forgeries. They do not, however, resemble Billys or Charleys so far as I know and must be something from another "factory." (February 1954, BMNH).

Abbott explored kitchen middens below Hastings Castle. He reported that he had found mesolithic flints with the pottery; this implied that the pottery was also mesolithic. No mesolithic pottery had ever been found in England. In 1937, E. Cecil Curwen reexamined the find, then at the Hastings Museum. He ascertained that the pottery was of historic times, mostly medieval. He did not speculate as to how mesolithic flint tools had gotten mixed up with medieval rubbish. I will so speculate. I think that Abbott planted the mesolithic flints as a false index to the age of the pottery. I think that he brought the fossil ivory Kennard alludes to to the site. I wouldn't be surprised if the amulet forgeries came not from Billy's or Charley's but from Abbott's factory. As we'll see, Abbott was talented at fabricating artifacts.

"RESULTS OF QUITE A STARTLING NATURE":
SATISFACTION OF THEORY

No one among the suspects was as adamant, years before Piltdown, that England was host to Pliocene (or Plateau or Eolithic or Forest Bed) Man.

Kitchen midden. This picture appeared in Abbott's "Primeval Refuse Heaps at Hastings" (1897). On the ledge below cavern is the kitchen midden. The bearded gentleman to the left holding a pickax may be Lewis Abbott. (From archives, Wellcome Institute Museum.)

A. S. Kennard, who considered him "a born collector," repeated a colleague's remark: Abbott "is such a man. Put him in Trafalgar Square and he would find fossils in the granite basin." "Wherever he went," Kennard added, "he found." Abbott began publishing his discoveries and theories on the prehistoric races of Sussex and Kent in 1892; he wrote on pleistocene vertebrates, including walrus fossils in the Thames valley; on geology and gems; and especially on flint industries in England and elsewhere. For a find of Pleistocene vertebrate fossils, he shared the Lyell Award of the Geological Society (in 1897). He also was funded by the British Association for the Advancement of Science. He explored caves, barrows, tunnel-works, and middens at Kent, Sevenoaks, Hastings, the Cromer Forest, and many other sites.

Long before the Piltdown finds, Abbott had proposed that in the Pliocene, prehistoric English hominids had left mementos of their bodies in fossilized bones and of their culture in eolithic tools. Paleolithic and neolithic tribes followed the eolithic. As early as 1894, he published on Plateau Man, the thesis of the article that paleontology has found "it necessary to extend the dominion of the genus *Homo* into the geologic past to a degree that was previously undreamed of." Benjamin Harrison had so predicted.

Eighteen ninety-seven was a productive year for Abbott. Although he lost most of his money in West Australian bonds, he received the Lyell Award and published an important article in *Natural Science,* "Worked Flints from the Cromer Forest Bed," whose concluding rhetorical question is, "Are we not justified in admitting the existence of man in Britain in the Forest Bed period?" that is, the Pliocene. In "The Antiquity of Man in Britain," *Natural Science* commented on an Abbott discovery:

> In this country, at all events, no one has ever professed to find the remains of man at so low a horizon, although the opinion before now has been hazarded that if they occurred at this horizon at all, they would be found at the place where Mr. Abbott has actually discovered them.

Eighteen ninety-eight's contribution was "The Authenticity of Plateau Implements," also in *Natural Science.* At a lecture to the Eastbourne History Society in 1908, Abbott directed his audience to forget Kent and look to Suffolk and Sussex for evidence of Plateau Man. He reported that Reid Moir, taking his advice, had conducted researches in Suffolk that "led to results of quite a startling nature, and which have since been the object of discussions all over the civilized world." The flint implements that Reid Moir found, and sent to Abbott, showed that primitive human beings living in the same area had "sufficient intelligence to chip flints into desired forms quite early in the Pliocene period." Other articles followed, elaborations of Abbott's central theory that a tool-making Pliocene hominid had existed in England. Exploring, he said, would uncover more paleontological and eventually anatomical evidence of that existence.

We're creeping up to the Piltdown pit. It's time to pause for a moment and reflect on where Louis Abbott was circa 1911. He had published at least twelve papers, most of them before the turn of the century (1892, two; 1893, two; 1894, one; 1895, two; 1897, two; 1898, two); then a gap until 1911, one. He would publish throughout the rest of his life fewer papers than he had from 1893-1898. But he kept on writing them and kept on complaining that though (or because) he was far ahead of his time, a real pioneer, they were not readily accepted. Everybody kept on carping about eoliths not being tools and kept on ignoring him. He had dedicated his life, and would continue to dedicate his life, to the proposition that a toolmaking hominid had existed in England. As 1911 approaches, W. J. Lewis Abbott is an angry middle-aged man.

Nothing in the weald would be better than for someone to find a hominid obviously ancient (say, with a jaw bone very like an ape's), the bones accompanied by flints that were unquestionably tools.

"A FINGER IN THE PIE": THE SKULL FORGERY

Lewis Abbott guided Dawson to the pit, defined the remains as human, and adulterated them.

Abbott suggested that ancient hominids had lived not just in the weald, not just in Sussex, but in Piltdown. Sending his regrets to Woodward that business would not allow him to attend the forthcoming December meeting of the Geological Society, he explained that he had

> paid such a lot of time to the Wealden gravels, bringing to light a new set of facts which will fit in no where with the old ideas, but find a place for the flint bearing gravels of the weald a necessity & also because I feel that my work in this line has stimulated Mr. Dawson, without which, it is quite possible that these important things would never have been brought to light as Mr. Dawson knew of the existence of the gravel many years, without following it up. (December 15, 1912, BMNH)

Four years later, in early 1916, he said that it was his having described a drift in a St. Leonards valley that induced Dawson to look to the gravel pits around Uckfield, the village where Dawson had his law office and contiguous with Piltdown. A month after Dawson's death, Abbott informed Woodward that he had told Dawson that, before anything was found there at all, "these gravels are so important and contain so many patches of the old Pliocene drifts that they deserve working inch by inch" (October 13, 1916, BMNH).

It is possible (I feel that many of my colleagues would say inescapable) that Abbott was lying, taking undue credit after the fact, that is, in December 1912 and October 1916, for Dawson's having looked around Uckfield in 1911. But saying that he lied imposes something extraneous. Nothing exists to contradict his version, and much exists in what he wrote before the finds that he anticipated Pliocene Man being discovered in the weald.

The first fossil fragment found was part of a human cranium. I don't know whether it had been planted (as Weiner and the first team of investigators maintained) or had been there originally (as Costello and Thieme and others of the post-Weiner team maintain). It seems plausible to take one's stand with those who identify the left parietal fragment as having been there originally (perhaps a relic of a victim of the Black Death, according to Costello, or of someone who had been decapitated, according to Burkitt). Then this story unrolls: Dawson brought that fragment, found sometime around 1908, to Abbott, who had to tell him what it was. (Abbott told that to Sir Richard Gregory in a letter dated November 30, 1930—maybe; the date reads 1936, but Abbott had been dead three years in 1936.)

W. D. Lang wrote in 1953 that Abbott had informed people visiting him either that

> he had found the Piltdown skull and gave it to Dawson, or he saw Dawson with it, and in either case persuaded Dawson that it was an interesting fossil and not to be thrown away, as Dawson was inclined to do. I do not think that on this alone one can form any valid opinion, except that Abbot [sic] claimed to have a finger in the pie at about the time that the skull was found. (December 14, 1953, BMNH)

If the skull fragments had always been in the pit, why did it take the diggers almost twenty-four months to retrieve all nine of them? It might have been the case that someone had planted the first piece and then sequentially over those twenty-four months of 1911 and 1912 put in the rest.

Another piece of the puzzle that's hard to fit in anywhere is a letter Abbott wrote to Woodward in the fall of 1912. Dawson had visited

Abbott to discuss the fragments and, in June 1912, to discuss the tools. Dawson wrote to Woodward about that visit, Abbott saying "They are man, and man all over!" The spring season's dig at the pit had launched the jawbone. As 1912 drew to a close, Abbott wrote to Woodward:

> I am sure you are inundated with enquiries for information about the skull which I hear you had on view; you will fully realize what special interest this is to me, since I have been workng these Sussex gravels, and trying to awaken an interest in them in others. Did Mr. Dawson show you the fragments of the one he has got. I have been trying to make him realize how wrong our old ideas of Wealden geology are, and the startling nature of some of these gravels! and I have no doubt that some of the flints he has brought me are really man's work, while the fragment of the skull was very remarkable, thicker than anything I have ever seen before. If you can possibly spare me a minute or two to tell me anything of your new addition, I shall be very much obliged to you. (November 24, 1912)

Abbott here asks Woodward for information about the skull, which he knew had come from the Piltdown pit. Then he tells Woodward that Dawson had shown him a fragment of a very thick skull. One reading of the letter is that Abbott did not know that the pieces Dawson brought him and those in Woodward's possession were the same. But surely Abbott would have inquired of Dawson as to the provenance of the cranial fragments and tools Dawson had brought him. How could Abbott not have realized the identity of the fossils Dawson brought him and those Woodward had? He could have been engaging in subterfuge, streaking a red herring across his trail, dissociating himself from the finds, but it would have been obvious to Woodward that the pieces Abbott had seen and those Abbott was inquiring about were the same.

Abbott also took credit for recommending that Dawson consult with Arthur Smith Woodward about the fossils. If we wanted to revel in paranoia, we could assume that Abbott chose Woodward as the consultant on hominid fossils because Woodward's specialty was fish fossils.

According to Abbott, he and Dawson gave the fossils a bath. F. H. Edmunds, in the letter quoted, said that he "had every reason to believe" that Abbott had soaked the skull fragments in bichromate. Any of the suspects could have picked up potassium bichromate at any chemist's. Abbott's letterhead listing offers a clue to expose how and where the staining of the fossils took place:

All the latest productions of the gem world
Old family jewels remounted and modernized
Every description of gem cut, re-cut and polished
Designs and estimates prepared
Sterling silver plate
Silver novelties for smokers
Trophies and badges and medals
Electro plate and re-plating
English keyless levers
Presentation clocks
Optical: All kinds of spectacles, eyeglasses and lenses
Repairs: By selected skilful men under my own personal supervision

I should like to focus on the eighth item: "Electro plate and re-plating." Before rhodium came to the jeweler's aid in the late 1920s, chromium compounds were used by jewelers for decorative plating, for polishing metals to a fine blue-white finish, and for testing the carat of gold and silver. The compound for that testing was potassium bichromate.

"A LIKELY SOURCE": THE JAWBONE FORGERY

I believe, with J. S. Weiner, that Abbott was probably the source for the jawbone. The forged teeth present us with a number of clues leading to Lewis Abbott.

Abbott anticipated that the prehistoric wealden hominid would have apelike features and, before the canine was found, that it would possess that tooth in apelike form. Sometime in the winter season of 1913, Abbott lectured to the East Sussex Art Club. He exhibited tables of geological formations on which were pictured skulls, bones, and flints found in those formations. In this survey, he emphasized the evolutionary principle that as we "descend the ladder of time" we find ancestors who are so different from us as to constitute a different species and that, as we go still further back, we come to ancestors who belong to a different genus, "one which, while it had a claim to the genus Homo, had nearly as great a claim to characters not found in man today, but only in the higher apes."

That as we go back in time, we find hominids with ape characters is the thesis of his "Pre-Historic Man: The Newly-Discovered Link in His Evolution," a short article published on February 1, 1913, in the *Hastings and St. Leonards Observer*. "The recent discoveries in Sussex have a special bearing" upon the evolutionary principle. The pit's geological formation is just what he had expected, and the fossil fauna just what he had expected, and the cranium and jawbone most exactly what he had expected in the combination of humanoid, chimpanzoid, and gorilloid features. The jawbone is, as it should be, more like that of a chimpanzee than of a human being. Unfortunately, the part of the jawbone that carries the canine was missing, but if there had been a canine, it would "in all probability" be "essentially chimpanzoid." Abbott concludes: "We have at last discovered the Pliocene ancestor of at least one branch of modern man."

How could Abbott have known about the jawbone in January 1913 when he wrote this article? He hadn't attended the Geological Society December meeting; he could not have read the Dawson-Woodward paper because that would not be published until March; he could not have had a cast because casts would not be distributed until April; he could not have seen the chimpanzoid canine because Teilhard would not find that until August. The jawbone could, however, have been in his collection before it ended up in the pit.

In the article, he mentioned "a chimpanzee jaw now before me," "a row of human jaws now before me," and "thousands" of jaws in his collection. The Wellcome Institute purchase included a skull of a macaque, with the note, "The only fossil monkey skull found in England—complete with lower jaw." Few paleontologists other than Abbott would have labeled any primate skull as coming from an animal indigenous to England. This is the skull that Dawson refers to in a letter to Woodward:

> I have come to the conclusion that our friend at St. Leonards is a dangerous person! He wrote to Keith the other day and told him some yarn about my having said something about the Ipswich skeleton which shocked poor K. considerably. I told Abbott his skull was a comparatively modern Barbary ape . . . but you will see from his letter enclosed that he has no idea of being taught. (March 10, 1913, BMNH)

Although contrary views continue on whether the cranial pieces had been there originally or put there, there's a clear consensus that the jawbone had been planted—it came out from the gravel already adulterated (unless some British Museum wag gave it a bath in bichromate and then in sulfate after Woodward had brought it to the museum). The jawbone, which had once hung out in a Dyak hut in Borneo, could have been an unregistered item from the Everett Collection (the BMNH had a hoard of collateral items not thought good enough for itemizing). But it did not have to come from there. Abbott had thousands of jaws; he would have been on the lookout for something like that on the fossil market. He knew that market well and was unusual among the suspects in knowing the monetary as well as the paleontological value of prehistoric commodities. He not only studied fossils; he sold them.

Abbott might have exhibited the very orangutan jaw before its brief interment in the pit. One of the items Abbott prepared for a 1909 Hastings Museum exhibition consisted of human jaws and teeth. His note for this read: "Some worn down by gritty food, some jaws show abnormal dentition. In one case the last molar is more than twice the size of the first—an essentially pre-human character." To J. S. Weiner, who quotes this, this "one case" refers to a child's milk dentition, Abbott unable to tell the difference between milk teeth and permanent teeth.

"Pre-human" could mean a hominid earlier than *Homo sapiens*—but Abbott could not have had any of those (he could well, however, have imagined he did). "Pre-human" in his lexicon would mean ape. If it were an ape's jaw, it wasn't that of a chimpanzee. Gerrit Miller noted that the Piltdown teeth were larger than those of a chimpanzee. The American Museum of Natural History's William King Gregory wrote in 1914 of the third alveolus of the eoanthropine jaw that it would have been a suitable receptacle for a very large molar. An orangutan jaw has such large molars. The jawbone displayed in Hastings, then, could have been the same as the one exhumed from the pit three years later.

I wonder if reasoning along these lines accounts for Weiner's spinning another of the tantalizing leads to Abbott. In a letter to W. N. Edwards, curator of geology at the BMNH during the time of the exposé, Weiner wrote that it would be "worthwhile" to visit Abbott's daughter, have a "look around" to see what had happened to Abbott's collections. "In a catalogue of 1909, Abbott has some amusing exhibits of different types of skull and teeth, which makes one think!" (December 3, 1953, BMNH). Weiner might have made the connection made here. That doesn't mean he thought Abbott was in on the hoax, just that Abbott (innocently) gave the jawbone to Dawson. Harrison Matthews thought that, while the skull was Dawson's (given to him by Mr. Burley), the jaw came from Abbott's collection of curios. (Matthews, May 14, 1981). I think the jawbone did come from Abbott's collection and that it was already imperfect, lacking condyle and symphysis.

Like almost all the other suspects (Teilhard is the exception), Abbott had a place in which to work the transformation of a common human cranium and an orangutan jaw into the earliest Englishman. Alone among the suspects, he used in his profession the tools and supplies effecting that transformation—pliers, tweezers, hammers, gravers, files, burrs, grinding tools, a handsaw and a delicate jeweler's saw, abrasives and acids, polishing compounds, rotten stone, rouge. A jeweler's saw could be used to cut wedding rings and semi-mineralized bones; abrasives to buff silver trays and to lower molar occlusal levels; nitric acid and aqua regia to smooth out roughly abraded surfaces; potassium bichromate to put a chrome finish on trophies or a patina on fossils. All the tools and supplies needed for the chemical and anatomical forgeries were right at hand, though they were not always used with consummate skill.

Knowing less about anatomy than Smith, Sollas, or Doyle, Abbott could have made such errors as filing the molar surfaces at too sharp an angle, scratching them, and misaligning their planes. The grossest error the hoaxer made in the whole enterprise of fabricating an ape-man was his choice of the canine tooth. Not of a canine tooth, but of the special one that Teilhard found. The hoaxer selected the wrong tooth—a young canine incommensurate with a mature jawbone. Then he proceeded to abrade it too much, puncturing a hole into the juvenile pulp cavity. A piece of metal alloy was found sticking to the canine tooth. Abbott was the only one who would use metal alloy in his work and could make a gratuitous mistake like that.

The next point is more tentative. He repaired clocks. Paints had to be available for the refinishing of dials, marking of numbers, renovation of woodwork. He could have used artist's paints. An oven would have come in handy for melting, joining, casting metal alloys, and baking paint onto tooth enamel.

A week after the Geological Society meeting, Abbott wrote a letter to Woodward. The letter begins with an attack on E. Ray Lankester's notion that the skull was similar to those of inhabitants of Sussex a mere 1,000 years ago and Lankester's equally appalling notion about how such diverse fossils could have come together: water had dissolved the ground, freeing bones and allowing them to move downstream where they assembled. That hypothesis would have dissolved Abbott's theory that the skull was hundreds of thousands of years old and that the fossils had been found together because the animals from which they came had lived and died together.

In the letter, he disclaims anatomical knowledge. And then he counsels that he "should not be so mad as to 'father' that big-chinned, beetle-browed, receding-foreheaded, Roman-footed athlete of the *Illustrated London News!*" (December 27, 1912, BMNH).

"ALL THE UNIQUE SPECIMENS":
THE MAMMALIAN FOSSILS FORGERY

Abbott had immediate access to fragments of the specific mammalian fossils found at Piltdown.

Abbott's museum at 8, Grand Parade, St. Leonards-on-Sea, included tens of thousands of gemstones, which he advertised at the end of his 1898 article on "The Pre-Historic Races of Hastings": sapphires, spinels, alexandrites, berylonites, turquoises, "imitative and artificial gems," and "proxy diamonds guaranteed to natural gems the closest yet produced." He also had a large supply of mammalian fossils, especially of Pleistocene vertebrates, "All the unique specimens discovered by Mr. Lewis Abbott." He sold lantern slides illustrating prehistoric anthropology. He sold fossils as well as gems, traded them, wrote about them, lectured on them, displayed them in museum exhibits.

If access to fossils is to be a high criterion of hoaxmanship, then Abbott comes out first on this as well as on other criteria. Some of the fossils were of animals native to England. The Cromer Forest Bed, which Abbott explored in 1897, contained these, the inventory from that year's *Natural Science:* cave-bear, rhinoceros, hippopotamus, elephant, and deer. Abbott retrieved fossils of rhinoceros, hippopotamus, elephant, and deer from St. James Park. And also, from that site, fossil pelecypods and a leaf-shaped flint implement.

After Abbott's death, some of his collection went to W. J. Sollas, most to museums. The Wellcome Institute had the monkey skull already mentioned; and, in addition to that, fossil fragments of a horse; mammoth molars; "two incomplete right third upper molars" of a rhinoceros; part of "unciform of distal carpal row" of a hippopotamus; and an Elephas tusk and its upper and lower limb bones. I think the claim is supportable that he had specimens of all the extinct species represented in the pit's assemblage, even of the elephant femur bone.

"MAN ALL OVER": THE FLINT IMPLEMENTS FORGERY (1)

If the flint tools were paleolithic, anyone could have bought the handful and salted the pit with them. Abbott comes out a little ahead of the other suspects in knowing so well what gravel bed to select and what index fossils and tools (flint and bone) from his large collection to plant.

The shop offered for sale "Plateauliths, Palaeoliths, Mezzoliths, Neoliths, Palaeolithic types." In the letter disclaiming anatomical knowledge,

Abbott does "with all modesty assert a claim" to knowledge about stratigraphy and flint industries. Others agreed with that self-appraisal. Dawson visited Abbott to check out the Piltdown flints, after which meeting Dawson wrote to Woodward that Abbott was in no doubt about their being artifacts. "They are man, and man all over!"

The Plateauliths, or eoliths, caused a good deal of trouble in Edwardian paleontology in general and between Abbott and Dawson specifically. Abbott insisted that the Piltdown pit had originated in Pliocene times. Assuming that the cranial fragments, jawbone, and mammalian fossils had been swept down into the pit with Pliocene gravel ensured the conclusion that the flint implements were more recent came in for an Abbott insult. Abbott asked Woodward to tell him who had dared to date them as Chellean or Pleistocene. He wrote to the *Morning Post,* "Of all the mystifying libels that have been circulated in connection with Piltdown man, and the one that is calculated to prevent his true age and nature being understood, it is the one which makes him of Chellean age" (January 1914). His whole plan would have been nipped in the bud if those he wanted to con had rejected the great antiquity of the remains. Lankester had rejected that antiquity. So had Dawson.

Dawson thought the deposit Pleistocene and its eolithic objects only rocks. A fight between Abbott and Dawson on eoliths was imminent. It broke out when Dawson conducted the experiment in which he showed that starch fragments could be made to look like tools simply by being shaken in a bag. The experiment shook Abbott so much that in 1914 he wrote Dawson abusive letters. The antagonism between Dawson and Abbott included Abbott's thinking Dawson too ignorant to tell the difference between a human cranial fragment and an eolith and Dawson's thinking Abbott too ignorant to tell the difference between an extinct monkey's skull and a modern one.

In 1915 another quarrel broke out between them, again on dating deposits, this time on whether certain strata had been laid down in the age of mammoths or in the age of Victoria. Dawson informed Woodward:

> Lewis Abbott has been lecturing at Hastings on new strata he had discovered—Pliocene. I went and had a look on my own but there is no doubt the so called *Pliocene* deposit is only a recent surface soil affair with modern beach stones such as you see on the cultivated areas all around the coast. The beach is put on the roads and farm yards and gets scraped up and put on the land as "road-scrapings". . . . We shall soon hear of prehistoric bombs discovered at Ipswich and laid at the feet of the East Anglian Scientific Society. (April 30, 1915, BMNH)

These road scrapings, Dawson explained in another letter, were put on the land for manure. No Pliocene river bed. Then Dawson expresses his anticipation that members of the Geological Association will be "rather furious to be brought down over such nonsense" (May 22, 1915). A dangerous person like Lewis Abbott would be even more furious at Dawson's pulverizing his Pliocene river bed into manure.

The flint implements found in the pit are generally assumed to have been from paleolithic cultures. In that case, Abbott had an abundance from which to choose. Just how many of what flint tools were found where does not shine through any stage of the Piltdown history. The original 1913 and 1914 papers to the Geological Society specify four flint implements, each of which received a BMNH number and analysis by Kenneth Oakley (Weiner, 1955). But Woodward's listing (*The Earliest Englishman,* 1948) doesn't correlate with either of those. The first problem is trying to figure out how many flint tools were in or near the pit—four, five, six, or none. Woodward lists a handax, a small pointed triangular tool, a squarish heavy tool, a flint borer, and a leaf-shaped flake of flint.

The handax found by Teilhard was shown by the Weiner team to possess the telltale chromium coat. Abbott analyzed the process of natural staining in his "Worked Flints from the Cromer Forest Bed" (1897), where he wrote of iron giving flints "a brown colour with various amethystine tinges," of what manganese does to color fossils, of amythystine tinges. In "On the Classification of the British Stone Age Industries" (1911), he expresses a gemologist's aesthetic pleasure in the "beautiful red-yellow-brown" of plateau flints and the "old brown" of iron-oxidized flints. He also develops a new and extremely, if not excessively, detailed taxonomy of flint types and explicates the physics of fracturing flints into implements.

Working out a credible connection between something found in the pit and something that had been in Abbott's collection would be a smoking gun in this inquest. (1) The jawbone. If the jawbone had come from Abbott's collection, that could indicate that he had a finger in the pie—but it could also indicate that Dawson got it from him and planted it. (Although the question would then be, Wouldn't Abbott have recognized it? To which the reply is, Abbott and Dawson collaborated. To which the reply is, Abbott so disliked Dawson, he wouldn't have collaborated on anything.) (2) The elephant femur slab. If that had come from the collection, it would be a clearer clue to Abbott's guilt. Chris Stringer, of the BMNH Palaeontology Department wrote to me that the color of the Piltdown slab "does not closely match" that of the elephant bones in the

Abbott collection of the BMNH. The slab "was probably produced from a chunk of fossil bone as found, i.e., of similar size to the pieces as now preserved, rather than cut from a larger bone." Stringer thinks that the finds at Site II are the major reason "to implicate Dawson as at least a co-conspirator" (October 28, 1985). (3) The leaf-shaped implement. Abbott found this at St. James Park. The Dawson-Woodward paper describes a "foliate implement." (4) The fossil pelecypod. Abbott found such a fossil in a flint at the St. James Park site. The Dawson-Woodward paper of 1914 illustrates a flint in which is embedded a fossil pelecypod; it is also illustrated (#7) in Woodward's *The Earliest Englishman*. Perhaps the flint in which *Inoceramus inconstans* resides is the one that Abbott found in the park.

"AN IMPLEMENT OF ANY PATTERN": THE FLINT FORGERY (2)

The hoaxer may have made the paleolithic implements from fresh flint or from neolithic implements. The only one among the suspects who could have done that is Lewis Abbott.

Abbott discussed flint industries in "Plateau Man in Kent" (1894); in "Worked Flints from the Cromer Forest Bed" (1897), which—a relevant point—discusses at length how natural oxidation stains fossils; and in "On the Classification of the British Stone Age Industries" (1911). In this he drew a new taxonomy of flint tool types—celoclastic, clinoclastic, and so on, for a total of fifteen. He wrote of artisans who copied models from the past, as children copy adult productions, and requested due respect to the French, Irish, English, and other flint artisans who demonstrated the dexterity required in the striking of a blow that would hit the flint in such a way as to split it perfectly. He also observed that he could easily detect whether a flint tool had been reworked. In an 1895 paper, in one three years later, and in other places, Abbott reported finding such flints and flakes, paleoliths boldly "reworked and polished by neolithic man and again subsequently rechipped."

Reid Moir and others who have tried it have informed us that it is difficult to make tools out of rock.

> To those who have never attempted to make a Chellean implement it may appear a most easy thing to produce; but having many times attempted this task I know that it requires an immense amount of practice and much thought and care in flaking.

The prehistoric artisans knew how to remove flakes, Abbott wrote, not with a rounded hammer-stone, but by battering "in a way which can be imitated today." Abbott has so far told us that Pliocene Man could rework older flints into newer models and that he could recognize a flint that had been so reworked. What we could use is a statement that he could do it himself.

In the Cromer Forest Bed article, he said that before one could talk about differences between natural forces and artificial manufacture, one should have years of actual and practical experience

> not so much in rummaging amongst second-hand collections, nor even in visiting pits and buying implements from workmen, but in making them oneself. When one understands so much of the working of flint as to be able to set out and make an implement of any pattern and style of work desired, and also is able to tell a modern forgery at sight, then one is qualified to say what man or nature can or cannot do.

He is, he confides seventeen years later in "On the Classification of the British Stone Age Industries," "one who has spent his days and years in practical flint-working." And again, in his January 1914 letter to the *Morning Post:* one must know the physics of flint fracture "so as to be able to say what form will result from a flint being struck in this, that, or the other way. . . ."

It was no secret that Abbott could make flint implements. *Natural Science* wrote of him as a modern imitator of the stoneworkers. Abbott counterfeited tools not only for his own amusement and edification, but for others as well. W. R. Butterfield wrote that in a pageant "the clubs and axes carried by the 'Ancient Britons' were made by Mr. Lewis Abbott, and all who saw them will agree, I think, that they were remarkable well made" (Butterfield, 1913).

The flint tools could have been immaculate paleoliths that had come from other English sites; or made from pieces of untouched flint; or, the last supposition open to us, made from neolithic tools. In *The Piltdown Forgery,* Weiner agreed with E. Ray Lankester that the flints were "unlike any known or defined industry"—in other words, not normal paleoliths, and he praised the forger's skill at this: "Making the tools pre-Chellean, and therefore much ruder and definitely early, was a good stroke. The flints, we now believe, were really rejects off a Neolithic block."

The hoaxer may, then, have made them look like precursors of neolithic industry and therefore appropriate to a hominid older than neolithic. That operation would have demanded some virtuosity. If Abbott were the hoaxer, he could not only have done what he theorized prehistoric man had done, reworking old flints to make them look modern; he could have modified neolithic material to make it look older. A phrase that applies to prehistoric and historic flint makers comes from another article: "As time went on, he progressed in the art of chipping them, copying and improving upon the prototypes supplied to him by nature" (Abbott, 1912).

"PILTDOWN MAN WAS MADE IN MY SHOP": CONFESSIONS

Abbott came closer to confessing his role as Piltdown hoaxer than did any of the other suspects. Negative, and feeble, evidence supporting this claim is that he most surprisingly avoided public identification with the Piltdown pit; positive, and stronger, evidence appears in his articles and letters.

Abbott's failure to visit the Piltdown pit may be taken as tantamount to a confession of involvement. Usually it is unwise to take the non-existence of an event as proof of culpability—such as in pointing to Teilhard's not talking much about Piltdown as affirmation that he must have been thinking about it all the time, alternately conscience-stricken and chuckling; or to Sollas's absence from the Royal Academy portrait in 1915 as a sign of his having been the hoaxer. But I think Abbott's absence from the pit requires a little discussion.

Flint artisan and her mate. Prehistoric tool-making hominids were depicted before Abbott wrote about them. This is a reproduction of a gilt picture on the cover of Jno. Allen Brown, *Palaeolithic Man in N. W. Middlesex*, 1887.

Consider his general interest in such digs and his particular interest in those concerning prehistoric hominid relics. He dug at Galley Hill, at Boyn Hill Terrace, and other terraces of the Thames, at Whitehall, King's Cross, St. James Park, and other London sites, at Clapton, Essex, at the Cromer Forest Bed, at Kent's Cavern and other sites in Kent, in Suffolk, in Sussex. Had he merely heard about the Piltdown discovery, he should have been there promptly, leading the pack.

His interest in Piltdown should have been much keener than at any other site. By his own admission—and in this context, it doesn't matter if he wanted to grab credit, the admissions indicate how important the Piltdown dig should have been for him: (1) he pointed Dawson to gravel pits, urging him to look around Uckfield; (2) he convinced Dawson that the fragments were not iron oxide concretions or eoliths, but parts of a human cranium; (3) he took part with Dawson in staining the fossils; and (4) he comforted Dawson by stamping the flints as implements. In the December 27, 1912, letter to Woodward, he wrote:

> There are over a dozen patches of gravel, within half as many miles of Piltdown that require working out. I hope now as the pressure of Xmas is over that I shall be able to give a little more time to them.

Instead, he visited the pit publicly only once or twice. He went there with Geological Association tourists. In the January 1914 letter to the *Morning Post*, he refers to having visited the pit when the regulars were there, which might mean a second time. Converting this negative into positive support of his guilt is easy, if not facile. Abbott stayed away, deliberately avoiding public identification with the site, because he had been there in private. Perhaps some better explanation is available for his not digging at or even visiting the site that so urgently invited a romp on his hobby horse.

A few days after Woodward's announcement of Site II, Abbott wrote to his friend Yates, "Oh, did you see that those other fragments of a second Piltdown skull were described last Wednesday by Smith Woodward at the Geological?" (February 25, 1917, BMNH). That's it for his recorded comments on Site II, within the three miles of exploratory terrain he mentioned in his letter to Woodward. I wonder if Abbott could have been the "friend" who accompanied Dawson to Site II.

In the letter to Woodward of late December 1912, Abbott protested that he had not fathered the big-chinned, etc., athlete of the *Illustrated London News*. Why did he raise such a possibility only to knock it down?

Nobody had accused him of paternity. He had been raising possibilities for a long time, and not only in private letters. Before you can talk authoritatively of eoliths, you have not only to be able to tell a modern forgery at sight, but make such a forgery, an "implement of any pattern and style of work desired."

A letter from Abbott to A. Rutot started Oakley thinking of Abbott as a guilty party. Here's the heart of that letter:

> We are still in the thick of the controversy over the Piltdown man. . . .
> Dawson behaved very badly to me over the whole affair, for as my
> principal assistant said when he saw no reference to me in the report, "It
> is very certain no Lewis Abbott, no Piltdown man." (January 7, 1914,
> BMNH)

The letters he wrote toward the end of his life are the most pathetic documents in the Piltdown history. The saddest of that sad lot is a letter to Sir Richard Gregory. Since Gregory had shown some kindness to him, Abbott told him of his financial position (miserable) and health (moribund). He reminded Gregory that he had made "the big discoveries" of Pleistocene vertebrate fossils in 1890, that he had almost lost his life several times while excavating the Ightham fissures, that while others had made fortunes in the jewelry business he had not, and that he would have to close down. He wanted to sell his collection to some "establishment or private gentleman" and be hired as its curator.

Part of his plea that he deserved help was his having contributed to Piltdown Man.

> It was at my earnest entreaty that Dawson took to him [Woodward]
> what I had pronounced to be a fragment of a protohuman's skull, which
> he picked up for an "eolith" and realizing it was not one was about to
> throw it away. It is not everyone that knows that Piltdown Man was
> discovered in my shop, but it was.

"THE CROWNING JEWELL": MOTIVE

This scenario is a tissue of argument susceptible to being poked full of holes: Dawson found a piece of a human skull that had lain in the pit for hundreds of years. His bringing Abbott the first piece started Abbott thinking about doing a hoax. Abbott induced Dawson to collaborate in soaking that and later cranial fragments in bichromate and sulfate solutions. Later Abbott, in two or three unheralded visits to the pit, planted

the mammalian pieces, the jawbone, the simulcra of paleolithic implements he had converted from neolithic, and the elephant femur slab. Most
of these items did not require planting—they were just dropped near
hedges or on spoil heaps. In January 1915 and later in July, he took
Dawson to Site II and allowed Dawson to take credit for discovering
Piltdown Man, Jr.

Why go to all that trouble? Part of the motive was proving to the
opponents that they were fools. He considered himself the world's authority on flint tools; how dare they, Reid Moir, Ray Lankester, Boyd
Dawkins, Abbé Breuil, William Cunnington, oppose him on eoliths being
tools or on the antiquity of his and others' finds. Always distrustful, that
establishment, about his finds of bones, flints, other things. Once he called
upon someone to witness his picking up a flint tool in situ and explained
in the article relating the occasion that he had to have a witness since
"opposition would be raised by a certain section of anthropologists to a
Forest Bed implement" (Abbott, "Worked Flints from the Forest Bed,"
1897). It would have been demeaning to anyone; to a person as ego-
maniacal, as assertive, as obsessed as Abbott, it must have been maddening to need a witness who would confirm that he had picked up what he
said he had. The witness, by the way, was his wife.

And then there was Dawson. Abbott and Dawson were inspired by
imperatives about the same turf. Dawson's having the cheek after the finds
to reduce eoliths to mere rocks and river beds to manure suggests, as do
the abusive letters, that he and Abbott had their differences. It would have
been a pleasure enlisting the good-natured Dawson as an unaware accomplice. Brooding for years on inadequate recognition, on the success of
the rival Wizard of Sussex (who had had a plant as well as other things
named after him; who had a thriving business; who got along well with
everyone), on the ignorant arrogance and tedious pace of the professionals, Abbott hatched the Piltdown coconut.

But I don't think revenge was the only motive, or even the central
one. Abbott had a history of giving a nudge to reality. No one had ever
found any pottery from the mesolithic period; Abbott knew there had to
be pottery from then; and so there was, until Curwen's examination. He
couldn't help himself from pulling fast ones, an amulet here, a piece of
ivory there, a photograph somewhere else. It's still not enough.

The central motive was to create Pliocene Man not so much for
revenge (although there's more on that coming up) but because it had to
be. He wrote on Pliocene Man throughout his career as an amateur
paleontologist (1892-1918), even in some respects—such as undertaking

dangerous tours and making tools the way they used to be made—reliving the life of Pliocene Man. He found mirror images in two childhood heroes who had gone through similar experiences, Benjamin Harrison and Boucher de Perthes.

In "Plateau Man in Kent" (1894), Abbott commiserated with a body of workers, "plodding along in various parts, gaining here and there a little," unsupported by state or science. Of these the most neglected was Benjamin Harrison, a tradesman of Ightham, an "indefatigable observer."

> His struggles and his perseverance; his fighting against want of encouragement and sleepless nights; his early risings and tramps to some spot four or five miles away, so as to be there at sunrise, and to hunt before opening his shop: all these are matters to be relished when the hero is no more.

Harrison received little encouragement in his lonely search for a tool-making Plateau Man. "For years he sought to make his finds known to the scientific world, but his converts were few." His poor plateau tools were derided.

Abbott reflects himself again through another surrogate, Boucher de Perthes, whose history brings us smack into the center of hoaxery. Boucher de Perthes had been involved in the Moulin Quignon hoax of 1863, not as the hoaxer, but as a gull who believed the finds authentic. Abbott aligned himself with Boucher de Perthes early. "As a lad," he wrote in "On the Classification of the British Stone Age Industries" (1911), "I had heard of the discoveries of Boucher de Perthes, and living in a flint country tried to make flint implements before I had ever seen one." De Perthes did good work for science; but that didn't ward off the vultures.

> The years were rolling by, and the great savant was nearly broken hearted at his fate; a powerful instrument, for good or evil in the State—shall we say what? had become possessed of the fact that a certain workman had chipped some of the stones that the unsuspecting enthusiast had accepted amongst others. It was enough; it was "proved" that Boucher de Perthes had been duped by a fraudulent workman. The Church through the confessional had triumphed! One of the retouched implements is now before me; it is an unquestionably well worked paleolith, but obviously had no point; this the workman attempted to put on, by removing a few more flakes. It is a thing that, not only in those early days, but even today, might easily deceive one.

Could he get away with it? He could make flint tools (and medieval weapons too) as well as any artisan of the past. He may have set up a challenge for himself, a craftsman testing the limits of his talent in fabricating a proxy hominid as he had fabricated proxy gems. I think he practiced what he had preached when he said he could make implements (I'd add fossils) of whatever pattern he wanted and that he could forge a thing that would easily deceive. The challenge was to get away with a hoax greater than that at Moulin Quignon, greater than any in the history of science before 1911—and, as it would turn out, after.

I think implicit in this presentation is the reason he didn't confess, but I'd like to make it explicit. Peter Costello wrote to me that, if Abbott were the Piltdown hoaxer, he would have sold his story "for a large sum to the more sensational newspapers." In his late years, his financial position tumbled from precarious to fatal. The Wellcome Institute for the History of Medicine kept letters Abbott wrote to them from 1929 to 1932, the year before his death. In that time, he attempted to get as much money as he could from selling his collections. He sold his fossils, his flints, his gems, crystals, some things used by Faraday, even Benjamin Harrison's watercolors and implements and a fossil pearl from the collection of Boucher de Perthes. His wife was a "helpless hopeless invalid." He suffered from several ailments, including blindness—he could no longer read (though he could still type).

There were few moments of fun. One such came about as a result of someone applying to him for a magical aid to winning at cards. "I did up a restorer of fortune—which was to defeat the gods or devils—in a box saying 'tell him if he sticks to this, and all it is supposed to stand for, he will never lose at bridge again.' It was a Jade Cross" (June 1930, WIHM).

Given the deplorable conditions, why didn't he sell his story to those newspapers? One reason he didn't was that he made more from selling his collections to museums than he could have from selling his story. For "the only COCO-NUT PEARL of the country," he asked 10 pounds. For his crystals, he also asked 10 pounds. That wasn't much money even then. But for his fossil and gem collections, he asked, and got from the Wellcome Institute, one thousand pounds. That was much money then, and would be today in its modern equivalent of $40,000. Had he sold the story, there's little chance anyone would have touched his valued collections.

I doubt that he would have considered revealing that Piltdown Man was a hoax even if selling the story had been the only option. We find in his late letters the same self-congratulatory tone as in the letters of his prime. "My esteemed colleague . . . , Sir Arthur Keith, often reminds me that I am a generation before my time"; "The anthropological collection is admitted by all who know it to be in almost every way the most complete of any known"; "The collection contains ALL the finest things ever got together from the Plateaux"; "There was a big international gathering a little while ago, & the biggest man in America wrote me & told me how enthusiastically hot the Abbe Breuil waxed over the splendid researchs & collection, & set them all longing to see it."

Before 1911, Abbott had indicated in his articles just what he intended to do and where; after 1911, he had indicated in his letters (to Woodward, Rutot, and Gregory) what he had done. I think he resisted confessing because he wanted something more than he wanted to prove his opponents dunces. In the worst circumstances, he had something more important than money to sustain him, a sense of indomitable pride in the continued acceptance of his proxy fossils, guaranteed to natural fossils the closet yet produced. The simple matter is that, if Lewis Abbott had created Piltdown Man, he would have been the last person to smash it.

On July 28, 1912, Abbott wrote to Woodward about the female Piltdown Man. A passage from that letter, reproduced with its spelling unviolated, serves as a proper romantic conclusion to the affair between the Hastings jeweler and his Galatea:

> I tell you it is not at all ease defending the young lady. To me it is the crowning jewell of my life's work, especially in the last 25 years! I am like a man in love. I cannot do without her!

CHAPTER FOURTEEN

PILTON MAN: GRAFTON ELLIOT SMITH

Erase Piltdown from their dossiers, and you erase also whatever little fame Abbott, Butterfield, Dawson, Hewitt, Hinton, Sollas and Woodhead have today. Erase the episode from the dossiers of Teilhard de Chardin and Conan Doyle, and their fame would be intact. Grafton Elliot Smith, like all of those mentioned (except Conan Doyle), made important contributions to scientific knowledge. Like Sollas and Teilhard de Chardin, he was also a theorist. His name is no better known than that of any of the other suspects, but some of his theories set the dimensions of our understanding of where we came from.

Smith enters the lineup because a few historians have selected him as the Piltdown hoaxer. It seems to me that the chance of Smith's being the Piltdown hoaxer is about the same as that of Butterfield's, that is, infinitesimal. He is of interest partly because he fell for the hoax and, of deeper injury to his reputation, because he obstinately continued advocacy of Piltdown Man in the period between the wars. His career as advocate well illustrates how addiction to theory can distort interpretation of evidence.

His biographers were also hooked on telling tales—about Smith's residence in Egypt, his study of primate evolution and human cultural diffusion, his relationship to a Torres Straits mummy and to an Australian aborigine skull, and his sense of humor. One humorous exchange, not enough to send anyone whooping it up in the aisles, is worth a quote. In the spring of 1914, Smith took time off from jousting with Arthur Keith about the eoanthropine reconstruction and journeyed to Sydney, arriving there on July 2. An interview with him on July 3 begins:

Professor Grafton Elliot Smith, M.A., M.D., F.R.S., Professor of Anatomy at the Manchester University, who has come out to Australia to take part in the British Association Congress, is at least fifty thousand years old. Some say he is a million years old, but he denies this—or, rather, he says there is no direct evidence that he is over fifty thousand.

With this present chapter, the inquest rises from the Piltdown pit to the nobler cosmos of human ascent and diffusion over the earth.

PROFESSIONAL ADVANCEMENT

In *The Piltdown Men* (1972), Ronald Millar remarks that Woodward and Teilhard de Chardin are beyond the "shadow of suspicion merely because of their respective standings in Science and the Church. Another, who I firmly believe was the hoaxer, is never mentioned at all." Some hundred pages later, the book mentions Smith. Why did he do it? As a native Australian in the backwater outpost of Cairo, Smith needed something impressive for advancement in his profession. But his career shows just the opposite and justifies the word J. S. Weiner used about Millar's accusation that Smith needed "advancement through malpractice": "ridiculous." This is what Millar says of Oakley's reaction to the news that Smith was the Piltdown hoaxer: "The naming of Smith did not bring any objection from him. He raised his eye-brows. Indeed, Oakley thought that I could be right." This is what Oakley said of this eyebrow-raising conversation: Millar correctly reported the admiration Oakley had for Teilhard de Chardin, but "completely misrepresents me as supporting his absurd view that Elliot Smith might have perpetrated the Piltdown hoax" (Private communication, December 13, 1980).

Darwin's *The Descent of Man* hit the stands in February 1871. Half a year later and halfway round the globe, in New South Wales, was born one Grafton Elliot Smith, whose destiny it would be to validate the Darwinian theory that human beings had developed from primate ancestors.

In 1888, the year that a Melanesian mummy from Torres Straits was installed in the University of Sydney's Macleay Museum, young Grafton Elliot Smith enrolled. Seven years later, he was awarded the degree of Doctor of Medicine, his thesis being "On the Anatomy and Histology of the Non-placental Mammals," and a scholarship to England. When he arrived there, in June 1896, at the ripe age of 25, he had already authored a dozen papers on the brain and nervous system. The following year saw eight more of his papers published. A research assistantship at St. John's College, Cambridge, introduced him to teaching. In June 1897, he delivered a paper on the fornix to the Anatomical Society of Dublin; the next month, he attended a British Association for the Advancement of Science meeting in Canada; in the summer, he visited Australia. The British Medical Association gave Smith a scholarship of 150 pounds renewable annually.

In 1898, he read and admired a book that had just come out, *Outlines of Vertebrate Palaeontology*, by the assistant keeper of geology of the British Museum, Arthur Smith Woodward. In 1899, Smith took up a project already seventy-five years old, to catalogue the collection of brains at the Royal College of Surgeons—the catalogue completed and published three years later. He quickly became acquainted with all the major British and Irish anatomists, and had achieved so high a reputation in 1899 that the Government School of Medicine in Cairo, Egypt, invited him to take the post of professor of anatomy.

In the nine years of his stay in Cairo, Smith published close to one-hundred papers. In 1907, the year the Royal Society elected him fellow, he published sixteen papers on dentition, the cortex, corpus callosum, asymmetry of brains, relationship of lemurs to apes; in 1908, twenty-two; 1909, twelve. That output was kept up throughout his life— for example, the years chosen at random, 1923, seventeen; 1926, twenty-two; 1932, fourteen.

His professional career experienced no leaps. It's a record of steady achievement and recognition right from the beginning, when he and the Torres Straits mummy were freshmen at the University of Sydney, through his professorship at University College London, a record that includes the fact that his students fanned out over the world, many of them becoming famous in their fields, such as Raymond Dart, the discoverer of Australopithecus.

CULTURAL DIFFUSION

As further evidence of Smith's culpability, Millar emphasized the way in which Piltdown Man satisfied Smith's theories on the evolution of culture and the evolution of primates. Smith began to work out the theory of cultural diffusion during his stay in Cairo. Millar speculated that the Piltdown skull could have come from Egyptian skeletons Smith anatomized.

Malcolm Bowden also focuses on Smith's having taught in Cairo and on Smith's having had access to the hippopotamus and elephant molars that appeared in the pit, Malta and Tunisia just down the street. Furthermore, in that very city lived, at the very same time, Teilhard de Chardin. Bowden plays up this guilt-by-neighborhood, imagining that since Teilhard and Smith were in Cairo at the same time they must have met; and, if they met, they must have conspired. Perhaps Teilhard gave that Tunisian radioactive tooth to Smith, who then did the dirty work of planting it years later. Bowden concedes that his identification is "far from adequate. Nevertheless, it would seem that, at the very least, Smith was well aware of the hoax being carried out at Piltdown, and indeed may well have been the instigator."

But there is no reason to believe that, while he was at Cairo, Smith had special access to anything that turned up in the pit, fossils or Jesuit, or that he was aware of the hoax being tuned up in Sussex.

During the nine years of his professorship at Cairo, from 1900 to 1909, Smith participated in an archaeological survey of Nubia. He brought to this assignment useful anatomical training, the task requiring examination of 20,000 skeletons. In addition to having a hoard of ancient Egyptian bodies to work on, he also worked on modern Egyptian medical students, organizing the medical school. In 1906, he wrote the first of many papers on mummification.

His tour in Egypt introduced him not only to ancient techniques of mummification, but to the spread of those techniques throughout the world. In his 1911 *The Ancient Egyptians,* he traced the diffusion of culture from Egypt, where civilization was born, to the coast of Spain, and then to Malta, Sardinia, Great Britain, and the South Pacific (see his "Conversion in Science" for a synopsis of his views). Not only mummification, but other cultural inventions, such as the building of megalithic monuments, spread over the world from the Egyptian source. Similarities among different cultures had come about not because of some innate human tendency to do certain things in certain ways but because all the cultures either carried the original germ from Egypt or got infected by Egyptian modes.

In his 1912 Dundee address to the BAAS, Smith said that land connections existent in Tertiary times allowed our ancestors to wander all over the earth. The eoanthropine fossils at Piltdown and Site II, he would later add, were traces of this migration. The finding of a prehistoric tool-maker in Sussex therefore illustrated his theory that early man had wandered to the ends of the earth, that is, bonny England. Millar, in his fictional rendition of this fiction, explains this:

> He argued that as the new waves of culture spread from "somewhere in the Middle East" the exponents of the new learning so to speak, drove the more primitive occupants further out. A near-animal Piltdown Man as far west as Britain would lend admirable support to his view.

The Torres Straits mummy also illustrated that theory. This classmate of his freshman days was let out for Smith's investigation on his 1914 visit to his homeland. It was as dried as a smoked herring. While examining it before an audience, he pointed out features of the technology of mummification, how the fingernails were attached with threads, a hole through the occipital for the removal of the brain, slits in the flank. The Melanesians had obviously imported ways of mummifying from the Egyptians.

One observer of this autopsy wrote:

> The whole examination was most dramatic: the immediate discovery on the Torres Straits mummy of custom after custom of the Egyptian mummifiers, as they were described to us by Elliot Smith, made a vivid impression on my mind, and the whole picture remains in my memory. (Langham, "Talgai and Piltdown," 1979)

It seemed a tour de force, Smith apparently never before having seen the mummy and yet being so exact in knowing its lineaments.

According to Ian Langham, it was all a deception. If Smith had not seen that mummy when both entered the University of Sydney, he surely had known of it in the literature. Why then the pose? He may have been showing off, playing to the audience. Or just joking around.

Millar gives us a motive in addition to that of professional advancement for Smith's having executed the Piltdown hoax: "Smith would have loved a chuckle at the expense of what he thought, possibly correctly, was stick-in-the-mud paleontology and anatomy. Somehow the whole affair reeks of Smith." Richard de Mille noted of Smith that he was "a brilliant man of science given to playing mordant jokes on his colleagues." To this line of reasoning, or unreasoning, Glyn Daniel replied, "Stuff and nonsense."

PRIMATE EVOLUTION

The Cairo position held attractions—a good salary, a good pension, a schedule of teaching from October to June, which allowed Smith to peregrinate over the planet in his vacation months, and opportunity to analyze thousands of Nubian skeletons. But he found the duties too arduous, working in the museum, teaching, administrating, participating in the Nubian survey, and when an offer came to him from England he accepted it readily, migrating to England from Egypt like some ancient caveman.

To Millar, Smith plotted the Piltdown hoax before he left Egypt.

With his wife (he slipped marriage in between his busy affairs), Smith went on holiday to Australia in 1902. In 1904, he attended a meeting of the International Commission of Neurologists in London; in 1906, a summer meeting of the Anatomical Society in Dublin; in 1907, the Society's Birmingham meeting. On these visits in 1907 and 1908, Millar assures us, Smith manufactured and planted the fraudulent fossils that he would then research and with which he could make his mark in professional science. "His tumultuous appearances in England coincide remarkably with the turn of events in Sussex." Weiner said that tying these events to the Piltdown history is "incredible." Millar vies with van Esbroeck for high honors in fiction.

In 1909, he took the Chair of Anatomy at Victoria University in Manchester. In these first years in England, he worked out a theory of primate evolution: that the cerebrum developed from an appendage of the olfactory bulb in the lamprey to a center of visual impression in the reptile. This process of change from olfaction to vision, critical to the growth of the higher centers of the brain, he discussed further in an address he gave to the Anthropology Section of the BAAS meeting at Dundee.

Although the paucity of evidence permitted all kinds of opinions on our pedigree, there was enough to sketch that pedigree tentatively over a period of a million years. One factor stood out for Smith as of unquestionable certainty: "The steady and uniform development of the brain," especially of the neopallium, a term Smith invented to label the prefrontal area in which impressions are not only received but recorded, the organ of associative memory (now called neocortex). He pictures the emergence from mammalian stock of the tree shrew, progenitor of prosimians, from which evolved the shrewder monkeys, then simian intermediaries leading down one conduit to the modern apes and down another to human beings.

While the primates retained the generalized features of earlier mammals in, for example, their hands, they underwent specialization of the brain. Cerebral specialization came about through the insectivorous shrews launching into the trees. Terrestrial animals rely upon the sodden sense of smell for guidance to food, mates, and territory, and for recognition of enemies; but the sense of smell is less useful up in the branches. The small proto-primate looked down upon its terrestrial relatives and gave up keenness of olfaction for keenness of other senses, auditory and tactile as well as visual. The arboreal animals also had to be more agile, so there was a survival value in selection for a more efficient motor cortex than that possessed by the land-lubbers. Smith selects the prefrontal neo-pallium as the structure responsible for these functions of seeing, hearing, touching, moving, and the associative network linking them.

So what else is new? The reason this summary reads like a cliché is that Smith successfully worked it out and into the way we understand our development from tree shrew to suburbanite. On the next part of his theory, however, he was wrong.

He thought that the brain crossed the line to humanness before erect posture and speech. He asked, in opposing those who claimed that erect posture preceded enlargement of the brain, Why didn't the gibbon, which can walk erect, become man? Gibbons walking erect could use their hands. But that did not happen because the gibbon brain had not under-gone prior development. The brain made "skilled movements of the hands possible." And then a feedback mechanism went into action, the liberation of the hands opening the way for further cerebral complexity.

Smith's sequence, then, has the brain developing, growing larger and more intricate in its circuitry, until a primitive neopallium was achieved, and from that came the more advanced brain of modern human beings. After enlargement and complexity of brain came humanness of post-cranial anatomy. Smith discussed Pithecanthropus in his address to the Dundee BAAS. He didn't linger on the circumstance that Pithecanthropus fails to exemplify his sequence: its post-cranial anatomy is more human-like than its cranium.

It was in the paper summarized above, the address at Dundee, as Smith would later boast and as Malcolm Bowden and Ronald Millar and Chapter 2 of this inquest remind us, that Grafton Elliot Smith predicted just such a being as Piltdown Man.

PILTDOWN MAN

The discovery of Piltdown Man satisfied Smith's theory, but upset hopes for a consistent sequence. The humanlike Java pithecanthropine femur and jaw should have been found in association with the humanlike Sussex skull; and the apelike Java skull with the apelike Sussex jaw. Yet Piltdown Man's brain, which Smith estimated at 1,070 cc, and prominent prefrontal or neopallium region, in tandem with an ape jaw fit Smith's theory to a tee—for trouble.

A month before the Dawson-Woodward announcement to the Geo-logical Society, Smith (on November 21, 1912) notified a colleague:

I do not know whether you have heard that a very early (pre-Heidelberg, said to be Pliocene) skull has been found in England and I want to be able to compare the brain cast with your La Quina cast next week.

How often Smith visited the pit no one knows, though it is known that on one occasion his student Davidson Black found a fragment of rhinoceros tooth. Smith lived in Manchester, 250 miles from Piltdown, and did make a couple of visits in 1917. A few secret visits would have been enough for planting, and of course he would have known all about chemical staining and index fossils. But he certainly lacked the high degree of incompetence required to do the anatomical forgery. He also lacked a credible motive.

Smith's contribution to the creature was not in finding fossils, but in analyzing cranium and brain. He did so in August 1913 and then constructed a brain-cast, producing a replica of Eoanthropus's big (but not too big) brain. The first of his twenty-year barrage of notes, articles, and books on Piltdown Man, entitled "Preliminary Report on the Cranial Cast," appeared in the 1913 *Quarterly Journal of the Geological Society*. Here Smith complimented the Piltdown brain as being the most primitive and simian ever recorded, a fit companion for that fetching ape jaw. While skeptical anthropologists stressed the humanness of the brain lurking in that cranium, and the apeness of the jaw bone, Smith chose to stress the apeness of the brain and the humanness of the jaw bone, repeatedly, over twenty years.

In actual number of pages, Arthur Keith wrote more on Piltdown Man than anyone else; Smith wrote more papers than anyone else, many of those during his debate with Keith over the proper reconstruction of the skull. Smith's theory would accommodate better a brain of about 1,000 cc than Keith's bigger-brained reconstruction. Smith upheld the Woodward-Barlow model, which pleased Dawson no end.

The cranial cast article was followed by a note in *Nature* (October 2, 1913), "The Piltdown Skull." Though his full report was in process, he wanted to discuss the skull right away because of "present widespread misunderstandings" about Dawson's great discovery. Dawn Man is a primitive and generalized type, with some features like those of an ape, others more like those of a human being's than are the features of the Neanderthalers. It would be proper to fit out Piltdown Man's jaw with a set of large canines (Teilhard had found the canine four weeks earlier). Just as a young child uses his teeth to snap at a disagreeable parent, so in the dawn of human existence, primitive people used their teeth for offensive purposes long before the brain had crossed the line. The next few weeks saw more articles in *Nature,* in *Man,* in other periodicals, lectures to the Literary and Philosophical Society of Manchester, to the Royal Society, and elsewhere. Smith used Pycraft as a weapon, as Sollas did, to attack that American barbarian, Gerrit Miller. In 1924, Piltdown appears in Smith's *Evolution of Man;* in the second edition, 1927, the space increased from the original four pages to fourteen. Smith was tenacious. Far from loosening his adherence to Piltdown Man, the newly dug up hominids, the pithecanthropines and australopithecines, tightened it.

THE TALGAI SKULL

The last stories of our inquest relate the way in which a skull found in Australia was taken as confirmation of fossils found in England; and the way in which historians have used this skull to incriminate Grafton Elliot Smith. In reality, the skull confirms neither Piltdown Man's authenticity nor Smith's criminality.

Eighteen eighty-six was a wet year in Australia. A farmhand, Australian counterpart of Venus Hargreaves and Alfred Thorpe, laboring in the region of Talgai, spotted a cranium peeping out at him in a gully washed by the rains. He copped it, and it eventually ended up in the hands of a New South Wales auctioneer, Earnest H. K. Crawford. The relic consisted of a thick-boned human skull and jaw with large teeth, the largest human teeth ever found in a fossil. Hoping he was on to a good thing, Crawford offered it for sale to the Australian Museum and to the British Museum of Natural History.

Now, from 1892 to 1901, the assistant keeper of geology at the British Museum, and from 1901 on the keeper, was one Arthur Smith Woodward. The Australian connection becomes complex: Woodward had collaborated on an article with Robert Etheridge, Jr. This article described fossil fish from Queensland, Australia. Crawford communicated with Etheridge on the sale of the Talgai skull. He also sent a photograph. The British Museum didn't reply. It's Crawford to Etheridge to Woodward so far, and from Woodward to the Piltdown pit is a fast snap. Woodward blocked Etheridge from replying because (according to this fantasy), it was too early to have the Talgai skull confirm Piltdown Man since Piltdown Man was only a conception, not yet born.

Meanwhile, something equally suspicious was going on with Smith. In the summer of 1897, Smith visited Australia. He must have been aware

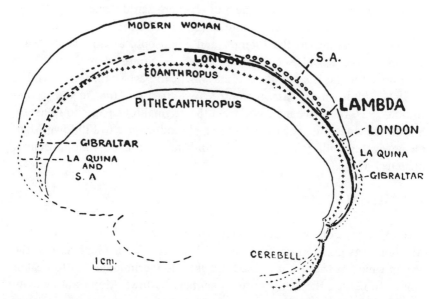

The Lady of Lloyds. Outline of Lady of Lloyds's skull in relation to five others. Modern woman, S. A. = Australian, La Quina, Gibraltar and Eoanthropus. Iambda, = site where sutures meet.) (From Smith [1925].)

of the Talgai skull. Yet he did not mention it in his letters back home. Of two surviving letters from September 1896 to February 1897, one "has had its concluding section torn away" (Langham, "Talgai and Piltdown," 1979). Perhaps that concluding section had harbored a discussion of the skull, and it was later ripped off as part of Talgaigate. In 1902, Smith undertook what Ian Langham terms a "hush-hush" visit to Australia. Maybe he returned there for a covert investigation of the skull, which he planned to use as a prototype for the coming hoax in Sussex—its thick bones and apelike dentition would be a suitable model.

I've already detailed the carelessness of the hoaxer in so filing the molars that their surfaces fail to align. But maybe he wasn't careless at all—Australian aborigine molars naturally exhibit the same misalignment of surfaces. The Piltdown cranium may have been that of an Australian aborigine—the Talgai skull is; and the Piltdown molars may have been modeled on the Talgai choppers.

By the time of Smith's 1914 visit to Australia, Piltdown Man had been discovered. This was the visit when Smith impressed everyone by his autopsy of the Torres Straits mummy. Smith gave an account of the

Australopithecus

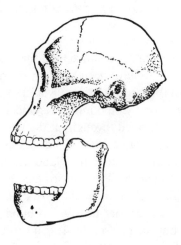

Homo erectus

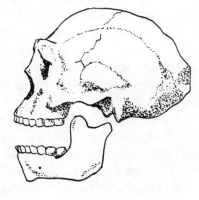

Eoanthropus

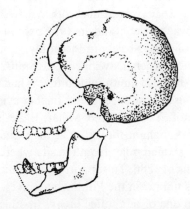

New finds and Eoanthropus. Eoanthropus became increasingly anomalous as the new australopithecine finds (such as *A. africanus*) and pithecanthropines (*Homo erectus*) were slotted into the human family. These new finds possessed a jaw more humanlike than the eoanthropicine under a skull less humanlike.

Piltdown finds and of his (incorrect) conclusion that the pithecanthropine jaw was even more primitive than the eoanthropine. He imagined the Piltdowner's life to have been like that of the Tasmanians, more recently extinct; reestablished his priority via the Dundee address in predicting what a Piltdown Man would look like; and summarized how and where Egyptian customs spread throughout the world, all this enveloped in his theory that the brain came first. It was time to bring the Talgai skull, which Woodward and Smith had collaboratively shelved, out of the closet.

The Talgai skull demonstrated its value upon presentation to the Anthropology Section of the BAAS meeting in Sydney on August 21. Langham tells us that nearly two hundred papers were delivered at that meeting, but the one on the Talgai skull stole the show. Piltdown was on everyone's mind. Smith, in a lecture at the Sydney Town Hall, drew the obvious moral: "The finding of the Talgai skull, with its great dog teeth" put to rest any doubts lingering about Piltdown Man. Through his brother, S. A. Smith, also an anatomist, G.E. put a value of 150 pounds on the skull and induced an affluent Australian to buy it for the Macleay Museum, where it could keep the Torres Straits mummy company. S.A. ranked the skull in importance with Piltdown. The brothers Smith enjoyed a family rapport in using both skulls as evidence that the brain led the way. Back in England, Dawson innocently observed that the pattern of Talgai tooth wear might support that of Piltdown dentition.

The Piltdown genus had sent envoys to two widely separated parts of the earth, Talgai and Sussex. Grafton Elliot Smith gave an illustrated lecture on it in February 1915, to the Manchester Literary and Philosophical Society; read his brother S.A.'s descriptive paper the next year to the Royal Society; and in 1917 exhibited the skull from down under to the Geological Society in Piccadilly.

Once, when Dawson asked Smith just where the Talgai skull had been exhumed, Smith replied that it had come from a village called Pilton. Millar used that anecdote as further evidence that Smith had a rich sense of humor. You see, said Millar, there isn't any place in Australia called Pilton. Langham looked at a map and found the Australian village of Pilton, sixteen miles from the site where the skull had been uncovered by the rains of 1886. To support an incrimination with a homonym, as Millar does, is unique in the Piltdown archives.

On one of our coffee breaks in June 1984, I asked Ian Langham if he still thought Smith the hoaxer; he laughed and said no, he had chosen someone else. He wouldn't tell me who. I have given his views from his 1979 paper not to make fun of him, but because I think it's a pleasant story with details about Smith's life and work that can be found nowhere else. Our conversation took place two months before his death in an accident in Sydney.

Smith's was a total system, an integration of physical and cultural evolution. His fondness for Piltdown Man detracts from his good work in tracing out the evolution of mentality from invertebrates through monkeys to, the concluding subject of this inquest, philosophers.

PART THREE

THE VERDICT

CHAPTER FIFTEEN

PILTDOWN MAN ON TRIAL

An inquest into Piltdown Man doesn't seem to offer much cheer to those of us who think that science is a legitimate enterprise that has drawn a credible chart of human evolution. Anyone conversant with the Piltdown history will readily, if not eagerly, agree that many of the researchers shaped reality to their heart's desire, protecting their theories, their careers, their reputations, all of which they lugged into the pit with them. As for the historians' search for the hoaxer, all the suspects were long dead before the assessments of their culpability began. Setting aside the Roman courtesy *de mortuis nil nisi bonum* hasn't harmed any of them. Their relatives, friends, and admirers may have been embarrassed into shame or stroked into resentment, but that seems a small price to pay for all the fun. Less fun is the more important part: what the Piltdown case signifies.

THE ATTACK ON PILTDOWN MAN

It is hard to know which particular mistakes we should pluck out of the cornucopia of error as examples of what went wrong. Dawson had a personal investment in enhancing his wizardry and, among other follies, invented ravenous bacteria to scavenge out out a pulp cavity; Woodward stitched a human condyle onto an ape's jaw; Keith and Smith tumbled into a macho confrontation over who was the better reconstructionist of crania; Abbott fell in love.

The fundamentalists generalize from Piltdown Man to the entire study of human evolution. McCann wrote in 1922: "The Piltdown remains disclose the ease with which 'missing links' between apes and men can be fabricated by resort to wide stretches of the imagination in support of pre-conceived theories." In 1967, the Watchtower's *Did Man Get Here by*

HEIDELBERG MAN
Built from a jaw bone that was conceded by many to be quite human.

NEBRASKA MAN
Scientifically built up from one tooth and later found to be the tooth of an extinct pig.

PILTDOWN MAN
The jawbone turned out to belong to a modern ape.

PEKING MAN
500,000 years old. All evidence has disappeared.

NEANDERTHAL MAN
At the Int'l. Congress of Zoology (1958) Dr. A. J. E. Cave said his examination showed that the famous Neanderthal skeleton found in France over 50 years ago is that of an old man who suffered from arthritis.

NEW GUINEA MAN
Dates away back to 1970 - - - This species has been found in the region just north of Australia.

CRO-MAGNON MAN
One of the earliest and best established fossils is at least equal in physique and brain capacity to modern man . . . so what's the difference?

MODERN MAN
This genius thinks we came from a monkey.

Professing themselves to be wise they became fools.
Romans 1:22

Big Daddies. (From *Big Daddy,* Chick Publications, 1972.)

Evolution or Creation? shoved Piltdown Man forward as Exhibit A of the way evolutionists manufacture facts. In 1979, Duane Gish, of the Institute for Creation Research, likewise wrote of Piltdown Man: "The success of this monumental hoax served to demonstrate that scientists, just like everyone else, are very prone to find what they are looking for." You can hardly blame the fundamentalist philosophers for occasionally whipping Piltdown Man, the bad boy of evolutionary theory.

The historians Broad and Wade support the view that scientists not only make mistakes but deliberately commit fraud, and not just now and then. Their *Betrayers of the Truth* (1982) divined that scandalous fudging is epidemic in science. They investigated thirty-four betrayals since the

Renaissance, such as Newton's tailoring data to suit his theories on optics, Mendel's making up statistics to prove particulate inheritance, and Piltdown Man. Thirty-four cases doesn't sound like a warehouse, but the authors calculated that, behind every one that becomes public, 100,000 others, major and minor, "lie concealed in the marshy waters of the scientific literature." That means that the waters of the marsh are clogged with 3,400,000 scientific frauds, 100,000 of which are of the Piltdown tribe.

Philosophers whose premise has it that science is irrational also give aid and comfort to fundamentalists. Karl Popper (1934) rejected science as a system that can attain truth or even probability. Science, argued Thomas Kuhn (1962), is dominated by theory. A given theory, or paradigm, acts like a magnet, orienting data into the direction it wants. The paradigm is discarded not because it is found to be untrue but because it grows too cumbersome, or tiresome, or homely. Science is not incremental; it doesn't bring us any closer to any "true account of nature." Paul Feyerabend (1975) went beyond Kuhn as Kuhn went beyond Popper, as though in a contest to see who could be most corrosive. "Science knows no 'bare facts' at all," he declared. Scientists are dogmatic, and their method is "putrid."

Once in a while, the ideas of philosophical irrationalists drift down to flavor the rhetoric of philosophical fundamentalists. Henry Morris, director of the Institute for Creation Research and an incorrigible exponent of creationism, wrote, "The proper term is not 'scientific theory' or even scientific hypothesis,' but 'scientific model' or 'paradigm' or some such title" (Morris, 1981). The paradigm that our ancestors had a large brain and an ape's snout directed Edwardian researchers to find specimens with a large brain and an ape's snout. Today's paleontological paradigm directs researchers to find fossil anthropoids with a small brain and a human jaw. And they're found.

Dr. Gary E. Parker, also of the ICR, focused on Piltdown Man as an example of how fleeting evolutionary paradigms are:

> At least Piltdown Man answers one often-asked question: "Can virtually all scientists be wrong about such an important matter as human origins?" The answer, most emphatically is, "Yes, and it wouldn't be the first time." Over 500 doctoral dissertations were done on Piltdown, yet all this intense scrutiny failed to expose the fake. Students may rightly wonder what today's "facts of evolution" will turn out to be in another 40 years. (Parker, 1981)

The anti-evolutionist Francis Vere wondered whether, forty years from now, opinion will reverse itself and Piltdown Man will once again be high on the tree. The evolutionist Earnest Hooton also wondered if that could happen.

The resolution of the question whether science does map the truth of reality or whether it is just another myth has consequences for us in our daily lives. In the 1920s, fundamentalists wanted to outlaw the teaching of evolution in public schools; today, they want to give creationism equal time with evolution, which change in attitude itself testifies to a sort of evolution toward tolerance or smarter strategy. They appeal to the Bill of Rights guarantee of religious freedom and to a sense of fair play.

For their two-model program, they can find support in Popper: science isn't objective; in Kuhn: science isn't incremental; and especially in Feyerabend, who warned that the scientists want to take over and not give a chance to those who hold other ideas (such as the ideas that people can levitate and change into wolves). Though an epistemological anarchist whose heart belongs to Dada, Feyerabend nevertheless pled for state intervention. "We must stop the scientists from taking over education and from teaching as 'fact' and as 'the one true method' whatever the myth of the day happens to be." In that, he touches on a political program which, though frivolous in prose (the Dadaist is "utterly unimpressed by any serious attitude"), is potentially dangerous.

For close to forty years, *Eoanthropus dawsoni,* a.k.a. Piltdown Man, was taught as fact. His australopithecine and pithecanthropine relatives are still taught as fact. If they are really as mythical as he was, then it seems the just thing to do would be to give equal time to competing facts or myths. If science is nothing more than myth, then biblical stories are agreeable alternatives and render, serendipitously, more wholesome ethics.

The exposé incited criticism of evolutionary science. Earnest Hooton feared that its revelation of "calculated dishonesty" would have unpleasant consequences for biological science, heating up latent hostility to the theory of human evolution. "Already the press is flooded with accusations by anti-evolutionists that all the other evidence of man's origin from an ape-like ancestor has been deliberately faked by unscrupulous scientists" (Hooton, 1954). He pushed the Piltdown case aside as unique; but the creationists pulled it back as typical of what evolutionists always do, deceiving themselves and others, by turning apes into people.

A DEFENSE OF PILTDOWN MAN

But, quite to the contrary, the Piltdown inquest can be seen as validating science in general and evolutionary science in particular. First of all, to go on the attack, it is possible that those advising us to beware of fudge are themselves in the concoction business. I don't know where Broad and Wade got the multiple of 100,000 submerged hoaxes for every known one, perhaps from the same well Parker dipped into for his 500 doctoral dissertations. Broad and Wade's accepting Harrison Matthews's conspiracy fiction does not advance one's confidence in the good sense of those savants of fraud.

Gertrude Himmelfarb, in *The Darwinian Revolution* (1959), wrote that Piltdown Man was a disaster for evolutionary theory because so many scientists either welcomed it or rationalized it into harmony with their prejudices.

> However earnestly scientists may now dissociate themselves and their theory from Piltdown man, they cannot entirely wipe out the memory of forty years of labour expended on a deliberate and not particularly subtle fraud.

Now that he has been kicked out of the family, evolutionary theory is left without "the much desired link, and even without such antiquity as Piltdown offered." Actually, the present inventory of links (or twigs) stores thousands of prehistoric hominid specimens, from frontal bones down to footprints. Her conviction that whatever is there lacks antiquity is incorrect: australopithecines lived long before Lewis Abbott's Pliocene Man.

Suffering from an insatiable hunger for myth, fundamentalists concoct stories in comparison to which Piltdown Man emerges as solid reality. An apeman who trod the weald is a being more believable, really more imaginable, than, say, a spare rib that became a woman, a prophet who inhabited a whale, a virgin impregnated by a ghost. The hundreds of biblical stories fundamentalists serve up as literal truth are no less childish because they are familiar. These stories have generated a literature far vaster than the Piltdown bibliography; and an influence often unhealthy in the history of militant Christendom. Fundamentalists sift Mount Ararat for splinters of Noah's ark, they penetrate deepest Africa in the hope of sighting the brontosaurian Mokele Mbembe grazing by the shores of Lake Tele, and they smile and smile as they cordially invite others to join them in a giddy flight from rationality.

Secondly, much of what went on before the exposé, and all of what went on in and after it, reminds us of the legitimacy of the scientific method even when applied to the study of the past. The investigators of the pit were biased. Edwardian culture did in fact anticipate the likes of Piltdown Man and, within the narrower confines of the scientific community, many defenders did seize the opportunity to hammer the fossils into malleable fit with their theories. But the figure of the scientist emerging on the scene with no view at all, commencing to gather facts and press them into theory, is a parody of the scientific method. Charles Darwin penned his opinion about this important issue of curving evidence to the template of theory. The passage providentially foreshadows Piltdown:

> About thirty years ago there was much talk that geologists ought only to observe and not theorise; and I well remember some one saying that at this rate a man might as well go into a gravel-pit and count the pebbles and describe the colours. How odd it is that anyone should not see that all observation must be for or against some view if it is to be of any service! (Darwin to Henry Fawcett, September 18, 1861)

Sherwood Washburn wrote:

> No matter how many fossils are found, what we see in them will depend on our theories and our experience. The purpose of experiment is to enrich that experience so that we may see more clearly. (Washburn, 1954)

Le Gros Clark perceptively advised that the facts known at that time achieved an integrity: "All the lines of collateral evidence appeared to be mutually confirmatory"—the geological proof that the terrace was Pleistocene, the index fossils, the fact that simian and human characteristics had been found conjoined in other hominids.

Evidence convinced. Conviction and even conversion were based at least as much upon that awful four-letter word "fact" as upon cultural bias, paradigms, deep inner longings, and rhetoric. Keith initially could not accept a human mandibular fossa hinging with an ape's condyle; but then the canine was found; it was real; and he capitulated. Osborn was pummeled into agreement by the reinforcements brought from Site II. But many were convinced by their study that Piltdown Man was unreal.

We do come across an absolutist like Pycraft here and there in the history. Pycraft translated script into scripture with this:

> The remains thus far uncovered leave no possible doubt that they represent not merely a fossil man, but a man who must be regarded as

affording a link with our remote ancestors, the apes, and hence their surpassing interest. (Pycraft, 1912)

Equally—or more—representative of attitude is what William Wright editorialized in his review of Keith's *The Antiquity of Man*. The most important aspect of that book was

> the forcible and persistent plea which the author makes for the consideration of evidence on its merits, with a mind untrammeled by tradition and unclouded by pre-conceived ideas. It is a plea well worth making, for a narrow dogmatism is not in these latter days the peculiar prerogative of the theologians.

After the exposé, Hooton managed to say, while eating crow, that the great lesson of the Piltdown case is this: It's wrong to fix on scientific discoveries as irrevocable. Certitude is out of place in the empirical statement.

First, then, anti-Piltdown brigades mount attacks from bunkers constructed of thin glass. Second, the total Piltdown history, from initial exploration of the pit through the exposé, legitimizes the study of evolution as a science. A third point is the way the Piltdown case suggests that fraud is not epidemic in science. Frauds, Lewis Thomas wrote, can, if you like,

> be made to seem all of a piece, a constantly spreading blot on the record of science. Or, if you prefer (and I do prefer), they can be viewed as anomalies, the work of researchers with unhinged minds, or, in the cases of Newton and Mendel, gross exaggerations of the fallibility even of superb scientists. (Thomas, 1983)

Thomas quotes the physicist John Ziman, who asserted, "Deliberate, conscious fraud is extremely rare in the world of academic science. The only well-known case is Piltdown Man." Culling the history of the study of human evolution will produce many mistakes like Nebraska Man. The only other hoax of even minimal consequence is that of Moulin Quignon.

A last point. Himmelfarb concluded that forty years of labor had been wasted time. The *London Times* drew a different conclusion:

> That the deception—whoever carried it out—has, though cunning and long successful, at last been revealed is a triumph to the persistence and skill of modern palaeontological research. ("Piltdown Man Forgery," 1953)

Others have been similarly enheartened by the case. Earnest Hooton was proud of the detectives, who did "honor to science by their fearlessness and their candor; they reflect credit upon anthropology by their skill and thoroughness." H. V. Vallois, a paleontologist who had been skeptical about Eoanthropus, was glad that the hoax had stimulated the development of new techniques.

The two surviving members of the Piltdown episode also affirmed the usefulness of the exposé. We have already seen what Teilhard thought about it—investigation of the find led to refinement of technology. The tests will continue to be important in dating and establishing unity or disunity of fossil assemblages. Keith, upon being told of the exposé, responded that his labor had not been wasted nor had the story of human evolution been damaged. The discarding of Piltdown Man made that story simpler (*London Times*, January 9, 1955).

The tenacity of Piltdown Man for forty years shows—no surprise here—that the science of human evolution was imperfect. Yet no scientist in 1913 would have mistaken a labyrinthrodont skeleton for that of a drowned lecher and none in 1953 would have been conned by a new Piltdown Man. The science of human evolution is still imperfect, but getting better all the time, which is more than we can say about a lot of things. The entire case is something to cheer us up after all, after all the swiping today at evolution, at science, at rationality.

A PERSONAL NOTE

The excavating I did at the gravesite of the Piltdown pit recovered an eolith, which now squats on a shelf next to a cast of the Piltdown skull. Although I have never sifted through gravel to exhume fossils, I have sifted through archives to exhume footnotes and have felt an excitement like that the diggers felt as they came upon one treasure after another. I have enjoyed putting textual relics together to recreate the history of Piltdown Man and to identify a hoaxer rather than a hominid, though the reconstruction may be a creature as fanciful as that unlamented monster, *Eoanthropus dawsoni.*

What impresses me most is not the mistakes everybody made all over the place about fossils and culprits, but the way these people we have met, the defenders of Piltdown Man and the opponents, were dedicated to an intellectual idea: charting the course of human evolution. In defining where we came from, they illuminated where we are now.

BIBLIOGRAPHY

Abbott, W. J. Lewis. Letters. Archives, British Museum (Natural History) Palaeontology Library.

———. Letters, Archives, Wellcome Institute for the History of Medicine.

———. *Gemmographical Tables for the Use of Diamond and Gem Merchants.* London: Heywood & Co., n.d.

———. "The Section Exposed in the Foundations of the New Admiralty Offices." *Proceedings of the Geologists' Association,* 12 (November 1892): 346-356.

———. "On the Occurrence of Walrus in the Thames Valley." *Proceedings of the Geologists' Association,* 12 (November 1892): 357.

———. "A New Reading of the Highgate Archway Section." *Proceedings of the Geologists' Association,* 13 (August 1893): 84-90.

———. "Excursion to Basted and Ightham." *Proceedings of the Geologists' Association,* 13 (October 1893): 157-163.

———. "Plateau Man in Kent." *Natural Science,* 4 (April 1894): 257-266.

———. "The New Oban Cave." *Natural Science,* 6 (May 1895): 330-331.

———. "The Hastings Kitchen Middens." *Journal of the Anthropological Institute,* 25 (1895): 122-145. Includes "Notes on a Remarkable Barrow at Sevenoaks" and "Notes on Some Specialised and Diminutive Forms of Flint Implements from Hastings Kitchen Midden and Sevenoaks."

———. "Worked Flints from the Cromer Forest Bed." *Natural Science,* 10 (February 1897): 89-96.

———. "Primeval Refuse Heaps at Hastings." Part 1, *Natural Science,* 11 (July 1897): 40-44; Part 2 (August 1897): 94-99.

———. "Authenticity of Plateau Implements." *Natural Science,* 8 (1898): 111-116.

———. "The Pre-Historic Races of Hastings." Privately distributed by Abbott. Reprinted from *Saint Paul's Magazine* (1898).

———. "On the Classification of the British Stone Age Industries, and Some New and Little Known, Well-Marked Horizons and Cultures." *Journal of the Royal Anthropological Institute,* 41 (1911): 458-481.

———. *The Geology and Prehistoric Races of the Hastings District.* Oxford, 1912.

———. "Pre-Historic Man: The Newly-Discovered Link in His Evolution." *Hastings and St. Leonards Observer,* February 1, 1913.

————. Letter to the Editor of the *Morning Post,* January 1914.

————. Letter to A. Rutot, July 1, 1914. Archives, Institut Royal des Sciences Naturelles de Belgique.

————. "The Discovery of British Palaeoglyphs." *The Sphere,* January 31, 1914.

————. "Implements from Cromer Forest Bed and the Admiralty Section." *Proceedings of the Prehistoric Society of East Anglia,* 3, Part I (1918-1919): 111-114.

————. Abbott Collection: Report on Some Quaternary Mammalian Remains in the Wellcome Institute Museum. London, 1974.

Abbott, W. J. Lewis, and R. Ashington Bullen. "The Authenticity of Plateau Implements." *Natural Science,* 12 (February 1898): 106-116."

Anthony, R. "Les restes humains fossiles de Piltdown (Sussex). *Revue Anthropologique,* 23 (September 1913): 293-306.

"The Antiquity and Evolution of Man." *Nature,* 92 (October 9, 1913): 160-162.

"The Antiquity of Man in Britain." *Natural Science,* 10 (January 1897): 12-13.

"Arthur Conan Doyle Is Piltdown Suspect." *New York Times,* August 2, 1983, Cl, C6.

Bergounioux, F. M., and André Glory. *Les Premiers Hommes.* Paris: Toulouse Didier, 1943.

Bergounioux, R. P. *La Préhistoire et ses Problèmes.* Paris: Librairie Arthème Fayard, 1958.

Berry, Thomas. "The Piltdown Affair." *Teilhard Newsletter,* 13 (July 1980): 12.

Big Daddy? Chino, Calif.: Chick Publications, 1972.

Blinderman, Charles. "The Curious Case of Nebraska Man." *Science 85,* 6 (June 1985): 46-49.

————. "The Great Bone Case." *Perspectives in Biology and Medicine* (Spring 1971): 370-393.

————. "Research in the Pits." *Clark Now* (Clark University), 13 (Summer 1983): 38-41.

————. "Unnatural Selection: Creationism and Evolutionism." *Journal of Church and State,* 24 (Winter 1982): 73-86.

————. "The Piltdown Problem Solved." *Journal of Irreproducible Results,* 31 (February/March 1986): 2-6.

Bobys, Richard S. "Research Frauds, Factors and Effects." *Free Inquiry in Creative Sociology,* 11 (May 1983): 44-48.

Boule, Marcellin. "La Paleontologie Humaine en Angleterre." *L'Anthropologie,* 26 (1915): 1-67.

————. "The Fossil Man of La Chapelle-aux-Saints (Correze)." In Leakey, L. S. B., et al., *Adam or Ape.* Cambridge, Mass.: Schenkman, 1971.

Bowden, Malcolm. *Ape-Men—Fact or Fallacy?* Bromley, Kent: Sovereign Publications, 1978. Second edition, 1981.

————. *The Rise of the Evolution Fraud.* San Diego: Creation-Life Publishers, 1982.

Boylan, Patrick J. "The Controversy of the Moulin-Quignon Jaw." In Jordanova, L. J., and Roy S. Porter, eds., *Images of the Earth.* London: British Society for the History of Science, 1979.

Brace, C. L., and M. F. Ashley Montagu. *Man's Evolution.* New York: Macmillan, 1965.

Breuil, Abbé. "Silex Talles de Piltdown (Sussex)." *Bulletin de la Societé Préhistorique Française*, 46 (1949): 344-348.

British Broadcasting Corporation. Program on Piltdown Man: "Buried Treasure" series, May 30, 1955; interview on Piltdown, "Newsnight" series, November 22, 1985.

Broad, William, and Nicholas Wade. *Betrayers of the Truth*. New York: Simon and Schuster, 1982.

Broom, Robert. "Summary of a Note on the Piltdown Skulls." *Advancement of Science*, 6 (1950): 344.

Brown, Jno. Allen. *Palaeolithic Man in N.W. Middlesex*. London: Macmillan, 1887.

Burkitt, M. C. *Prehistory: A Study of Early Cultures in Europe and the Mediterranean Basin*. Cambridge: Cambridge University Press, 1921.

Buttel-Reepen, H. v. *Man and His Forerunners: Incorporating Accounts of Recent Discoveries in Suffolk and Sussex*. Trans. by A. G. Thacker. London: Longmans, Green and Co., 1913.

Butterfield, W. R. Untitled article in *Hastings and St. Leonards Observer*, August 9, 1913.

Chamberlain, A. P. "The Piltdown Forgery." *New Scientist*, 40 (November 28, 1968): 516.

Cockburn, Alexander. "A Skull for Scandal." *London Sunday Times Magazine*, March 8, 1970, 30-34.

Cohen, D. "Is There a Missing Link?" *Science Digest*, 58 (September 1965): 96-97.

"The Controversy over the Discovery of 'Dawn Man.'" *Current Opinion*, 55 (December 1913): 421-422.

Costello, Peter. "Teilhard and the Piltdown Hoax." *Antiquity*, 55 (March 1981): 58-59.

———. "The Piltdown Hoax Reconsidered." *Antiquity*, 59 (November 1985): 167-171.

"Crowborough, Home of the Creator of Sherlock Holmes." *Crowborough Informer*, 66 (January 22, 1983) and 67 (January 29, 1983).

Cuénot, Claude. *Teilhard de Chardin*. Baltimore: Helicon Press, 1958. Second edition, 1965.

Cunnington, William. "The Authenticity of Plateau Man." *Natural Science*, 11 (November 1897): 327-333.

Curwen, E. Cecil. *The Archeology of Sussex*. London: Methuen & Co., 1937.

———. *Prehistoric Sussex*. London: The Homeland Association Ltd., 1929.

Daniel, Glyn. Editorial on Louis Leakey. *Antiquity*, 49 (September 1975): 165-169.

———. Editorial. *Antiquity*, 55 (March 1981): 2-4.

———. "Piltdown and Professor Hewitt." *Antiquity*, 60 (March 1986): 59-60.

Dart, Raymond A. "Australopithecus africanus: The Man-Ape of South Africa." In Leakey, L. S. B., et al., *Adam or Ape*. Cambridge, Mass.: Schenkman, 1971.

"Darwin Theory Is Proved True." *New York Times*, December 22, 1912, 1.

"Dawn Man of Piltdown." *Scientific American Supplement*, 78 (November 7, 1914): 296-299.

Dawson, Charles. Letters. Archives, British Museum (Natural History) Palaeontology Library.

———. *History of Hastings Castle,* 2 vols. London: Constable & Co., Ltd., 1909.

———. "The Piltdown Skull." *Hastings and East Sussex Naturalist,* 2 (1913): 73-82; 4 (1915): 182-184.

Dawson, Charles, and Arthur Smith Woodward. "On a Bone Implement from Piltdown (Sussex)." *Quarterly Journal of the Geological Society,* 71 (March 1915): 144-149.

———. "On the Discovery of a Palaeolithic Skull and Mandible in a Flint-Bearing Gravel overlying the Wealden (Hastings Beds) at Piltdown, Fletching (Sussex)." *Quarterly Journal of the Geological Society,* 69 (March 1913): 117-151. With appendix by Grafton Elliot Smith, "Preliminary Report on the Cranial Cast," and discussion.

———. "Supplementary Note on the Discovery of a Palaeolithic Human Skull and Mandible at Piltdown (Sussex)." *Quarterly Journal of the Geological Society,* 70 (April 1914): 82-99. With appendix by Grafton Elliot Smith, "On the Exact Determination of the Median Plane of the Piltdown Skull," and discussion.

Dawson, Warren R., ed. *Sir Grafton Elliot Smith: A Biographical Record by His Colleagues.* London: Jonathan Cape, 1938.

de Mille, Richard. "Of Piltdown Men and Don Juan Forgeries—The Surprising Costs of Scientific Hoaxes." *Human Behavior,* 8 (March 1979): 68-69.

de Vries, Hugo, and K. P. Oakley. "Radiocarbon Dating of the Piltdown Skull and Jaw." *Nature,* 184 (July 25, 1959): 224-226.

Dewey, H. Obituary of W. J. Lewis Abbott. *Proceedings of the Geological Society,* 90 (1934): 50-51.

Did Man Get Here by Evolution or by Creation? New York: Watchtower Bible and Tract Society, 1967.

"Did Theologian Have a Hand in Great 'Missing Link' Hoax?" *Boston Herald American,* July 20, 1980, A7.

Dixon, A. F. "Note on the Fragment of a Lower Jaw from Piltdown, Sussex." *Nature,* 99 (July 12, 1917): 399.

Dodson, Edward O. Letter to the editor. In Gould, Stephen Jay. "Piltdown in Letters." *Natural History,* 90 (June 1981): 16-21.

Doyle, Arthur Conan. "The Captain of the 'Pole-Star.' " *The Works of Arthur Conan Doyle.* New York: Walter A. Black, Inc., n.d.

———. *The Lost World.* London: John Murray, 1934.

———. *Memories and Adventures.* Boston: Little Brown, 1934.

Dubois, Eugene. "Pithecanthropus erectus—A Form from the Ancestral Stock of Mankind." In Leakey, L. S. B., et al., *Adam or Ape.* Cambridge, Mass.: Schenkman, 1971.

"The Earliest Man?" *Manchester Guardian,* November 21, 1912, 8.

"The Earliest Skull." *Manchester Guardian,* December 19, 1912, 6.

"Early Man." *London Times,* November 24, 1953, 9.

Eastman, C. R., Gregory, W. K., and Matthew, W. D. "Recent Progress in Vertebrate Paleontology." *Science,* 43 (January 21, 1916): 103-110.

Edmunds, Francis H. "Note on the Gravel Deposit from which the Piltdown

Skull Was Obtained." *Abstracts, Proceedings of the Geological Society*, no. 1457 (1950): 39-40.

———. Letter to K. P. Oakley. Archives, British Museum (Natural History) Palaeontology Library.

Ehrich, Robert W. and Gerald M. Henderson. "Concerning the Piltdown Hoax and the Rise of a New Dogmatism." *American Anthropologist*, 56 (June 1954): 433-436.

Elliot, G. F. Scott. *Prehistoric Man and His Story*. London: Seeley, Service & Co., 1915.

Emerson, Joyce, and J. S. Weiner. "The Piltdown Mystery." *London Sunday Times*, January 9, 1955, 4; January 16, 1955, 4; January 23, 1955, 4.

"England's Most Ancient Inhabitant." *The American Review of Reviews*, 47 (February 1913): 229-230.

"An English Ape-Man." *Literary Digest*, 46 (January 25, 1913): 176-177.

Essex, Robert. "The Piltdown Plot: A Hoax that Grew." *Kent and Sussex Journal*, 2 (July-September 1955): 94-95. Reprinted in Bowden, Malcolm, *Ape-Men—Fact or Fallacy?* Bromley, Kent: Sovereign Press, 1978.

"The Famous Piltdown Hoax." *Chemistry*, 42 (October 1969): 21-22.

Farrar, R. A. H. "Sollas and the Sherborne Bone." Letter to *Nature*, 277 (January 25, 1979): 260.

"Features of Piltdown Skull 'Deliberate Fakes.' " *Manchester Guardian*, November 23, 1953, 16.

Feyerabend, Paul. *Against Method: Outline of an Anarchistic Theory of Knowledge*. Britain: Verso, 1975. Second edition, 1978.

"50,000—not 500,000—Years Old?" *Manchester Guardian*, November 23, 1953, 16.

Friederichs, Heinz F. *Schaedel und Unterkiefer von Piltdown ("Eoanthropus dawsoni Woodward") in neuer Untersuchung*. Zeitschrift für Anatomie und Entwicklungsgeschichte. Band 98. Berlin, 1932, pp. 199-262.

Fuller, Curtis. "The Piltdown Hoax." *Fate*, 32 (May 1979): 10-11.

Geikie, James. *The Antiquity of Man in Europe*. Edinburgh: Oliver and Boyd, 1914.

Gish, Duane T. *Evolution: The Fossils Say NO!* San Diego: Creation-Life Publishers, 1979.

Giuffrida-Ruggeri, V. *L'uomo attuale una specie collettiva*. Milan-Rome-Naples, 1913.

Gould, Stephen. *Ever Since Darwin*. New York: W. W. Norton, 1977.

———. "Piltdown Revisited." *Natural History*, 88 (March 1979): 86-97.

———. "Smith Woodward's Folly." *New Scientist*, 82 (April 5, 1979): 42-44.

———. "The Piltdown Conspiracy." *Natural History*, 89 (August 1980): 8-28

———. *The Panda's Thumb*. New York: W. W. Norton, 1980.

———. "Piltdown in Letters." *Natural History*, 90 (June 1981): 12-30.

———. *Hen's Teeth and Horse's Toes*. New York: W. W. Norton, 1983.

———. Letter to *Science 83*, 4 (November 1983): 22-23.

Greene, John C. *The Death of Adam: Evolution and Its Impact on Western Thought*. Ames, Iowa: Iowa State University Press, 1959.

Gregory, William King. "The Dawn Man of Piltdown, England." *American Museum Journal*, 14 (1914): 189-200.

———. "Note on the Molar Teeth of the Piltdown Mandible." *American Anthropologist*, 18 (1916): 384-387.

———. *Our Face from Fish to Man.* New York: G. P. Putnam, 1929. Second edition: Capricorn Books, 1965.

Haddon, A. C. "*Eoanthropus dawsoni.*" *Science*, 37 (January 17, 1913): 91-92.

Haeckel, Ernst. *The History of Creation or the Development of the Earth and Its Inhabitants by the Action of Natural Causes*, 2 vols. New York: D. Appleton, 1906.

Halstead, L. B. "New Light on the Piltdown Hoax?" *Nature*, 76 (November 2, 1978): 11-13.

———. "The Piltdown Hoax: Cui Bono?" *Nature*, 277 (February 22, 1979): 596.

Hammond, Michael. "A Framework of Plausibility for an Anthropological Forgery: The Piltdown Case." *Anthropology*, 3 (1979): 47-58.

———. "The Expulsion of the Neanderthals from Human Ancestry: Marcellin Boule and the Social Context of Scientific Research." *Social Studies of Sciences*, 12 (February 1982): 1-36.

Harrison, Geoffrey A. "J. S. Weiner and the Exposure of the Piltdown Forgery." *Antiquity*, 57 (March 1983): 46-48.

Head, J. O. "Piltdown Mystery." *New Scientist*, 49 (January 14, 1971): 86.

Heim, J. S. "Le Professeur Henri-Victor Vallois et la Paleontologie Humaine." *Bull. et. Mém. de la Soc. d'Anthrop. de Paris*, t. 9, série 13 (1982): 109-122.

Heizer, Robert F., and Sherburne F. Cook. "Comments on the Piltdown Remains." *American Anthropologist*, 56 (February 1954): 92-94.

Himmelfarb, Gertrude. *Darwin and the Darwinian Revolution.* London: Chatto & Windus Ltd., 1959.

Hinton, M. A. C. "The Pleistocene Mammalia of the British Isles and Their Bearing upon the Date of the Glacial Period." *Proceedings of the Yorkshire Geological Society*, 20, Part 3 (November 1926): 325-348.

"Holy Hoaxer?" *Time*, July 28, 1980, 73.

Hooton, Earnest A. *Up from the Ape.* New York: Macmillan, 1931. Second edition, 1946.

———. "Comments on the Piltdown Affair." *American Anthropologist*, 56 (April 1954): 287-289.

Howells, William. *Mankind in the Making.* New York: Doubleday, 1959.

Hrdlicka, Ales. "The Piltdown Jaw." *American Journal of Physical Anthropology*, 5, no. 4 (1922): 337-347.

———. "Dimensions of the First and Second Lower Molars with Their Bearing on the Piltdown Jaw and on Man's Phylogeny." *American Journal of Physical Anthropology*, 6, no. 2 (1923): 195-216.

———. "The Skeletal Remains of Early Man." *Smithsonian Miscellaneous Collections*, 83 (July 1930): 65-90. Smithsonian Institution, Washington, D.C.

H.R.H. "The Sussex Skull." *Hastings and St. Leonards Observer*, February 15, 1913.

Huxley, Leonard, ed. *The Life and Letters of Thomas Henry Huxley*, 2 vols. New York: D. Appleton, 1901.

Irving, Rev. Dr. A. "The Piltdown Horse 'Grinder.' " *Nature*, 91, no. 2287 (August 28, 1913): 661.

———. "The Piltdown Skull." *Morning Post* (January 1914).

Jahn, Melvin E. "Dr. Beringer and the Wurzburg 'Lügensteine.' " *Journal for the Society for the Bibliography of Natural History,* 4 (1963): 138-146.

Jahn, Melvin E., and Daniel J. Woolf, eds. *The Lying Stones of Dr. Johann Bartholomew Adam Beringer, being his Lithographiae Wirceburgensis.* Berkeley, California: University of California Press, 1963.

Jefferson, E. A. Ross. Letter on Sherborne Horse's Head. *Nature,* 117 (March 6, 1926): 341-342.

Jessup, Ronald. *South East England.* New York: Praeger, 1970.

Johanson, Donald C., and Maitland A. Edey. *Lucy: The Beginnings of Humankind.* New York: Simon and Schuster, 1981.

Keith, Sir Arthur. "The Piltdown Skull and Brain Cast." *Nature,* 92 (November 6, 1913): 292.

———. "The Piltdown Skull and Brain Cast." *Nature,* 92 (November 20, 1913): 345-346.

———. "The Significance of the Discovery at Piltdown." *Bedrock: A Quarterly Review of Scientific Thought,* 2 (January 1914): 435-458.

———. "Note on Arthur Keith's Reconstruction." *Nature,* 92 (January 29, 1914): 624.

———. "Note on Arthur Keith's Reconstruction." *Nature,* 94 (October 29, 1914): 240-241.

———. *The Antiquity of Man,* 2 vols. London: Williams and Norgate, Ltd., 1915. Second edition, 1925.

———. Review of Osborn. *Man,* 17 (May 1917): 82-85.

———. *New Discoveries Relating to the Antiquity of Man.* New York: W. W. Norton, n.d. (1931).

———. "Obituary on Lewis Abbott." *London Times,* August 12, 1933.

———. "A Re-Survey of the Anatomical Features of the Piltdown Skull with Some Observations on the Recently Discovered Swanscombe Skull. Part I." *Journal of Anatomy,* 75 (1938); Part II, 75 (1939): 234-254.

———. Introduction to Woodward, Arthur Smith, *The Earliest Englishman.* London: Watts, 1948.

———. *An Autobiography.* New York: Philosophical Society, 1950.

Kennard, A. S. "Fifty and One Years of the Geologists' Association." *Proceedings of the Geological Assocation,* 58 (1947): 271-283.

King, Thomas M., S.J. "Teilhard, Gould and Piltdown." *America,* 148 (June 18, 1983), 471-472.

King, Thomas M., and James P. Salmon, S.J. *Teilhard and the Unity of Knowledge.* New York: Paulist Press, 1983.

Krogman, Wilton Marion. "The Planned Planting of Piltdown: Who? Why?" In Washburn S. L., and Elizard R. McGown, eds., *Human Evolution: Biosocial Perspectives.* Menlo Park, Calif: Benjamin Cummings, 1978.

Kuhn, Thomas S. *The Structure of Scientific Revolutions.* Chicago: University of Chicago Press, 1962.

"Lake Tele Expedition." *Acts and Facts,* 14 (January 1985): 3, 5.

Lang, W. D. Letter to K. Oakley. Archives, British Museum (Natural History) Palaeontology Library.

Langham, Ian. "Talgai and Piltdown—The Common Context." *Artefact,* 3, no 4 (1978): 181-224.

──────. "The Piltdown Hoax." Letter to *Nature,* 277 (January 18, 1979): 170.

──────. "Sherlock Holmes, Circumstantial Evidence, and Piltdown Man." *Physical Anthropology News,* 3, no. 1 (Spring 1984): 1-5.

Lankester, Edwin Ray. *The Kingdom of Man.* New York: Henry Holt, 1907.

──────. *Diversions of a Naturalist.* New York: Macmillan, 1915.

"Last Home of 'Swanscombe Man.' " *Manchester Guardian,* December 24, 1953, 12, U.S. edition.

Leakey, L. S. B. *Adam's Ancestors.* New York: Longmans, Green and Co., 1935.

──────. *By the Evidence. Memoirs, 1932-1951.* New York: Harcourt Brace Jovanovich, 1974.

Leakey, L. S. B., and Anne Morris Goodall. *Unveiling Man's Origin.* Cambridge, Mass.: Schenkman, 1969.

Leakey, L. S. B., and Jack and Stephanie Prost, eds. *Adam or Ape: A Sourcebook of Discoveries about Early Man.* Cambridge, Mass: Schenkman, 1971.

Le Gros Clark, W. E. "The Exposure of the Piltdown Forgery." *Proceedings of the Royal Institution of Great Britain,* 20 (May 1955): 138-151.

──────. *The Fossil Evidence for Human Evolution.* Chicago: University of Chicago Press, 1964.

──────. *History of the Primates.* Chicago: University of Chicago Press, 1965.

──────. *The Antecedents of Man.* New York: Quadrangle Books, 1971.

Lukas, Mary. "A Playful Prank Gone Too Far? Or a Deliberate Scientific Forgery? Or, as It Now Appears, Nothing at All." *America,* 144 (May 23, 1981): 424-427.

──────. "Gould and Teilhard's 'Fatal Error.' " *Teilhard Newsletter,* 14 (July 1981): 4-6.

Lukas, Mary, and Ellen Lukas. *Teilhard.* New York: Doubleday, 1977.

──────. "The Haunting." *Antiquity,* 57 (March 1983): 7-11.

Lyne, H. Courtney. "The Significance of the Radiographs of the Piltdown Teeth." *Royal Society of Medicine Proceedings,* 9, no. 3 (Februry 1916): 33-62.

MacCurdy, George Grant. "Ancestor Hunting: The Significance of the Piltdown Skull." *American Anthropologist,* 15 (April-June 1913): 248-256.

──────. "The Man of Piltdown." *Science,* 40 (April 1914): 158-160.

──────. "The Revision of *Eoanthropus dawsoni.*" *Science,* 43 (February 18, 1916): 228-231.

──────. *Human Origins: A Manual of Prehistory.* New York: D. Appleton, 1924.

"Man Had Reason Before He Spoke." *New York Times,* December 20, 1912, 1.

"Man of the Dawn," Interview with Grafton Elliot Smith, *Sydney Morning Herald,* July 3, 1914.

Marston, Alvan T. "Preliminary Note on a New Fossil Human Skull from Swanscombe, Kent" (1936). In L. S. B. Leakey et al. *Adam or Ape.* Cambridge, Mass.: Schenkman, 1971.

──────. "The Relative Ages of the Swanscombe and Piltdown Skulls, with Special Reference to the Results of the Fluorine Estimation Test." *British Dental Journal,* 88 (June 2, 1950): 292-299.

──────. "Reasons Why the Piltdown Canine Tooth and Mandible Could Not Belong to Piltdown Man." *British Dental Journal,* 93 (July 1, 1952): 1-14.

Matthew, W. D. "Recent Progress and Trends in Vertebrate Paleontology." *Smithsonian Annual Report for 1923.* Washington, D. C.: Smithsonian, 1925.

Matthews, L. Harrison. "Piltdown Man: The Missing Links." *New Scientist,* 90 (April 30, 1981): 280-282; (May 7, 1981): 376; (May 14, 1981): (May 21, 1981): 515-516; (May 28, 1981): 578-579; (June 4, 1981): 647-648; (June 11, 1981): 710-711; (June 18, 1981): 785; (June 25, 1981): 861-862; (July 2, 1981): 26-28.

McCann, Alfred Watterson. *God—or Gorilla: How the Monkey Theory of Evolution Exposes Its Own Methods, Refutes Its Own Principles, Denies Its Own Inferences, Disproves Its Own Case.* New York: Devin-Adair Co., 1922.

McCulloch, Winifred. "Some Remarks on Teilhard and the Piltdown Hoax." *Teilhard Newsletter,* 14 (July 1981): 1-2.

———. "A Reader's Guide to S. J. Gould's Piltdown Argument." *Teilhard Perspective,* 16 (December, 1983): 4-7.

Medawar, Peter. *Pluto's Republic.* Oxford: Oxford University Press, 1983.

A Medical Scientist. *Evolution: A Handbook for Teachers and Students.* Washington, D.C.: Truth-for-Youth Crusade, n.d.

Migeod, Frederick. *Earliest Man.* London: Kegan Paul, 1916.

Millar, Ronald. *The Piltdown Men.* New York: Ballantine Books, 1972.

Miller, Gerrit S. "The Jaw of the Piltdown Man." *Smithsonian Miscellaneous Collections,* 65 (November 24, 1915): 1-31.

———. "The Piltdown Jaw." *American Journal of Physical Anthropology,* 1, no. 1 (January-March 1918): 25-52.

———. Reviews. *American Journal of Physical Anthropology,* 3, no. 3 (July-September 1921): 385-386.

"The Missing Link: Professor Boyd Dawkins on the Piltdown Skull." *Manchester Guardian,* January 12, 1914, 10.

Mitchell, P. Chalmers. Letter to *Nature,* 96 (December 30, 1915): 480.

Moir, J. Reid. Letter to *London Times,* December 25, 1912, 8.

———. "Pre-Palaeolithic Man." *Bedrock: A Quarterly Review of Scientific Thought,* 2 (July 1913): 165-176.

———. "Pre-Palaeolithic Man in England." *Science Progress,* 12 (1917/1918): 465-474.

———. *The Antiquity of Man in East Anglia.* Cambridge: Cambridge University Press, 1927.

Montagu, M. F. Ashley. "The Barcombe Mills Cranial Remains." *American Journal of Physical Anthropology,* 9, no. 4 (1951): 417-426.

———. "The Piltdown Mandible and Cranium." *American Journal of Physical Anthropology,* 9, no. 4 (1951): 464-470.

———. *An Introduction to Physical Anthropology.* Springfield, Ill.: Charles C. Thomas, 1960, 3rd ed.

———. "Artificial Thickening of Bone and the Piltdown Skull." *Nature,* 187 (July 9, 1960): 174.

Moore, Ruth. *Man, Time, and Fossils.* New York: Alfred A. Knopf, 1953.

"More Doubts on Piltdown Man." *London Times,* November 23, 1953, 8.

Morris, Henry. *The Bible and Modern Science.* Chicago: Moody Press, 1951.

———. "An Answer for Asimov." Impact Series #99. California: Creation-Life Publishers, 1981.

Nelkin, Dorothy. *Science Textbook Controversies and the Politics of Equal Time.* Cambridge, Mass: MIT Press, 1977.

"1906 Skull Was Not the Piltdown Find." *Sussex Express & County Herald,* January 1, 1954, 6.

Nordon, Pierre. *Conan Doyle: A Biography.* New York: Holt, Rinehart, Winston, 1967.

North, Jessica. *Mask of the Jaguar.* New York: Coward, McCann & Geoghegan, 1981.

Nuttall, T. E. "The Piltdown Skull." *Man,* 17 (May 1917): 80-82.

Oakley, Kenneth P. "Relative Dating of the Piltdown Skull." *Advancement of Science,* 6 (January 1950): 343-344.

———. "Royaume-Uni." In Vallois, Henri V., and Hallam L. Movius, eds., *Catalogue des Hommes Fossiles.* XIX Congrès Géologique International, Algiers, 1952.

———. "Dating Fossil Human Remains." In Kroeber, A. L, ed., *Anthropology Today: An Encyclopedic Inventory.* Chicago, Ill.: University of Chicago Press, 1953.

———. "Artificial Thickening of Bone and the Piltdown Skull." *Nature,* 187 (July 9, 1960): 174.

———. "The Problem of Man's Antiquity." *Bulletin of the British Museum (Natural History),* 9, no. 5 (1964).

———. "The Piltdown Skull." *New Scientist,* 40 (October 17, 1969): 154.

———. "The Piltdown Problem Reconsidered." *Antiquity,* 50 (March 1976): 9-13.

———. "Piltdown Stains." *Nature,* 278 (March 22, 1979): 302.

———. "Piltdown Man." *New Scientist,* 92 (November 12, 1981): 457-458.

Oakley, Kenneth P., and Colin P. Groves. "Piltdown Man: The Realization of Fraudulence." *Science,* 169 (August 21, 1970): 789.

Oakley, Kenneth P., and C. Randall Hoskins. "New Evidence on the Antiquity of Piltdown Man." *Nature,* 165 (March 11, 1950): 379-382.

Oakley, Kenneth P., and J. S. Weiner. "Piltdown Man." *American Scientist,* 4 (October 1955): 573-583.

Obermeier, Hugo. *El hombre fosil.* (Comisión de investigaciones. paleontológicas y prehistoricas, Mem. No. 9), Madrid, 1916.

O'Connor, Gerald. "The Hoax as Popular Culture." *Journal of Popular Culture,* 9 (1976): 767-774.

"The Oldest Human Fossil." *Dublin Daily Express,* August 13, 1913.

Osborn, Henry Fairfield. *Men of the Old Stone Age: Their Enviroment, Life and Art.* New York: Charles Scribner's Sons, 1915.

———. "The Dawn Man of Piltdown, Sussex." *Natural History,* 21 (November-December 1921): 577-590.

———. *Man Rises to Parnassus.* Princeton, N.J.: Princeton University Press, 1927.

———. "Recent Discoveries Relating to the Origin and Antiquity of Man." *Palaeobiologica,* 1 (1928): 189-202.

Osborne White, H. J. *The Geology of the Country Near Lewes: Memoirs of the Geological Survey England.* London: H. M. Stationery Office, 1926.

Page, James K., Jr. "Phenomena, Comment and Notes." *Smithsonian,* 9 (March 1979): 30-34.

"Palaeolithic Man." *Nature,* 90 (December 19, 1912): 438.

"A Palaeolithic Skull." *London Times,* December 19, 1912, 4.

"Palaeolithic Skull Is a Missing Link." *New York Times,* December 19, 1912, 1.

Parker, Gary E. "Origin of Mankind." Impact Series. #101. San Diego: Creation-Life Publishers, 1981.

Parliamentary Debate on Piltdown. *Parliamentary Debates* (Hansard), 5th. Ser., vol. 521 (November 26, 1953): 527-529. House of Commons Official Report Session 1953-1954. London: Her Majesty's Stationery Office, 1953.

Peacock, D. P. S. "Forged Brick-stamps from Pevensey." *Antiquity,* 47 (June 1973): 138-140.

Pearsall, Ronald. *Conan Doyle: A Biographical Solution.* London: Weidenfeld and Nicolson, 1977.

"Piltdown: How Fake Was Found." *London Observer,* 8, no. 477 (November 22, 1953).

"Piltdown Man, A Re-examination." *Nature,* 142 (October 1, 1938): 621.

"The Piltdown Man Discovery: Unveiling of a Monolith Memorial." *Nature,* 142 (July 30, 1938): 196-197.

"Piltdown Man Forgery." *London Times,* November 21, 1953, 6.

The Piltdown Man Hoax. Palaeontology Leaflet #2. London: British Museum (Natural History), 1975.

"Piltdown Man Hoax Is Exposed: Jaw an Ape's, Skull Fairly Recent." *New York Times,* November 22, 1953, C1.

"Piltdown Man Hoax: Protest Against 'Attacks.'" *London Times,* November 26, 1953, 5.

Piltdown notes. Brief, unheaded notes on the Piltdown finds are in *Nature,* 95 (June 24, 1915): 460; 97 (June 8, 1916): 309-310; and 99 (July 12, 1917): 399; and on the exposé in *Antiquity,* 30 (March 1956): 1-2.

"Piltdown Redux." *Life,* January 1984, 154.

"The Piltdown Skull." *London Times,* November 25, 1912, 8.

"The Piltdown Skull." *Nature,* 92 (September 25, 1913): 110-111.

"The 'Piltdown Skull' a Forgery." *Manchester Guardian,* November 26, 1953, 1, U.S. ed.

"Piltdown Skull or Piltdown Man." In Brewer, E. Cobham, *Brewer's Dictionary of Phrase and Fable.* New York: Harper & Row, 1981

"Piltdown Won't Down." *Scientific American,* 241 (July 1979): 80-82.

Popper, Karl R. *The Logic of Scientific Discovery.* New York: Basic Books, 1959. 1st ed., 1934.

Postlethwaite, F. J. M. Letter to *London Times,* November 25, 1953, 9.

Puccioni, Nello. "Appunti intorno al frammento mandibolare fossile di Piltdown (Sussex)." *Archivo per L'Antropologia e la Ethnologia,* 43 (1913): 167-175.

Pycraft, W. P. "The Most Ancient Inhabitant of England: The Newly-Found Sussex Man." *Illustrated London News,* 141 (December 28, 1912): 958.

———. "Ape-Man or Modern Man? The Two Piltdown Skull Reconstructions." *Illustrated London News,* 163 (September 20, 1913): 444.

————. "The Jaw of the Piltdown Man: A Reply to Mr. Gerrit S. Miller."
   *Science Progress in the Twentieth Century: A Quarterly Journal of Scientific
   Work and Thought,* 11 (1916-1917): 389-409.
Quenstedt, Werner. *Hominidae Fossiles.* 's-Gravenhage: W. Junk, 1936.
Ramstrom, M. "Der Piltdown-Fund." *Bulletin of the Geological Institute, Univer-
   sity of Uppsala,* 16 Denmark: Uppsala, 1919, 261-304.
Ray, John E. Letter to K. Oakley. Archives, British Museum (Natural History)
   Palaeontology Library.
Raymond, Ernest. *Please You, Draw Near: Autobiography 1922-1969.* London:
   Cassell, 1968.
Reader, John. *Missing Links: The Hunt for Earliest Man.* Boston: Little, Brown,
   1981.
Rosen, Dennis. "The Jilting of Athena." *New Scientist,* 39 (September 5, 1968):
   497-500.
Rudwick, Martin J. S. *The Meaning of Fossils: Episodes in the History of
   Palaeontology.* New York: Neale Watson Academic Publications, 1976.
Salzman, L. F. "Piltdown Mystery." Letter to *London Times,* January 23, 1955,
   2.
Schaaffhausen, D., and T. H. Huxley. "On the Human Skeleton from the
   Neander Valley." In Leakey, L. S. B., et al., *Adam or Ape.* Cambridge,
   Mass: Schenkman, 1971.
Schmitz-Moorman, Karl. "Teilhard and the Piltdown Hoax." *Teilhard News-
   letter,* 14 (July 1981), 2-4.
Schrier, Eric. "The Case of the Faked Fossil." *Science 83,* 4 (September 1983): 5.
Sergi, G. "La Mandibola Umana." *Revista di Antropologia,* 19 (1914): 119-168.
Shapiro, Harry L. *Peking Man.* New York: Simon and Schuster, 1974.
Smith, Grafton Elliot. "Man's Hairy Covering." *Nature* (April 22, 1909): 211-
   212.
————. "The Evolution of the Brain." *Nature,* 82 (January 20, 1910): 349-350.
————. "Fossil Remains of Man." *Nature,* 85 (January 26, 1911): 402-403.
————. Presidential Address. *Nature,* 90 (September 26, 1912): 118-126.
————. "Preliminary Report on the Cranial Cast." *Quarterly Journal of the
   Geological Society,* 69 (March 1913): 145-147.
————. "The Piltdown Skull." *Nature,* 92 (October 2, 1913): 131.
————. "The Piltdown Skull and Brain Cast." *Nature,* 92 (October 30, 1913):
   267-268; 92 (November 13, 1913): 318-319.
————. "The Controversies Concerning the Interpretations and Meaning of the
   Remains of the Dawn-man Found Near Piltdown." *Nature,* 92 (December
   18, 1913): 468-469.
————. "On the Exact Determination of the Median Plane of the Piltdown
   Skull." *Quarterly Journal of the Geological Society,* 70 (April 1914): 93-97.
————. "New Phases of the Controversies Concerning the Piltdown Skull."
   *Memoirs and Proceedings of the Manchester Literary and Philosophical
   Society,* 60 (February 1916): 28-29.
————. "The Cranial Cast of the Piltdown Skull." *Man,* 82 (September 1916):
   131-132.
————. "On the Form of the Frontal Pole of an Endocranial Cast of *Eoanthro-
   pus dawsoni.*" *Quarterly Journal of the Geological Society,* 73 (1917): 7-8.

———. "The Problem of the Piltdown Jaw: Human or Sub-Human?" *Eugenics Review*, 9 (1917): 167.

———. "Hesperopithecus: The Ape-Man of the Western World." *Illustrated London News* (June 24, 1922): 942-944.

———. *The Evolution of Man.* London: Oxford University Press, 1924. Second edition, 1927.

———. "The London Skull." *Nature*, 116 (November 7, 1925): 678-681.

———. *Search for Man's Ancestors.* London: The Rationalist Press, 1931.

———. "The Discovery of Primitive Man in China." *Antiquity*, 5 (March 1931): 21-36.

———. "Human Palaeontology." Review of Keith. *Nature*, 12 (June 27, 1931): 963-967.

———. "Conversion in Science." *Huxley Memorial Lectures.* London: Macmillan and Co., 1932.

Smith, Grafton Elliot, notes. Brief, unheaded notes on Smith are in *Nature*, 92 (December 18, 1913): 468; 92 (February 26, 1914): 729; 97 (March 2, 1916): 26; and in *Antiquity*, 46 (December 1972): 262-264.

Sollas, W. J. *Ancient Hunters and Their Modern Representatives.* London: Macmillan, 1911. Second edition, 1915. Third edition, 1924.

Sollas, W. J., and C. J. Bayzand. "The Palaeolithic Drawing of a Horse from Sherborne, Dorset." *Nature*, 117 (February 13, 1926), 233.

Speaight, Robert. *Teilhard de Chardin: A Biography.* London: Collins, 1967.

Spencer, Frank. "The Neandertals and Their Evolutionary Significance: A Brief Historical Survey." In Smith, Fred H., and Frank Spencer, eds., *The Origins of Modern Humans.* New York: Alan R. Liss, 1984.

Stern, Philip Van Doren. *Prehistoric Europe from Stone Age Man to the Early Greeks.* New York: W. W. Norton, 1969.

Stibbe, E. P. *An Introduction to Physical Anthropology.* London: Edward Arnold & Co., 1930.

Stove, D. C. "Popper and After." *Four Modern Irrationalists.* Oxford: Pergamon Press, 1982.

Straus, William L. "The Great Piltdown Hoax." *Science*, 119 (February 26, 1954): 265-269.

"Swanscombe." *Antiquity*, 10 (December 1936): 480-481.

Tarnoky, A. L. "Genetic and Drug Induced Variation in Serum Albumin." In Latner, A. L., and M. K. Schwartz, eds., *Advances in Clinical Chemistry*, 21, pp. 101-146. New York: Academic Press Inc., 1980.

Teilhard de Chardin, Pierre. "Le Cas de l'Homme de Piltdown." *Revue des questions scientifiques*, 77, 149-155. Louvain: Societé Scientifique de Bruxelles, 1920.

———. "On the Zoological Position and the Evolutionary Significance of Australopithecines." *New York Academy of Sciences Transactions*, 14 (February 1952): 208-210.

———. *L'Apparition de l'Homme.* Paris: Editions du Seuil, 1956.

———. *Lettres d'Hastings et de Paris, 1908-1914.* Aubier: Editions Montaigne, 1965.

———. "The Idea of Fossil Man." In Kroeber, A. L., *Anthropology Today: An Encyclopedic Inventory.* Chicago: University of Chicago Press, 1953.

———. *L'oeuvre Scientifique*, vol. 10, ed. by Nichole and Karl Schmitz-Moorman, pp. 4561-4567. Olten: Walter-Verlag, 1971.

———. *The Phenomenon of Man.* New York: Harper & Row, 1959.

Thacker, A. G. "Human Palaeontology and Anthropology." *Science Progress,* 10 (July 1915): 264-269, 312-314, 461-464, 468.

Thomas, Lewis. *Late Night Thoughts on Listening to Mahler's Ninth Symphony.* New York: Viking Press, 1983.

Thorne, Guy [Real name: Cyril Arthur Edward Ranger Gull]. *When It Was Dark: The Story of a Great Conspiracy.* New York: G. P. Putnam's Sons, 1905.

Thuillier, Pierre. "Une supercherie exemplaire: l'Homme de Piltdown." *La Recherche,* 3 (November 1972): 998-1002.

Tobias, Phillip V. "The Child from Taung." *Science 84,* 5 (November 1984): 99-100.

"The Tragedy of Piltdown: Sir Arthur Keith's Opinion Revealed." *London Sunday Times,* January 9, 1955, 1.

Underwood, A. S. "The Piltdown Skull." *British Dental Journal,* 56 (October 1, 1913): 650-652.

Vallois, Henri V. "La Solution de l'enigma de Piltdown," *L'Anthropologie,* t. 57 (1953): 562-567.

———. "Encore la fraude de Piltdown." *L'Anthropologie,* t. 58 (1953): 353-356.

Vallois, Henri V., and Hallam L. Movius, eds. *Catalogue des Hommes Fossiles.* XIX Congrès Géologique International. Algiers, 1952.

van Esbroeck, G. *Pleine Lumière sur l'Imposture de Piltdown.* Paris: Les Editions du Cedre, 1972.

Vere, Francis. *The Piltdown Fantasy.* London: Cassell and Co., 1955.

———. *Lessons of Piltdown.* London: The Evolution Protest Movement, 1959.

von Koenigswald, G. H. R. Letter to the editor. In Gould, Stephen Jay. "Piltdown in Letters." *Natural History,* 90 (June 1981): 21-25.

Wade, Nicholas. "Voice from the Dead Names New Suspect for Piltdown Hoax." *Science,* 202 (December 8, 1978): 1062.

Washburn, Sherwood. "The Piltdown Hoax." *American Anthropologist,* 55 (December 1953): 259-262.

———. "An Old Theory Is Supported by New Evidence." *American Anthropologist,* 56 (June 1954): 436-441.

———. "The Piltdown Hoax: Piltdown 2." *Science,* 203 (March 9, 1979): 955-957.

———. Letter to the editor. In Gould, Stephen Jay, "Piltdown in Letters," *Natural History,* 90 (June 1981): 12-16.

Waterston, David. "The Piltdown Mandible." *Nature,* 92 (November 13, 1913): 319.

Waterton, Charles. *Wanderings in South America.* London: B. Fellowes, 1828. Reprinted by the Gregg Press, Upper Saddle River, N.J., 1969.

Weidenreich, Franz. *Apes, Giants and Man.* Chicago: University of Chicago Press, 1946

Weiner, J. S. *The Piltdown Forgery.* London: Oxford University Press, 1955.

———. "Grafton Elliot Smith and Piltdown." *Symposium, Zoological Society of London,* 33 (1973): 23-26.

————. "Piltdown Hoax: New Light." *Nature,* 277 (January 4, 1979): 10.

Weiner, J. S., and K. P. Oakley. "The Piltdown Fraud: Available Evidence Reviewed." *American Journal of Physical Anthropology,* 12 (March 1954): 1-7.

Weiner, J. S., K. P. Oakley, and Wilfred Le Gros Clark. "The Solution of the Piltdown Problem." *Bulletin of the British Museum (Natural History),* Geology Series 2, no. 3. London: British Museum, 1953.

Weiner, J. S., K. P. Oakley, Wilfred Le Gros Clark, et al. "Further Contributions to the Solution of the Piltdown Problem." *Bulletin of the British Museum (Natural History),* Geology Series 2, no. 6. London: British Museum, 1955.

Weinert, Hans. *Das Problem des "Eoanthropus" von Piltdown.* Zeitschrift für Morphologie und Anthropologie. Band XXXII, pp. 1-76. Stuttgart, 1933.

Weinstein, Deena. "Fraud in Science." *Social Science Quarterly,* 59 (March 1979): 639-651.

Wendt, Herbert. *In Search of Adam.* Boston: Houghton Mifflin, 1956.

West, Anthony. "Darwinitis: A Literary Complaint." *New Yorker,* October 10, 1959, 188 ff.

"When It Was Dark." *Manchester Guardian,* November 26, 1953, 6.

Whitcomb, John C., and Henry M. Morris. *The Genesis Flood: The Biblical Record and Its Scientific Implications.* Phillipsburg, N.J.: Presbyterian and Reformed Publishing Co., 1961.

Wilder, Harris H. *The Pedigree of the Human Race.* New York: Henry Holt, 1926.

Wilson, Angus. *Anglo-Saxon Attitudes.* New York: Viking, 1956.

Windle, Bertram C. A. *Remains of the Prehistoric Age in England.* London: Methuen, 1904.

Winslow, John, and Alfred Meyer. "The Perpetrator at Piltdown." *Science 83,* 4 (September 1983): 32-43.

Woodward, Arthur Smith. Letters. Archives, British Museum (Natural History) Palaeontology Library.

————. "On an Apparently Palaeolithic Engraving on a Bone from Sherborne (Dorset)." *Quarterly Journal of the Geological Society,* 70 (April 1914): 100-103.

————. "On the Lower Jaw of an Anthropoid Ape (Dryopithecus) from the Upper Miocene of Lerida (Spain)." *Quarterly Journal of the Geological Society,* 70 (December 1914): 316-320.

————. "Description of the Nasal Bones and Lower Canine Tooth of *Eoanthropus dawsoni,* and Some Associated Mammalian Remains." *Quarterly Journal of the Geological Society,* 70 (April 1914): 86-93.

————. "Fourth Note on the Piltdown Gravel with Evidence of a Second Skull of *Eoanthropus dawsoni,*" with an appendix by Grafton Ellliot Smith, "On the Form of the Frontal Pole of an Endocranial Cast of *Eoanthropus dawsoni*" and discussion. *Quarterly Journal of the Geological Society,* 73 (1917): 1-10.

————. "The Palaeolithic Drawing of a Horse from Sherborne, Dorset." Letter to *Nature,* 117 (January 16, 1926): 86.

————. "The Second Piltdown Skull." *Nature,* 131 (February 18, 1933): 242.

————. *The Earliest Englishman.* London: Watts, 1948.

Wright, William. Review of Keith's *The Antiquity of Man. Man,* 16 (August 1916): 124-127.

————. "The Endocranial Cast of the Piltdown Skull." *Man,* 16 (October 1916): 158.

Wymer, John. *Lower Palaeolithic Archaeology in Britain.* New York: Humanities Press, Inc., 1968.

INDEX